LIFE BEYOND PERSONALITY

Part One

THE STORY of 'YOU'

Author's Note

In this book certain key words are capitalised because I am using them in a specific way. Words mean different things to different people; the effectiveness of language depends on a consensus of meaning between speaker and listener. To communicate this material effectively I have had to be clear on exactly what I mean when using these key words in the context of this enquiry.

Once the book begins I explain and define these capitalised words as they arise. For easy reference they are also summarised in the Glossary.

Conversations have been edited for clarity and simplicity. Other people's personal details have generally been changed for privacy reasons.

Jez Alborough
London, August 2018

LIFE BEYOND PERSONALITY

Part One

———

THE
STORY
of 'YOU'

Jez Alborough

In discussion with Matthew Wherry

Still Point Press

Dedicated to my beautiful wife,
who shared much of this journey with me
and whose love and support
has been such a blessing.

———————————————

I would also like to thank my friend Matthew
whose probing questions and incisive editing skills
have been invaluable in the creation of these books.

Second Edition

Published by Still Point Press 2018

Copyright © 2018 Jez Alborough
This edition published 2020

Cover art from a painting by Jez Alborough

ISBN: 978-1-9993541-1-4

www.lifebeyondpersonality.com

CONTENTS

*

BEGINNINGS

Before energy becomes something, it starts out as the
undivided, potential energy of everything

When Oneness manifests as Two-ness

The interplay of two levels of reality

*

THE NATURAL STATE

Before we relate to any human, our primary relationship
is with life itself

How the Original Relationship to Life manifests in a person

*

THE WORLD OF MAN

*

CHILDHOOD

*

PERSONALITY

OUTCOMES

*

PERSONAL GROWTH

*

LIFE BEYOND PERSONALITY

The Story of 'You'

Introduction

In my younger years I experienced a series of what I call 'Openings'. These took me beyond the perspective of a teenage boy into a place of stillness, peace and heightened awareness and set me on a search to understand what they meant: What was the implication of that perspective to the Personality who seemed to be living this life when the Openings were not there?

Unlocking the secret of these Openings seemed to be the most important endeavour I could undertake in this life, much more important than anything I could learn at school or university. This questioning has sometimes set me apart from those around me. Socrates said: 'An unexamined life is not worth living.' It seems to me that many people would disagree because they find asking deep questions about who we think we are, and how we live, to be too confronting. The fact that you are reading this book could mean that you are not one of these people. Perhaps you have experienced an Opening, or maybe you just have the sense that there is something more to life, something the society you live in does not acknowledge.

In this book and its sequel, *The Infinite Journey,* I share the answers I have found to the questions posed by the Openings. Each chapter takes the form of a discussion with my friend Matthew. Together we drill down into each topic and take the reader on a journey to a place beyond belief, hope and desire: a place beyond Personality, and its suffering, that is everyone's birthright.

This book discusses the 'Natural State of Being' in which we are born, how we lose it as we come to identify as our Personality, and the outcomes of that identification. The next book, *The Infinite Journey*, covers what it means to wake up from the dream of Personality, how it differs from the image of enlightenment that has been passed down to us, and how life beyond Personality relates to the sometimes-confusing world of spiritual seeking and teaching.

I feel absolutely blessed to have been given these glimpses into my true nature, for the journey they took me on, and the answers I was given. These books are my way of sharing the gift that life gave to me. May they be a mirror in which you glimpse the wonderful and mysterious truth that we all hold inside.

Jez

My Story

My first ever memory was of having my nappy changed. I can still remember the pattern of the black and white fabric I was lying on because it was right near my face. I also remember looking at my Mum and thinking: 'What are you doing down there?' It was as if, for a split second, I had the consciousness of an adult even though I must only have been about one or two.

I am the youngest of three children. We were brought up in a leafy suburb of southwest London. From a young age I had quite severe asthma; during attacks there were moments when I had to fight for every breath. It is a frightening situation: You need to breathe to live, but your body is somehow working against you taking in air efficiently. Because of the severity and danger of what was happening I would be intensely focussed on my next breath; it was like an enforced meditation practice. I was surprisingly calm; panicking would have made a dangerous situation worse. Not that I did anything to be in that calm state; I *had* to be calm – so I was.

A few years before my Mum passed away, she confessed to my wife that she was post-natally depressed for at least a year after having me. She said that, all those years later, she still felt guilty about being unable to show her love for me at that time. Apparently when my Dad came home from work my Mum would sometimes say to him: 'You have to hold the baby – he's been crying and I haven't been able to pick him up all day.' When my wife told me this I was rather relieved because it explained a lot about my psychology: As a baby I obviously did not know what love was, but I felt its absence acutely and I know that this left a deep wound in me, a place of pain and dislocation.

As I grew up and my character developed I became a sensitive, confident and artistic child. I had two great loves: football and drawing. Both these activities were the source of unending joy. I played football before and after school, and in the breaks. When I was indoors I was never far from some paper and a pen, sketching, drawing likenesses of celebrities from photos in the newspaper and copying cartoons from the comics I read. Comics showed me how to place drawings in a series of frames to represent time passing, and how you could make a character talk by adding a speech bubble beside its head. This made characters come alive and opened up the possibility of them having a story created about them. From then on, storytelling became a central part of my artistic life. At primary school the blank exercise books with one side of plain paper opposite a page of lined paper were my favourites: an invitation to write stories on one side and draw on the other.

When anyone asked me: 'What do you want to be when you grow up?' the answer: 'An artist,' came without hesitation. I did not really know what sort of artist, I just knew that life had cast me in that role and there was great joy in playing it out. It was as if all I had to do was follow the inspiration, follow the joy and become what I was meant to be. However, I was aware of two sides to my life: the creative, outgoing character who loved and enjoyed his life and, deep down underneath, the traumatised, damaged side which came from starting out with a mother who was very depressed.

My damaged side was mostly hidden away but occasionally it would show its face and I would be confronted with it. For example, my parents were normally placid, quiet people who generally kept their occasional disagreements behind closed doors. However, there was an alarming period in my early teens when problems in their marriage started to show themselves in the form of explosive arguments. When these rows filled the house, my early trauma was activated and I experienced deep anxiety. (I now know that this came from the feelings that were recorded in my body from babyhood.) At times like this, when the hidden trauma was exposed, it was like an old nemesis saying: 'You don't think you've got rid of me do you? I'm still here, I'm not going anywhere.'

Around this time I began experiencing something that had no relation to my background or my everyday life. I would be cycling by the river Thames and, as I swerved along the twisting path, I would occasionally have experiences that I now call 'Openings'. Physically there was the sensation of golden light in my spine. That light, or energy, had an effect on my brain too: It put my thinking process in neutral and I was released into a state of bliss. During these Openings I could observe my life but there was a distance to it, almost as if it was happening to someone else. Whenever an Opening happened I did my best to make it stay, but it never did.

The Openings showed me that there was another point of view

to the one that society and my parents had taught me, a perspective totally beyond the trauma that I had inside. This was not a belief; it did not come from me *wanting* another viewpoint to make my life better. It just felt like life saying: 'Here, look at this – there's more to this life than the model that's been handed to you.' These Openings continued sporadically into my thirties.

***

After Art School I tried my hand as an editorial illustrator and spent quite a few years with barely any commissions or money coming in. One day I was in the bath in my bedsit when, out of nowhere, a rhyming couplet popped into my head:

> *'To keep warm in the Arctic air,*
> *a polar bear wears polar wear.'*

I had the feeling these words were important so, not wanting to forget them, I rushed out, dripping from the bath, and scribbled them on a piece of paper. Those words were the origins of my first ever picture book, which was published in 1984. I had finally found a use for my writing and drawing skills; I knew what sort of artist I was going to be: a picture book artist. Some picture book artists write, some illustrate; I joined a smaller band of artists who do both. However, it was not until 1992 that I created a book that actually sold well – in fact, it is still selling today. Over the last thirty or so years I have created about 45 picture books and sold over eight million copies.

To write a story you have to create characters, move them around and have them say, feel and do things. The dialogue, characters and plot points all work together, like an encrypted code, to generate and serve the telling of the story. As a reader you do not need to know the code to enjoy the story it is creating; if you drive a car, you do not need to know what is happening under the hood to appreciate the ride. But, like a mechanic, the storyteller needs to know exactly what is going on under the hood. His craft and art bring all the elements together to tell the story in the most engaging, entertaining way.

While my career took off the trauma from my childhood retreated into the background, but I knew that no amount of success could ever take it away. The only real freedom from that pain was in the Openings I had experienced. This left me in what seemed to be an impossible position: I had found a place beyond suffering but I did not know where it was; I had no control over my access to it.

In an effort to understand myself and find the answer to this impossible problem I began a regular practice of observing and recording my experiences, feelings and insights in a journal. I examined my present and my past, laying out the details of my emotional landscape in forensic detail. Then I applied the same inquisitiveness of mind that I used in cracking the code of a story. This boiled the problem down to a series of questions: 'How did the Openings fit with the Personality that seemed to run the rest of my life?' 'What *is* Personality?' 'What is Suffering?' 'Am I the one who has the trauma or the one who has the Opening?' I gained a lot of insight into the workings of my Personality but this did not deliver me from the shadow of the trauma from my childhood.

Around this time a friend gave me a book to read by the Indian guru Bhagwan Shree Rajneesh called 'I am the Gate'. If anyone knew the answers to my questions I thought this charismatic, wise guru would. I began going to his organisation's London centre and engaging with his followers and teachings. Soon I was taking part in a weekly 'encounter group' where I found myself getting in touch with feelings I did not even know I had. It was frightening and exhilarating: I believed that I had found a path that would lead me to the answers I sought. Gradually I immersed myself more and more in the teachings of this guru; I wore the red colours and took on a new name.

When the commune broke up I was still looking for answers and sought out many other teachers, went to lectures and meetings, and read countless books. Although I learned a lot, no one seemed to be able to answer the questions that my Openings had posed.

***

One day several years later I was giving a talk to teachers and librarians to promote my books. Just before I began the talk I started to feel strange: My hands turned icy cold and my heart started racing. It was as if something in me did not want to be where I was, giving that talk, because I did not have the ability to fulfil that role. My mind said: 'Come on, just get on with it, you've done this hundreds of times before,' but the body does not care about what your mind wants. The body just expresses whatever is going on in the only way it can, in the form of physical symptoms and mental stress. Somehow I managed to pull myself together enough to give the talk but I was severely shaken. There were a few episodes like this over the following months; each time I was greatly disturbed. Something was seriously wrong: The primal trauma, which ran like an underground seam through my life, had started to break through and reach the surface.

These episodes began to interfere with me carrying out my job so it was a period of mounting stress. Four months after that first disorientating episode I was driving to the southwest of England with my wife for a holiday, a chance to get some relaxation that would hopefully put right whatever was wrong with me. After about thirty miles I pulled into a service station for some petrol. On the way back to the car my knees buckled beneath me and... the best way I can put it is my whole Personality just fell apart.

This time there was no coming back from it; I could not pull myself together. The centre from which I had previously operated just was not functioning. As you can imagine, this was accompanied by tremendous anxiety. People around me were staring at this grown man, collapsed on the ground, sobbing.

Someone called the paramedics. They had no training to deal with this situation; they did not know what to do except take me to the local hospital to be checked out. The doctor there was the same: I think because I did not have any serious physical problems, he thought I was wasting his time with some kind of panic attack.

We went home and I just hoped that it would stop, but it did not. As the months passed by I found a way to function, to a much lesser degree, in the safety of my own home but only by becoming a virtual recluse. I became very sensitive to stimuli; for example, I could not watch TV because it overloaded my senses. Silence was the only thing I could deal with; the world of people, thought and busyness was beyond my capacity. I used to see people through my window, waiting at bus stops, going to work and think: 'I used to be able to do that.' It was as if I had forgotten how to be me, at least, the 'me' I had been living for forty-odd years.

My personality always had a lot of willpower. That is part of what brought me success in my career, but when it came to the breakdown those qualities meant nothing. I would try to go out in the world, try to be that 'me' who I used to know. The fear all just became worse, so much so that these attempts to break back into my old life took days to recover from.

The months rolled by; my life shrank to a limited existence of trying to sleep, eat and just get through another day. One night, about six months later, the torment intensified and reached a point where I did not know if I could bear it. And then... something happened. In my desperation and exhaustion I somehow let go into the pain; I entered it more fully. This triggered some sort of primal release, and in the middle of all that terrible, writhing emotion... It stopped. A light broke through the dark night; a distance appeared between the pain and me.

I thought that this event would surely mark the end of my suffering but after a day or so the perspective I had glimpsed in that 'Awakening' passed and this left me back in the shell of this broken-down life.

As the years went by I thought maybe that freedom I had glimpsed in the Openings and Awakening was *never* going to be a permanent experience for me; eventually there was a giving up of the hope that it would be. The spiritual hopes and expectations had gone; the only ones left were practical. All I wanted now was to get back into my previous life, the one I had lived before the breakdown in which I could function and operate in the world, do my job and be like other 'normal' people.

By now the extreme cathartic stage of the breakdown had lessened, and I tentatively tried to get back into my life as an author, working on new books and doing promotional events. It was like putting on an old suit; I had been doing that job for 30 years. I knew how to do it, I was good at it, and at least it gave an outlet for my creativity. I did this for a few years, but something felt wrong. I found I was not as at ease in the role as I had once been; I was not really 'in it' the way I had been before.

Over time I felt more and more uncomfortable carrying out that role; I started to feel like a fraud, like I was playing a part that did not suit me any more. This was all I had left, this semblance of a life as it was, and now that was being taken away! I tried to get it back for years but just as with everything else, I had to surrender any idea of having control over it. I can see now that the life I had been trying to force my way back into was the last stand of any identification with Personality. When I let go of that, or rather, when that dropped away, it seemed to be the last straw. It was a death, not the death of the Personality but the death of *identification* with it. That was what I call the Shift, in which the answers to all my questions posed by the Opening were finally revealed to me. These books are my opportunity to share those answers with you.

Prologue

Matthew: It would be useful to start with an overview of the main theme we'll be discussing in these talks and books. Can you summarise it for me?

Jez: Put simply, we enter this world as the experience of Oneness, or Being, but we lose our perception of this as we grow up and become identified with Personality. After that identification, the suffering of Personality overshadows the stillness and love of our natural state. What I'm proposing is that it's possible to return to the experience of this natural state, while being and operating as an adult.

Matthew: It's a pleasing thought, but isn't that just your belief? How do you know it's true?

Jez: I know because it's happened to me. I'm not sharing any beliefs here; I'm simply describing the view from a different perspective to yours. If you asked me if I *believed* there was any money in this box on my desk I'd say: 'No. I don't *believe* there's any money in it, I *know* there is, because I've opened the box and seen it in there.'

Matthew: How can I be certain you know what's in the box? How do I know what you're saying about Oneness has any validity?

Jez: You don't, but you don't need to know it in order to engage with my proposition that it's true. If you do that, it's possible that you might open the box and see for yourself. That's what these talks are about: encouraging you to open the box.

Matthew: There are a lot of big words in your summary. What, for example, do you mean by 'the experience of Oneness'?

Jez: We'll go into what I mean by each of these words in more detail as they arise in future talks but for now I'll give you a shorthand to point to what I mean by the experience of Oneness: Imagine a newborn baby in a state of rest.

Matthew: OK...

Jez: Well, that's it.

Matthew: (Laughs.) Oh! OK, that gives me a vague sense of what you mean.

Jez: That's all you need for now. That feeling you're tuning into when you picture a baby at rest goes much deeper than any concepts we could come up with about it. This is because that feeling arises not just from the memory of being around a baby but also from having once *been* a baby yourself. After all, this is how we all started.

So we come into the world in the experience of Oneness but we need to develop something else that acts like a spacesuit and allows us to operate within the world where there is the appearance of the opposite of Oneness; where there is separation. (Let's call this the 'World of Separation'.) And that something which enables us to operate in this World of Separation is a sense of self. So gradually we become an 'I' and we identify with a name and a body which this 'I' apparently lives inside.

The self is a practical necessity for operating in the World of Separation. But the thing is, the sense of self doesn't remain neutral and purely functional: As we grow up it collects beliefs, opinions and emotions. Gradually it builds into a Personality, an identity based on the things you've done, the places you've gone to and the successes you've achieved. Somewhere along the line suffering and unhappiness enter the picture, then one day you end up as the person you are today, locked into your own particular spacesuit. You've forgotten that, at your centre, you're not this conglomeration of experiences from your past, you're the Beingness that you came into this world with, which always exists 'now'.

Matthew: This is an interesting theory, but aren't these all just abstract, fancy words?

Jez: It's unavoidable that words sometimes start sounding grand and pompous when you discuss this subject – language strains to describe these issues because what we're discussing is beyond the usual reaches of the mind. Having said that, what I'm describing is not some abstract idea or belief. As I said, just sit beside a newborn baby. You can see and feel that potential we all have inside us: the experience of Oneness that we came with. I call this the 'Natural State'.

Matthew: How did this realisation come into your life?

Jez: It began when I was a teenager. I used to experience Openings, breaks in the domination of the Personality's viewpoint.

Matthew: Will you tell me about your experience of Openings? And also, what you were like back then?

Jez: I was a middle-class kid living in the suburbs of London; I have an older sister and brother. My parents were Christians but not particularly devout. It was a fairly happy household but there were some problems in my parent's relationship and some unhappiness in my mum that trickled down into the family.

I had a friend called Erhard who I loved being around. He possessed a confidence and enthusiasm that no one else I knew had, and I think these qualities mirrored aspects of myself that I wasn't always in touch with. Erhard had the unheard-of luxury of owning his own table tennis table. In the summer he would set this up in his small suburban garden and we'd play for hours on end. Our tournaments were an amazing mix of competitiveness, excitement and sharing as we pushed each other to improve our fast-spinning returns.

In between matches we would eat unlimited amounts of ice cream scooped from a selection of huge tubs in his outside freezer cabinet. When it came to food, there was a sense of abundance round Erhard's house that was lacking in my own. Due to my mother's occasional depression, that lack of abundance would sometimes be felt as an absence of joy. Looking back I can see that my hours spent at Erhard's place, where there were no limits on fun, friendship or ice cream, gave me a respite from the influence of my mother's unhappiness.

After exhilarating afternoons spent at Erhard's place I would cycle home by the river Thames and, as I swerved along the twisting paths, I'd occasionally have these experiences, these Openings. Physically I felt them as the sensation of golden light in my spine, but that light or energy had an effect on my brain too: It put my thinking process in neutral and I was released into a state of bliss. I remember that, during these Openings, I could observe my life but there was a distance to it, almost as if it was happening to someone else. Whenever this Opening happened it was like an old friend returning and I did my best to make it stay. Who wouldn't?

Matthew: Did it work?

Jez: No, it never worked. It was almost as if the effort to hold onto it actually caused it to pass. Usually by the time I'd cycled home it was just a memory. But what a beautiful memory!

Matthew: So what was the effect of these Openings in your daily life?

Jez: In my daily life, not much. They couldn't help me pass an exam or chat up girls but in my inner life they were invaluable. They showed me that there was another point of view to the one that society and my parents had taught me.

It wasn't a belief; it didn't come from me *wanting* another viewpoint to make my life better. It just felt like life was saying: 'Here, look at this: there's more to this life than the model that's been handed to you.'

Matthew: I suspect lots of people have experienced something like this in their lives.

Jez: I agree, but the Opening itself is just the beginning; it's what happens next that's the key factor. The thing is, even if you've had such a shift in perception like this, the pull of the Personality's viewpoint is so strong, so habituated, that the experience of the Opening can be repressed and pushed into the subconscious. Many people forget they even have them.

Matthew: Why do you think that is?

Jez: The Personality has a function of self-preservation: It's programmed to maintain its sense of absolute authority. These sorts of experiences undermine the ultimate sovereignty of the Personality and so they are dangerous to it. By being consigned to the subconscious they're no longer a threat.

Matthew: But this isn't what happened in your case?

Jez: No, the Openings started when I was quite young; my Personality hadn't fully developed yet. Perhaps that's why I had no resistance to them. I welcomed them but, like I said, that didn't make them stay. Afterwards I just returned to the everyday trials and tribulations of being a teenager.

Matthew: You didn't tell anyone about them?

Jez: No. It's odd really: You'd think when something so wonderful happens that I'd have wanted to share it with my family or friends. But it was a secret I kept to myself; it was between life and me.

Matthew: Did the Openings continue?

Jez: Yes, intermittently. I still had them in my twenties but they'd changed by then. They'd become more instructive; they were like lessons, understandings of my true nature. My Personality was well formed by then; I'd had my share of suffering, mostly in the form of periods of depression, so I needed those lessons.

Matthew: Was this related to your mother's depressions?

Jez: It's not hard to see the link, is it? My basic character was very positive: I always felt that those negative moods weren't mine; I wasn't born with them in my makeup. They were learnt. The Openings were like a light shining, guiding me back to my original nature. I don't want to give the impression that they were mystical, divine events though.

Matthew: No religious figures appeared before you?

Jez: (Laughs.) No, it was much more mundane than that: It happened when cycling, when sitting by the Thames, before an exam, lying in a field near my parent's house. One was even triggered by the gentle voice of an Indian lady at the till in a department store. In some ways the Openings felt strangely ordinary to me because what I experienced in them seemed to be something that, deep inside, I'd always known. But they were extraordinary in so far as that they didn't happen that often.

Whatever the Openings were, wherever they came from, I knew that I trusted them above all else: above my parents, teachers or any religious authority. The only thing that bothered me about them was that they always went away. I couldn't understand why, after such enlightened certainty, I was always returned to the confusion and occasional suffering of my everyday life. It became my quest to discover both what the Openings meant, and why they always passed, leaving me without their ongoing guidance.

This quest is common to many people who have such experiences; something is awakened, a distant memory of their true nature. It kick-starts an enquiry into the nature of their identity by raising the questions: 'Who am I?' and 'Am I just the product of the family and society I was born into and their beliefs systems, or am I something more, something which existed before all of that was downloaded into me?' When this quest is activated, rather than being pushed down into the subconscious, the experience of an Opening is actively held onto as a beacon to shine light on the way back to who we really are. That's certainly how it's been for me.

Matthew: Can talking to someone who knows about this lead to the same effect as having such a transcendent experience?

Jez: It's possible. It depends on many factors. A lot of it is down to the readiness of the person listening. Most people's identification with Personality is so absolute, and so well defended that even to consider what I'm saying as having any truth would be preposterous. Many readers will have already discarded this book as airy-fairy twaddle after the opening paragraphs.

Matthew: Maybe it is airy-fairy twaddle! Perhaps the Openings are just the creations of your rich imagination.

Jez: That is of course a possibility. All these words could be just the mad ramblings of a deluded Personality, grasping at beliefs to stave off unhappiness. But maybe they're not! The question is, does the listener have enough curiosity, openness and willingness to carry on into this enquiry to find out?

When some people come across a new idea that challenges their worldview they retreat into a tight, rigid scepticism. There are so many crazy minds out there with equally crazy theories that, quite understandably, this has become a default setting for many.

Matthew: But not everyone's like that.

Jez: No. Some people, who are perhaps looking for answers beyond what's generally accepted in society, are more open: They respond with a willingness to believe what's being presented. As far as finding out what's true is concerned, both approaches miss, the first because it comes from a pre-existing decision to refuse what's being presented. The perspective being offered is simply used to further entrench and bolster up beliefs that are already held. The second response of willingness to believe seems more positive because there's openness behind it, but still nothing useful can come from it.

Matthew: Why not?

Jez: Because nothing useful is gained from blindly believing anything. Even if what's presented is truly valuable and insightful, a belief in it simply keeps the understanding of it at an intellectual or emotional level. For a new perspective to be useful an understanding of it has to take root in your own experience; believing in something simply keeps that possibility at bay. There's a quote from Nietzsche on this:

> *There are two different types of people in the world: Those who want to know, and those who want to believe.*

What I'm doing here is telling a story. Not just any story, it's a story about a really big subject: It's the story of you, the story of me, the story of everyone. Like I said earlier, you don't know if this story is true or not but you don't have to believe a story is true to get something out of it. When you watch a film you know it's not 'true', you know it's not 'real life'. It's just a narrative concocted by writers and acted out by actors, but that doesn't mean it can't affect you in all sorts of ways. Maybe it moves you, thrills you; perhaps the subject matter reflects something you're dealing with in your own life and it helps you think about it in a whole new way. The fact that you watch a film knowing it's *just* a story doesn't stop any of that engagement; you engage *despite* the fact that no belief is invested in it being true. So I'm not asking you to believe this story is true either; without belief you can still get a lot from it. If you're ready to hear this argument, and find out if it *is* true, then this enquiry could change your whole life in ways that you couldn't even imagine right now.

Matthew: OK, so if I've got this right, you're not asking me to believe anything you say is true but... just to be open to it?

Jez: Yes, it's possible to practice what one might call 'open-minded scepticism'. By this I mean being open-minded enough to be available to the possibility of encountering something beyond what you know, and finding, in your experience, it is true. And sceptical enough not to fall into the trap of belief, so that you test every argument you hear against your own experience. Aristotle said:

> *It is the mark of an educated mind to be able to entertain a thought without accepting it.*

To take that assertion and run with it: You might *not* accept a thought that your mind has 'entertained', but then again, you might also find that you *do* accept it. This would happen not through belief, but because you find it to be true in your own experience. If that were not the case, then you would reject it.

Matthew: I'm generally sceptical about this sort of thing but, having observed how you live and work, I'm interested to find out more about what's behind your different way of Being. So I'm open to the possibility that what you've learned about this could be true.

Jez: That's all you need, and then something of what I'm saying might reach you, not just on an intellectual level, but an energetic level. Sometimes we've talked about this subject and your mind has been in its normal busy mode, jumping erratically from subject to subject...

Matthew: That sounds like me!

Jez: ...But then I've said something in the course of our discussion and it suddenly changed your state dramatically. It's as if your mind had been tripped up; you experienced what I call the 'Stillness'.

Matthew: I remember feeling really peaceful – not like my normal self at all! (Laughs.)

Jez: It was almost like another 'you' had arrived. 'Normal' Matthew has a very busy mind that darts from one subject to another all day long. This Matthew was like sitting by a waterfall; there was space and depth in him. It was lovely to be around.

Matthew: So which is the real me?

Jez: I would say that both are aspects of you, but one aspect is informed by Being, the other by Personality. One has the peace of the infinite in it, and the other can be overcome by busyness and compulsive thinking.

Matthew: As you said, it's like there are two different versions of me.

Jez: Yes, it all depends who's running the show. In that Stillness, Being is king. In the Personality the mind is king and all of its thoughts, beliefs and emotions, which are mostly the product of your past, are in control of your life. When you truly experience the present you realise that you are so much more than the sum of your past.

Matthew: So can you learn to have access to that?

Jez: Our minds are used to the process of learning as a gradual assimilation of information until we possess knowledge. Naturally we apply this same model of learning to the 'goal' of finding this way out of our suffering. But this isn't like taking a course in accountancy or plumbing: There are no progressive steps; liberation can't be learned. How can you learn to be what you already are? If anything, you have to *unlearn* all that you think you are, all that you've taken to be you, which has covered up your innate understanding of this.

So, although this is an enquiry, it's not a process of learning; it's actually about uncovering, or remembering. Whatever I say in these talks isn't material that you need to learn – that's not what it's for.

*Matthew: So what **is** it for?*

Jez: It's to jog your memory, to penetrate the layers of mist that have shrouded your perception. To cut though the beliefs, thought patterns and emotions which, without your knowing, rob you of the attributes of the Natural State.

We'll start by covering a few basic principles and concepts that underpin this whole enquiry, and by examining exactly what I mean by the Natural State. Then we'll look at how we lose it, why we lose it and what replaces it. In the second book, *The Infinite Journey*, we'll discuss how it's possible to remember what, deep inside, you have always known.

BEGINNINGS

1

ONENESS

Before energy becomes something, it starts out
as the undivided, potential energy of everything

'Each one of us is part of the soul of the universe.' – Plotinus

Jez: When talking about huge metaphysical subjects, language quickly becomes less precise. It's easy to describe your hair fairly accurately as being black and curly, but when we start using words like 'Oneness', 'Being', 'love' or 'energy', meanings become more elastic. What this means practically is that the vocabulary I use in these discussions may have slightly different connotations and meanings for you. In order to communicate clearly it's necessary to agree on what exactly *I* mean by the use of such words in the context of this enquiry.

Matthew: Would it help, as these sorts of words crop up, if I look up the dictionary definition?

Jez: That will be a good starting point, then I'll apply that definition and refine it so you know exactly what I'm trying to express in the context in which I'm using it. The more we talk about the subjects, the more my interpretation of these words will become clear.

Matthew: You've suggested that most of our problems come about because of identification with our Personality. So let's start off with what you mean by the word Personality? Do you mean the ego?

Jez: A lot of connotations have become attached to the word 'ego', not least the idea that the ego is somehow bad or negative. I use the word 'Personality' because it's more neutral.

Matthew: OK, so according to you, what is the Personality?

Jez: The Personality is an idea of identity constructed of many aspects such as beliefs, desires and thought; its foundations are laid down in childhood and carried throughout life. We'll cover all of these aspects individually, but we have to set things up properly before we can do that.

Matthew: I'm quite impatient to get to the details of what Personality is...

Jez: The mind always wants to race ahead, to be anywhere but right here now. Like I said earlier, what I'm doing here is telling the story of Personality, the story of 'you'. An epic story such as this has many twists and turns; its overall arc is simple, but the details are intricate. My job is to tell this story as clearly as possible in manageable stages, revealing the plot points in the right order and releasing information at the right time. To make any sense of this story you'll need to hear it in the order it's told. If you jump in somewhere in the middle it will create confusion: The story won't make any sense to you because you won't have the set-up information you'll need to be able to follow it.

So we have to start by examining what existed *before* the Personality. That is: Where does the Personality come from? I don't mean childhood, I mean before that.

Matthew: For there to be a Personality there has to be a person.

Jez: Right, but let's keep going back: A person starts out as a baby, but where does the baby come from? I know it sounds like an obvious question, but bear with me.

Matthew: You mean the parents?

Jez: Yes, the baby is formed from the father's sperm, which comes from his testes, and the mother's egg, from her ovaries, her hormones, blood, nutrients etcetera. But if we go back another level, what's all this biological matter made from?

Matthew: Once you start looking under the microscope scientists talk about everything being made of atoms.

Jez: Yes, but it doesn't stop there; they also talk about dark matter, neutrinos and a more general term: energy. It seems the further scientists go into the question of what the universe is made of, the more they discover that they don't really know. All that happens is they keep inventing names for more stuff they don't understand.

Scientist are driven by an impulse to decode, pin down and understand life. It's almost as if, by categorising and naming it, they believe they can remove a bit more of the mystery of the unknown, and this makes us feel safer. 'Dark matter' can be identified and given a science fiction-sounding name, but that doesn't mean it can be understood. In the end, it's like chasing the horizon; the answer is always just beyond reach, but searching for it distracts us from the scary fact that we don't really know what the hell is going on, that it's all a mystery. Socrates said:

> *The only true wisdom is in knowing you know nothing.*

T.S. Eliot put it another way:

> *All our knowledge brings us nearer to our ignorance.*

Matthew: So we've come to a dead end?

Jez: As far as science is concerned, yes, but science isn't the only approach that man's mind can make to this question of where we come from. In this enquiry we lean towards a metaphysical approach. So we need to be clear exactly what 'metaphysics' is.

Matthew: I did a bit of Ancient Greek at school. Metaphysics is a combination of two words: 'Meta', meaning 'over and beyond', and 'Physics', 'the study of matter and energy'.

Jez: I'm sure most scientists would hate the proposition that the view we're looking from here is 'over and beyond' a scientific approach, but we can say it's certainly a very *different* approach. Let's see how the dictionary defines metaphysics...

Matthew: It says: 'A branch of philosophy investigating the fundamental nature of being.'

Jez: That's an accurate description of what we're getting into: 'The fundamental nature of Being.' I'm proposing that our fundamental nature of Being is not this life full of constant thought, emotion and suffering – it's the Stillness of the Natural State which we come into this world as.

Matthew: OK, so we're discussing where the baby comes from, in a metaphysical sense, how it comes into Being?

Jez: A metaphysical approach would agree with the scientists on the use of one word: 'Energy'. You can use all sorts of names like atoms, neutrinos and dark matter but an umbrella term for all of that would be 'energy'. How does the dictionary define energy?

Matthew: It says here: 'Matter in movement.' It makes me think of a rock falling down a mountain...

Jez: Yes, but there's another application of that definition, which is that energy is moving from one *form*, one state to another.

Matthew: You mean like water turning into steam?

Jez: Yes. That's energy (matter in the form of water) changing into matter of a different form (steam). But what about energy that hasn't taken form yet?

Matthew: What do you mean?

Jez: At one point, there isn't a baby; then there is a baby.

Matthew: So you're talking about energy in an unmanifested form?

Jez: Exactly, it exists as a potential to *be* something. At one point there's this potential, and then there's the manifestation of a physical embryo. Before that energy becomes something, it starts out as this undivided, potential energy. And because it's undivided, a more metaphysical word for describing that potential is 'Oneness.'

If you accept this metaphysical interpretation, then you can see it's logical to say that this Oneness is where everything comes from; it all arises from the same source. We can also call that the 'Absolute Level.'

Matthew: I presume this is what it means when you hear the phrase: 'We are all One' – they're talking about the Absolute Level.

Jez: Yes, it's a fairly new concept in mainstream culture. I think it really broke into mankind's consciousness in the 1950s with the discovery of psychedelic drugs. Following on from this you can find all sorts of oblique references to Oneness in music.

Matthew: There's that Joni Mitchell song 'Woodstock' with the line: 'We are stardust.'

Jez: Science has proved the hippies right: We're all part of the universe, different forms built from the same building blocks of life – carbon, nitrogen, oxygen, iron. John Lennon also pointed to this in the song 'I Am the Walrus' with the lyric:

I am he
As you are he
As you are me
And we are all together.

Matthew: It's quite poetic isn't it?

Jez: Definitely. You can see that, as we're stretching words beyond their capabilities to describe this subject, another form of language is creeping in; a more poetic form. When you're trying to express the inexpressible, poetry has a magical ability to point more eloquently in the direction of what is being described.

The word 'Oneness' is quite poetic in a way. It's not a scientific word, but I think you understand what I mean when I use it. 'Oneness' is one of those 'spiritual' words that start to make sense if you've had any experiences of life beyond Personality. It's what religiously minded people would call God, but the word 'Oneness' is beautifully free of any religious associations.

In 1954 Aldous Huxley wrote an essay about a transcendent experience that was stimulated by a mescaline trip. He said that the drug opened up the 'doors of perception'. (This phrase, previously used by William Blake, is where the band The Doors got their name.) You don't have to take drugs to glimpse through that door; that viewpoint of Oneness can be available without chemical stimulation. But we're getting ahead of ourselves. The point here is that when 'the doors of perception' are open, we glimpse a different reality; we perceive another level of existence: the Absolute Level.

Matthew: People often talk of these kind of experiences as being the outcome of reaching higher level of consciousness.

Jez: Yes, I wouldn't call it higher but it's certainly different. Consciousness is another one of those big words; we'll cover it in a later talk.

Matthew: When people try to describe psychedelic trips, religious experiences and Openings, you often hear another word: 'Love'.

Jez: Yes, we can't avoid the 'L' word. It's not a word that most scientists would use but... I'm not a scientist.

Matthew: No, but you seem apprehensive about using the word 'love'. Why is that?

Jez: There's a lovely quote from Rumi which answers that:

> *However much we describe and explain love,*
> *When we fall in love,*
> *We are ashamed of our words.*

Love is such a big word, it's come to have all sorts of sentimental meanings; it's been so devalued there's a danger that using it in this context will make what I'm saying sound trite. But there's no substitute for it so I can't do anything about that; I have to use the word in our vocabulary which, despite its limitations, comes closest to pointing in the direction of this. We'll talk later about what the word 'love' has come to mean in the world of man, but here I'll make a distinction from that and try to define the way I'm using it in relation to Oneness.

Matthew: OK.

Jez: Love, with a capital 'L', is what a human feels when they perceive Oneness. The more Oneness is perceived, the more Love is felt. This can't be proved, but it can be known.

Matthew: Oneness is an attractive concept: It sounds so poetic and appealing.

Jez: The question is: *Is* it just an attractive concept that our minds can entertain intellectually, or is it the truth at the core of human experience? A truth that can be known and lived consciously, which has far-reaching outcomes in the life of the knower? Can the wave remember that it's just a part of the ocean, even as it's rolling around on the surface looking very impressive and powerful?

Matthew: You're saying that it can.

Jez: I am, but we're getting ahead of the story; we're still in the set-up.

Matthew: It feels like we've come a long way from the question: 'What is Personality?'

Jez: Yes, but now we've discussed Oneness and introduced the subject of the Absolute Level we can start moving towards it. For now, just remember that whenever I use the words Love, Consciousness, or Oneness I'm referring to the Absolute Level.

2

DUALITY

When Oneness manifests as Two-ness

'Love is the bridge between you and everything.' – Rumi

Matthew: Another term for Oneness is 'Non–Duality', isn't it?

Jez: Yes, meaning the non-separated, non-divided.

Matthew: So we'd better define the word 'Duality'...

Jez: Duality is when Oneness becomes 'Two-ness'; it refers to all appearance, all manifestation.

Matthew: You mean form, objects... stuff? (Laughs.)

Jez: That's right. When Oneness expresses its potentiality, the 'everything' of Oneness becomes the 'something' of manifestation: you, me, this glass of water... Everything.

We've discussed the Absolute Level, which refers to the essential Oneness of all things; when we talk about Duality we're referring to the 'Relative Level', in which things relate *to* each other: That glass is in front of me, I am slightly taller than you, the moon is smaller than the earth etcetera.

Going back to the definition of energy as 'matter in movement', the Relative Level refers to that potential energy of Oneness manifesting as physical matter. It has 'moved' from the formless to form.

Matthew: And once it's manifested, that energy keeps moving. At school we learned about something called the 'kinetic theory of matter.' It says: 'All matter is made of atoms and molecules that are constantly moving.'

Jez: As we said in the last talk, molecules can also *change* form: When heat is applied they expand; if I were to pour boiling water into this glass it would probably shatter.

Matthew: That expansion happens because the atoms in the glass vibrate faster and the space between them increases.

Jez: But I'm not just talking about size... Once upon a time the glass was just sand, and that sand was once a rock; and so on, leading all the way back to the Absolute Level of potentiality, from where that rock manifested.

Matthew: So anything you can see – mountains, clouds, trees, cows – that's all Duality, all the Relative Level.

Jez: Yes, but it's wider than that: It includes sound waves, light, smells as well as lots of things we can't perceive. When the Oneness of potentiality has manifested, in any form whatsoever, that's the Relative Level.

Matthew: So if everything we see is the Relative Level, that includes us human beings who are seeing it...

Jez: Yes, we're observing this Relative Level, identifying it and discussing it, but this apparatus, this body, this brain is of course all part of the Relative Level as well.

Matthew: So the Absolute Level is discussing itself, through the Relative Level of our bodies and minds.

Jez: Exactly.

Matthew: You talked about the Absolute Level using the word Love; seeing as the Relative Level arises from the Absolute Level, are you saying that everything is a manifestation of Love?

Jez: Yes, in this story I'm relating, 'All is Made of Love.'

Matthew: So by association, as part of the Relative Level, we too are made of Love?

Jez: If you accept the notion that 'All is Made of Love', then you have to take on board that human beings are made of Love too; or you might say: We *are* Love. It would be pretty weird if we were an exception, if all manifestation in the Relative Level was made of Love, except human beings!

Matthew: (Laughs.) As if we were somehow made of... the absence of Love.

Jez: In fact we are the *presence* of Love, literally, the embodiment of Love.

Matthew: This all sounds very nice but, playing devil's advocate, how can we be the embodiment of Love when there's obviously so much violence in human beings? What I mean is, if this story you're telling is true, how can there be wars, for example?

Jez: When I say 'All is Made of Love' I'm talking about the Absolute Level, the core of who we are, what we're made of. Hatred is a psychological manifestation that arises in the Relative Level, in the emotional life of human beings.

As we know, in the Relative Level, Duality gets to play itself out; Oneness takes on all sorts of disguises. Hatred, just like grief or fear, is something that can take root in Personality. The Personality is a manifestation that arises in the Relative Level; but again, we're getting ahead of ourselves. We'll go into hatred and its origins in detail once we've defined what Personality is. All of this is leading us to answering that fundamental question.

Matthew: When you say 'We are Love,' I don't really understand how or why this is true, but I've always felt it is.

Jez: This can be felt and known by the human heart but it can't be measured or scientifically proven. Love will never be isolated under a microscope in a laboratory!

Matthew: No, but in the last discussion we talked about how people on psychedelic trips often describe experiencing this Love you're talking about.

Jez: That's why such experiences are called transcendent: because they transcend the Relative Level and allow at least a passing recognition of the Oneness in all things, which is the Absolute Level. In that recognition of Oneness, Love is felt. Love is the feeling and perception of Oneness.

Matthew: What do you mean?

Jez: Let's take Love in the form of relationship as an example. If you're really close to someone, you begin to feel this overwhelming Love; it's what all Love poetry is about. There comes a point when Love is so strong you transcend the Personality; the lovers disappear and only Love remains. That's an experience of two lovers, disappearing into Oneness.

As we've noted in the case of psychedelic trips, this can be experienced not just through bonding with fellow humans but also with the manifest world, by just looking at reality manifesting around you, for example as a field of wheat or a beautiful sunset.

Matthew: Are you advocating the use of psychedelic drugs?

Jez: No. I have nothing against their use, but they've never appealed to me. It's a bit like gatecrashing into heaven: You know you're going to get thrown out of the party when the drugs wear off. I was always more interested in arriving there without the use of drugs, probably because that was my early experiences of it in the Openings. What I'm saying is, if what I've described really is our Natural State then we shouldn't need foreign chemicals in the brain to induce it or to remain in it.

Matthew: You could argue that those chemicals – LSD, mushrooms, whatever – are natural too.

Jez: Of course, they are all part of the Oneness – how could they not be? But it seems that we're born with the capacity for our own perception of this naturally, without the need of foreign chemical stimulation to the brain. That's what I mean by 'natural'. Taking anything that isn't already part of our bodily equipment to induce this can lead to dependency and addiction, both of which are products of the Personality, not the Natural State in which we enter this life.

My experience is that if there's openness, anything can stimulate an experience of 'All is Made of Love'. There's a story of the Indian mystic Ramakrishna falling into a religious trance after watching a flock of swans flying in front of a bank of grey clouds.

Matthew: But it doesn't have to be as poetic as that, does it? You said you had an Opening just listening to a woman's voice in a department store...

Jez: Yes, that recognition of Oneness is always potentially available; the circumstances are just the excuse. Another Indian mystic, the poet Kabir, said:

'Wherever you are is the entry point.'

For me it used to be cycling by the river, or hearing a certain tone in a voice; you wouldn't normally ascribe such things to being the cause of what some people would call 'religious experiences'.

Matthew: People who haven't had such experiences might find the idea that 'All is Made of Love' simplistic, unscientific or perhaps even naïve.

Jez: I'm sure you're right, but as I've said before, there's a very direct way to experience what I'm talking about which anyone with friends or family who've recently become parents can have access to: Go and sit with a newborn baby that's at rest. They are manifesting that Love I'm talking about without filter; there's no mind yet, no emotions, no hatred or fear so there's nothing to obscure that Love. To use a religious term, newborn babies are fresh from heaven; that's why it's so lovely to be around them.

Did you know that the first organ that grows is the human heart? I think that says it all: The heart is the centre of Love in a human being. It's like a portal, a bridge that spans Duality, from the Relative, physical Level to the Absolute Level.

3

THE ABSOLUTE & THE RELATIVE

The interplay of two levels of reality

'There is another world, but it is in this one.' – W.B. Yeats

Jez: From the viewpoint of Non-Duality we're all made of Love, we are One, and yet as sentient beings we experience the appearance of separation. You're in that body, I'm in this one, and this feels very real to the self.

Matthew: It's confusing; how can both be right?

Jez: I know; how can two apparently opposite things be true at the same time? It seems to make no sense whatsoever.

Matthew: This isn't something we often encounter in everyday life is it? Usually it's either 'This is true', or 'That's true' – never both!

Jez: That's because in normal life we're focussing on the World of Separation – the Relative Level – and here we're discussing metaphysics and the Absolute Level. But you *can* see this phenomenon in the world: The metaphor of the wave and the ocean is often used to illustrate this.

Matthew: You mean how can a wave be both a wave and the ocean at the same time?

Jez: Yes, how can one thing be another thing at the same time? It's illogical. The wave looks separate from the ocean but in fact it's just the ocean in a particular form: the form of a wave. Which interpretation is true? They're both true. It all comes down to which perspective you're looking from: Is it the perspective of the wave or the ocean?

So to understand how we can be both One and separate at the same time, we have to realise there are different perspectives involved. When it comes to human life we have to take into account the fact that essentially, human beings are the interplay between two perspectives or, you could say, two realities. 'Reality' might not be the right word but it's the closest I've got.

Matthew: So what do you actually mean by these 'two realities'?

Jez: The simplest way to explain it is if we go back to where we began this enquiry: Remember we talked about the baby in the Natural State of Love? That state is a reality for the baby, it's not an abstract theory held in her brain. It's who she is. It's who we all are. If you try

44

to describe that state, words become inadequate. Perhaps the best we can do is to define *that* 'reality' as Oneness, Being or Love. All of that is summed up by the umbrella term: 'the Absolute Level'.

Matthew: But it's not really a Level, is it?

Jez: You're right, the 'Absolute' is the ground in which everything appears, including something called 'Levels', so technically the phrase is incorrect. But go with me on this: In order for us to be able to discuss this metaphysical subject, and to aid comprehension of the concepts I'm going to share with you, that phrase will be helpful.

Matthew: So it's just a concept you're going to share with me?

Jez: That's a loaded question! Yes, it's *just* a concept; but why use the word 'just?' Our talks are littered with concepts that I'm putting to you. What's wrong with concepts?

Matthew: I suppose I have this idea that concepts aren't the truth.

Jez: Oh no! (Laughs.) Now you've introduced another contentious word: Truth!

Matthew: I presume we're trying to get to the truth in these discussions?

Jez: Yes, let's agree that we're trying to get to something called 'the truth'. (We'll go into what I actually mean by the word 'truth' in a later talk). So you had the idea that concepts aren't the truth; I think we need to look up a definition of the word 'concept'.

Matthew: The definition here says: 'An abstract idea representing the fundamental characteristics of what it represents.'

Jez: Perfect, that's nice and clear. So you can see from this definition that you're absolutely correct: Concepts *aren't* the truth. What I'm going to share with you about this subject is not the truth, it's 'just' an attempt to *point* to the truth using abstract ideas. (In this case the idea of levels of reality.)

The thing is, through Being, humans have the ability to perceive the Absolute Level. Through our senses we can feel the Stillness, the peace, the joy – whatever form you perceive it in. But when it comes to thinking about and understanding the Absolute Level, our equipment falls short. Our brains have the ability to contain and understand what we perceive in the Relative Level, but they can't 'contain' the Absolute Level. It's a bit like looking directly into the sun. Our eyes are not built to do that, it's too much for them.

The fact that our brains can't fully 'contain' the Absolute is reflected in our inability to speak about it. Language can't accurately describe the Absolute Level but, using concepts, analogies and metaphors, it can point in its direction. That's the best we can do. Going back to our sun analogy; you can't look directly at the sun but you can look at it one step removed, as a reflection in a mirror or a body of water. The reflection isn't the sun, but it's a representation of it.

So the teacher employs concepts to point to life beyond Personality, because that's all he's got to use. There's a danger though that you take the concepts very literally and mistake the reflection for the real thing. So every now and then I have to remind you that the concepts I use are just thought formations trying to point to something beyond the scope of language. The concept is not the subject; it's a reflection of the subject.

Unless we're going to just sit in silence together, we only have words and concepts to point to Being and Oneness; that's the game we're playing. It's like trying to catch the sky in a butterfly net. If we agree on the language and definitions we're using, even pointing to 'the truth' can be a very powerful means of communicating it.

Matthew: It seems ironic to be using thought to point towards something that's beyond thought.

Jez: Yes, to point to what the Zen people call 'no mind,' or 'empty mind' by *using* the mind is kind of absurd. Imagine a Zen monk in a temple who spends his time immersed in 'no mind'. Then a visitor knocks on the temple door and asks: 'What's going on in this temple? What's the secret hidden inside these walls?' The Zen monk might take the visitor on as his student and assume the role of a teacher. Then he'll have to use thoughts to communicate what he knows of the Absolute Level because that's the only language the student will understand. Why? Because the visitor has forgotten the Natural State he knew as a baby, and like everyone else, has become located primarily in his mind.

The monk has remembered his original state of Being, which, when lived as an adult, spans the Absolute Level *and* the Relative Level, where thought arises. So the monk is able to use thoughts to try to communicate with the student and remind him what exists beyond thought. He will use mind to express no-mind. That's what all Zen koans do: They are riddles, using words to express the wordless. Some Zen koans have even become well known in mainstream society. The most famous is:

What's the sound of one hand clapping?

Matthew: It does kind of throw you beyond the mind doesn't it?

Jez: Yes, because the mind can't make sense of it. It speaks of a place beyond the mind's logic. Zen koans like this can have a strong effect, but only on someone who's ready and willing to penetrate their real meaning. Otherwise they become just wordplay, or gibberish.

Matthew: This is turning into a bit of a detour.

Jez: That's why I call these talks 'travelling conversations': You never know where they're going to lead you, but in the end, wherever that is can become another reflection back to the topic we're discussing. But to get *back* on topic, do you understand what I mean when I use the phrase 'the Absolute Level'?

Matthew: Yes, the name seems appropriate because all the words you ascribe to it – Love, Oneness, Being etcetera – we think of as being infinite.

Jez: OK, so this Absolute Level, the formless ground of everything, manifests as the phenomenal world, where there appears to be a *different* reality, in which there's time, space and form – where there appears to be a me and a you.

Matthew: I can't argue with that.

Jez: If you did, it would be a 'you' arguing so, in effect, you'd be proving my point! So that world, where there's appearance, form and separation, is the 'Relative Level'.

Matthew: So these are the two realities you're referring to: the Absolute and Relative Levels?

Jez: Actually, there's only the Absolute Level; what we mean by the Relative Level simply arises within that. But from the human perspective, and for the purposes of human beings talking about this subject, there appears to be these two levels, two realities, and the point is our existence as human beings spans both of them.

Matthew: What does that mean?

Jez: It means that, on the Absolute Level, we are Oneness, but on the Relative Level we appear as a person, an 'I' that's separate from the world 'out there'.

Matthew: So this is what you mean by two apparently opposite things being true at the same time: We're all essentially One, yet you and I are apparently two?

Jez: Yes. To express the conundrum mathematically: How can two equal one?

Matthew: It's impossible, isn't it?

Jez: Certainly to a mathematician! (Both laugh.)

Matthew: And to most people I should think!

Jez: Probably, but it's not a conundrum to life; it's just the way life does its thing! This is what we're built to do, to live as – and in – the Relative expression of the Absolute.

Matthew: We're part of the Two, which arises from the One.

Jez: Exactly. This is what we've forgotten: We've learned to focus on the 'Two', and we've lost our perception of the One. This enquiry is all about realising that we're locked into the perception of the wave and remembering the perspective of the ocean.

Matthew: The way you've explained these two realities makes it seem quite obvious; why do you think this isn't more widely known?

Jez: Because part of that manifestation of the Relative Level is man's mind and, as I said, man's mind is used to seeing logical divisions of opposites in the World of Separation: black/white, up/down, day and night. Man's mind knows only 'either/or', so it says: 'How can two opposing things be true at the same time? It's impossible: Either one is right or the other.'

We didn't always operate like this: Before we learned to divide the world in this way, there was a time when we perceived and lived only that Oneness that's the mother of all Duality; we didn't live as this idea of separation. Back then, as babies in the Natural State, we didn't have minds to conceptualise Oneness like we do now, we just lived it. So although to adults, we appeared to be separate beings, to us we were just part of the everything that was arising. So there's no division between the Absolute and Relative: They appear as both at the same time.

However, the longer we live in the world, the more we attune to the Relative Level, the more our developing minds learn to name it and then everything starts to become separate. Eventually we arrive at the decisive moment when *we* apparently become separate too. This is the moment when we identify as the self. From then on, through the development of the Personality, we're attuned mostly to the Relative Level, because what's real to the Personality is mind, matter, thought and logic. This means we experience a division, a dissonance, between the Absolute and Relative Levels in us, because we're operating as if there's only the Relative Level.

We pay a heavy price for this: Because we've forgotten that we are One, that we are Love, we suffer the illusion of thinking that we are separate. This manifests as neurosis, worry, emotional states, depression, addiction, self-hatred etcetera. This kind of Suffering, with a capital 'S', follows the Personality like a shadow. We'll look at Suffering in more detail later.

Matthew: Unless we have some sort of Opening – then we suddenly have an experience beyond the Relative.

Jez: Yes, then a more 'spiritual' life can sometimes begin, which recognises there's something more, beyond this rational, physical world of things and names. It's as if we start to remember the Absolute that lies behind the Relative. This can actually intensify the

Suffering and give it a more 'spiritual' dimension.

Matthew: What do you mean?

Jez: Quite understandably, the Suffering of the person becomes focussed on the loss of the stillness, peace and clarity of the Opening, and the quest of how to find it again. So although the Absolute has been experienced in the Relative Level, there's still a disharmony between them, because the Absolute perception is lost once the Opening has passed.

Matthew: But you're suggesting there's a way to live in which what is found in the Opening becomes available all the time.

Jez: Yes, then the dissonance between the Absolute and Relative Levels in human life, which causes all the Suffering of the Personality, disappears. Then we return to a synthesis of the Absolute and the Relative, just as we knew as babies in the Natural State.

This understanding of the Relative and Absolute Realities is a key that explains a lot of confusion which can crop us in this enquiry, because along the way many subjects arise in which opposite accounts are given of the same subject. This is because each side is looking from a different perspective, from a different reality, both of which can be true.

THE
NATURAL
STATE

4

OUR ORIGINAL RELATIONSHIP TO LIFE

Before we relate to any human, our primary relationship is with life itself

'I am nourished by the great mother.' – Lao Tzu

Jez: Now that we've talked about Duality we can look more closely at the human manifestation of it in the form of a baby. As I've said before, by looking at a newborn baby we can see clearly how we all begin this life before the Relative Level starts to influence us and develop our Personality. How does Oneness look, in the form of a baby, when it's still untouched by the world of man, by family, society and culture?

You can see how this is a logical, even scientific approach to the question of who we are. We're examining the evidence under a microscope to answer the question: 'What is our essence as human beings?'

Matthew: So, according to you, what's the answer?

Jez: I'm proposing it can be summed up under two headings: our Original Relationship to Life and our state of Being. Our Relationship to Life is the set up and dynamics of how humans exist in the world; our state of Being is how those dynamics actually manifest in the life of a baby.

Matthew: You're going to have to explain that a bit more.

Jez: Let's start with the Original Relationship to Life. Relationship requires Duality, because to have relationship you need two things which can relate to each other. There's no such thing as relationship in the Absolute Level, there's only Oneness; but in the Relative Level of manifestation, things are different. A baby is Oneness manifesting in the Relative Level, but it's not just *appearing* within the World of Separation – it's also *interacting* with it. The baby splashes water in the bath and the water makes the baby wet. That means there's a relationship between the baby and the water.

Duality is manifesting as the subject (the baby) and the object (the water). Between these two there can be all sorts of activity: The water can be seen, felt, moved, tasted etcetera. So in the World of Separation, there's the arising of an apparent difference between the splasher and the splashed, the seer and the seen, the experiencer and the experienced.

Matthew: OK, so to summarise, in the Relative Level there's Duality, and from that arises relationship...

Jez: Exactly. So having set that up, I'll explain what I mean by our Original Relationship to Life. This is one of those subjects that's so obvious, it's difficult to describe. It's like asking someone: 'How do you breathe?' It's a difficult question to answer. We all know how to breathe, but the knowledge is instinctive, it's before thought. In the same way, our Original Relationship to Life is there before the formation of the mind, so it's not something we're usually conscious of. But it can be seen clearly in babies because there's nothing obscuring it; the baby embodies it fully.

Matthew: When you use the phrase 'Original Relationship to Life' I immediately think about the relationship between the baby and the parents, but that's not what you're talking about, is it?

Jez: No, that's the first *human* relationship of course, but with this phrase I'm pointing to the relationship a baby has before that. It's a relationship to life itself, to the entire manifest world.

Matthew: That sounds very grand!

Jez: It may sound grand when I try to put it into words but it's not at all; it's the most obvious, simple, natural thing.

Matthew: I can't get away from the feeling that a baby's relationship with its parents is their Original Relationship. On a physical level, without the mother's womb there'd be no baby, and without her breasts there'd be no natural milk to feed it. On the emotional level there'd be no love to nourish it.

Jez: This is a bit like when we were talking about Oneness and I raised the question: 'Where does the baby comes from?' At first you said: 'The parents', then I asked you to go back one step, and we approached the question from a more metaphysical level. So that's what I'm also asking you to do now.

Everything you said about the mother's fundamental relationship to the baby is of course true, but I'm proposing that, if you go back one step, you'll see that our *Original* Relationship is to Life itself.

Matthew: Go on then, convince me.

Jez: Let's start at pregnancy. The baby manifests in the womb, it's receiving oxygen and nutrients through the blood of the mother. That means there's a relationship with its environment.

Matthew: Yes, a relationship with the mother!

Jez: But if you move back one step, did the mother create the womb which so perfectly protects and nurtures the baby? And is the mother wilfully sending blood into the baby in order to nourish it?

Matthew: I see where you're going with this; you're kind of trumping me by going meta.

Jez: I am, but this is not just a game of one upmanship: I'm making a vital point. *Through* that most intimate human relationship with the mother, the baby is being nurtured by life itself. Our parents and family are simply manifestations of Oneness in the Relative Level. They may be the physical source of our own manifestation, but ultimately, we are children of the infinite.

Matthew: I understand the broad strokes of this but I think you're going to have to go into it a bit further for me to really accept it.

Jez: When something is confusing and difficult to grasp it's always good to try approaching it from different angles. Let me give you an analogy: For an apple to grow on a tree it's given everything it needs; all the nourishment and energy is freely provided by the tree.

Matthew: So in this analogy the tree is the mother and the apple is the child?

Jez: Yes, there'd be no apple without the tree, but going one step further, there would be no tree to produce the apple without life, in which the tree grows.

Matthew: By life, in this case, you mean the earth, oxygen, carbon dioxide, rain and all that's necessary for the tree to grow?

Jez: Yes, so although the tree 'grows' the apple, the tree is not ultimately the source of that nourishment which allows that growth to happen; it's simply an instrument, a structure that passes it on. So from the Relative perspective you would say the Original relationship is between the apple and the tree, but from the Absolute viewpoint, the *Original* Relationship is between the apple and life itself.

Matthew: Let's bring this back to the human world. You're saying that in the bigger picture, as babies, life is supplying everything we need to survive, and our parents are just a part of that process.

Jez: Yes, in the mother, life provides the womb, the nourishment through the placenta, and the breast milk after birth. Then, as we grow, our parents teach us to be a human being, to eat, to bathe etcetera. But *before* all that relationship, we're *already* interacting and relating with life through the body. You could say that this begins with the baby's very first breath; life is filling its lungs and bringing energy into the body on a physical level. This is why yoga techniques use the breath: It's our primal connection to life, quite literally, because, in the exchange of oxygen, nitrogen and carbon dioxide, we're kept alive.

Then we have our relationship to food: Life produces the milk in our mother so that we receive the nourishment we need from the breast. But our relationship to life is not only found in what's necessary for our survival, it also manifests just in the experience of being a human in a body; it's functioning in everything we perceive through our senses. For example, light is entering our eyes, stimulating our optic nerve and producing vision, temperature is affecting our pores and skin, regulating heat. Life is interacting with us continuously.

Matthew: And we don't play any active part in this...

Jez: Exactly! All of this relating and interacting with life goes on without any conscious input from us at this stage. We don't need to do anything to breathe; the autonomic nervous system makes sure we keep breathing. Even when we're asleep, life breathes us. Likewise, we don't do anything to perceive light and turn it into an image on our retina, we don't need to concentrate and will our stomachs to digest. This relationship to life is just flowing through us, living us and it doesn't require our minds.

I met up with my nephew Tim and his one-year-old son Flynn yesterday. Flynn sat on Tim's knee but kept crawling off to explore the café we were in. I watched Flynn relating to, and interacting with, everything that appeared around him: the wooden floor he crawled on, the can of drinks he reached for in the freezer cabinet, the bowl of water left outside for dogs. In a sense, everything he encountered fed him. By stimulating his brain cells, by the touch, texture and temperature of his experience, life was flowing through him, nourishing him and growing him.

Tim, who kept having to retrieve Flynn from his wanderings, was just a part of the world he was relating to. A central part, that's vital for his safety and development in the world, but as far as Flynn was concerned at this stage, just another part of it.

The point is: Our Original Relationship to Life exists before any human relationships; it's our intimate connection to this life, which fulfils and sustains us. This is something most of us lose touch with as we grow up. As the Personality develops we start to think we're important, that *we* are running the show, which is as ridiculous as the apple thinking it's in charge of the tree.

By observing a baby we can see this Original Relationship to Life clearly; we can see we're totally at the mercy of life to breathe us, to make our bodies function etcetera.

Matthew: Isn't this perception at the root of most religious experiences?

Jez: Yes, to understand this as an adult changes the whole way you live. You no longer adopt a position of fighting life; you fall into a natural relationship of surrender to it. Religious people might substitute the word 'life' for God. I favour the way the great Taoist sage Lao Tzu put it:

> *I am nourished by the great mother.*

This sums up the Original Relationship to Life – the reality of our existence is that we are all children, and Life is the mother. This is our true place in the scheme of things, and the only natural response to knowing this is a position of surrender. This Original Relationship is, in the end, the only thing that can fulfil us because through it, we are receiving Love.

Matthew: What do you mean?

Jez: This brings us back to our discussion of the Absolute Level. If all is made of Love then our interaction with the world is an interaction with Love in other forms. By relating in the world of Duality, we're receiving Love. Flynn was filled up and fed by his relationship to life because he was receiving constantly; he was receiving Love in the form of whatever he encountered: the cold drink in his hands, or the mud on his sock.

Matthew: How lovely to be fulfilled by such simple pleasures...

Jez: It's a kind of passive receiving; the sky or the tree we look at doesn't have to do anything or give us anything to feed us, it just has to be what it is. In the adult world we're estranged from this feeling of being fed by life itself. Such 'passive receiving' is usually replaced with 'active receiving' in the form of stimulation of our minds.

Matthew: You mean in the way that most of us, like me, are technology junkies, always on our phones?

Jez: Yes. It wasn't always like this. If you look back at the start of your life you'd see that you didn't crave any mental stimulation, you were just able to look at the sky and be nourished.

Matthew: There's a backlash now against always being on our smartphones...

Jez: Yes, when people go off communing with nature it's this Original Relationship to Life they're seeking to rediscover: The sound of a campfire crackling, the stars at night, the dawn chorus and the dew sparkling on the grass in the morning. All of this is prior to any human relationship; it's our Original Relationship to Life, a nourishment that most people have lost connection with.

5

BEING

How the Original Relationship to Life manifests
in a person

'Limitless undying love which shines around me like a million suns
It calls me on and on across the universe.' – John Lennon

Jez: What's the dictionary definition of the word 'being'?

Matthew: It says: 'Existence, the state of existing', but when used in relation to people it means 'the nature and essence of a person'.

Jez: It's an interesting distinction; a rock exists but we wouldn't say that a rock *has* being.

Matthew: A rock has energy but it's not alive; I think that's the distinction.

Jez: So we *could* agree that a dog or a plant has being, because they're alive. So then, what does 'alive' actually mean? What are the defining characteristics of life?

Matthew: There are functions that all living things share, such as eating, drinking, excreting, respiring and reproducing...

Jez: So all living things have being – that state of aliveness – but the definition goes on to say that, when applied to people, the word means 'the nature and essence of a person'. For me, those words point to how we come into this world, rather than what we *become*. They're not referring to qualities of character, skills or talents that develop as we grow up; they're talking about how life is expressed through us *before* all that happens. So these are not attributes that make us different from each other, they're attributes which, when we're born, we all share.

Matthew: So you could call them attributes of our original state of Being?

Jez: Yes, but to use this phrase wouldn't be quite right, because Being, that essence of who we are, is not lost as we grow older; it's just that our connection, our experiencing of it is forgotten.

That Being can be rediscovered and lived at any moment. So whenever I use the word Being with a capital 'B', those primal attributes are what I'm referring to.

Matthew: So what would you say are these attributes that we start our lives with?

Jez: If you look closer and observe how the Original Relationship to Life manifests in a child, you find the attributes that add up to what I mean by Being. The first one we're going to discuss is Stillness. On one level you could define it as a lack of action, a sense of peace. What comes into your mind if I ask you to think about Stillness?

Matthew: A calm lake.

Jez: Yes, a calm lake doesn't have being, but it definitely has the quality of Stillness. That's why people often sit in nature, by a still lake or on a mountain when they meditate: to tune into that quality of Stillness, because it reflects back the Stillness in themselves. The same Stillness we have when we come into this world...

Matthew: It becomes a bit more elusive as you grow up.

Jez: Yes, often it has to be sought out. That's what meditation's for, but why is that? If it's part of who we are, part of our Being, what is it about growing up into adulthood that makes that Stillness less accessible?

Matthew: Our busyness I suppose: We get occupied with living this life.

Jez: But what drives that busyness? What sort of busyness is it? Where does it come from?

Matthew: The mind: It's mental busyness.

Jez: Yes, apart from lack of action, what constitutes that Stillness I'm talking about is a lack of thought. Babies have no thought about what they are, who they are or what they're experiencing. A baby doesn't think about what it does, it just grabs food, smiles, or crawls without thought going into those actions.

When out walking by the river yesterday I walked passed a toddler, a beautiful Spanish child with a dark complexion. It was obvious that she was still in the Original Relationship to Life. As I walked towards her she just stood still in the middle of the path staring at me. There were no thoughts, no self-consciousness or fear; she just watched as this giant adult approached. If you're around children who are in this Stillness, there's no need for words, no need to try to pull them into their virgin minds. Just look back at them and enjoy that Stillness, because it's mirroring back what's in all of us.

When I use the word Stillness this is what I'm talking about. I don't just mean being a bit quiet, I mean the deep Stillness that exists before thought. It's the core of who we are, on the Absolute Level. Stillness is one manifestation of Being.

Matthew: We may all start out with it, but as we grow up the function of thinking develops...

Jez: Yes, and what happens with most people is the Stillness, to a large extent, is lost. It's even forgotten about, as if they never had it.

Matthew: But you're saying this Stillness is not incompatible with having a mind and adult consciousness; we don't have to lose it?

Jez: Absolutely. Stillness is an attribute of Being. Being is what we are before thought in the same way that radio waves exist before they manifest as music coming through a radio. You can listen to the music, and forget that they are there, but without the sound waves, there'd *be* no music. Just because you're not conscious of something doesn't mean it's not there. In the Openings I experienced as a child, there was Stillness, but also awareness of it; I was watching it happening. Which brings us to the second attribute of Being: Choice-less Awareness.

There are two categories of awareness. When I said: 'Just because you're not conscious of something doesn't mean it's not there', I was referring to Personality Awareness, in which Personality chooses what awareness falls on – it selects what you become conscious of. If there's something you find confronting, something you don't want to acknowledge, Personality will turn awareness off; you'll look the other way.

Matthew: That makes me think of how I choose to look away when something violent or gory comes on television...

Jez: Yes, our minds often do this. You might find yourself turning away from the TV before you even realise what you're doing. We're not always consciously aware of what we're turning away from. But I'm not just talking about physically turning away, I mean metaphorically too.

Matthew: You mean repression?

Jez: Exactly. We can choose not to become aware of things by closing off our minds to them. In babies the mind is undeveloped, so at that stage awareness is not running through thought. In Being, a baby sees whatever is in front of it and becomes aware of it. If a dog comes up and sniffs the baby, that's what the baby becomes aware of: a sniffing wet nose and warm panting breath. It has no ability to choose what its awareness falls upon. This is what I mean by Choice-less Awareness: Life breathes you and lives you, while awareness watches it all happening.

Like all attributes of Being, Choice-less Awareness is available in adults too. It arises independently of Personality; it comes from consciousness. Unlike Personality Awareness it has no agenda, no prejudice; it sees with absolute clarity.

Matthew: OK, but getting back to the subject of Being in babyhood, babies aren't just passively lying, watching the world go by all the time. They do interact in the world; they could reach out and touch the dog...

Jez: Yes, there are passive aspects to Being (Stillness and Choice-less Awareness) and then there's a more active part. This brings us to the third attribute of Being: feeling.

Feeling is the medium through which we relate and interact in the world; it's how we participate in it. As we grow up, we learn that we can close down feeling. Personality Awareness doesn't just apply to what we see – if it says: 'I don't want to feel that,' then we can pull in, cut off from our experience by withdrawing from our feelings. In Being this isn't an option: There's no repression, only full-feeling engagement with life. Through feeling we interact with the world, and in response we have feelings, which are felt fully. Feeling is another one of those big subjects that we'll cover in a later talk.

The final attribute of Being is one particular feeling. It plays such an important part of our feeling experience in Being that it warrants a mention of its own. As babies we explore physical sensations through the body's senses, we also experience psychological feelings in relation to what we encounter in the world. In this story I'm telling, the original feeling is Joy; it's our primal feeling that arises as a response to the Original Relationship to Life. When Love engages with Love in other forms it provokes this primal feeling in our hearts.

Matthew: Like when we connect with friends?

Jez: That sense of connectedness, of intimacy, is a part of that Joy but it's not just with people. For example, babies don't only feel Joy when Mummy comes into the room; it could arise with anything: playing with a toy, eating mashed up banana, snuggling in a blanket.

   I'm not talking about the buzzing, euphoric happiness that adults feel when they've passed an exam or won the lottery; it's not linked to *gaining* anything. This Joy is generally quieter and more steady, although there can be an excited version of it – think of a baby ecstatically transfixed by the sound of a rattle or a simple game of peek-a-boo. Joy arises simply from the enjoyment of living what you are; it's a natural outcome of Being, interacting with life in all its different forms.

Matthew: I remember having that feeling as a child, lying in bed with my thumb in my mouth and rubbing brushed cotton sheets between my fingers.

Jez: Just interacting with life in the form of that texture of the cotton, or the warmth and shape of your thumb fitting perfectly in roof of your mouth... It's beautiful isn't it? When we're open to life we're so easily and simply fulfilled. Have you heard the Zen phrase: 'Chop wood, carry water'? A modern equivalent might be, 'Pay gas bill, buy groceries.'

Matthew: Not quite so elegant is it?

Jez: No, we'll stick with the original. 'Chop wood, carry water' basically means that, just by doing what you have to do to survive, to keep warm and drink, you engage with this life and that's rewarding and joyful in itself. It's another way of expressing the Original Relationship to Life.

Matthew: So you're talking about a kind of contentment.

Jez: Yes, but it's more than that, it's an expression of Love. Joy is the best word I have for it but I'm using it in a very broad sense because, as I said, this Joy can be expressed in different forms. As a baby you might feel excited about the stimulation of a new toy, or bold in an exploration of an unfamiliar place. Or you could feel peaceful and calm lying in a pram as the sky above you reflects back the infinity that you are. These are all aspects of that same Joy which arises as Being interacts in the world.

Matthew: But not all babies appear joyful. What about when they're screaming and crying?

Jez: That's true, other experiences of life are available, such as stress. As babies we're dependent on adults to look after us. If we're denied our basic needs of food, water and shelter, or if we feel threatened in any way, we experience a different type of feeling – distress. Distress is our survival instinct's alarm bell, an outward directed forceful energy that rises up to gain control of any threat in the only way it can. By having us draw attention to ourselves, nature provides a way for our needs to be recognised by those around us who can act on our behalf.

Stress can also arise when babies suffer birth traumas and, in those cases, the expression of the stress in their systems can be more ongoing. In those cases the attributes of Being can be interrupted very early on.

Matthew: It's upsetting to see a baby feeling distress.

Jez: Mostly that's just the adult's projection of his or her own distress which comes from their emotional life. As I said, in babies distress is usually just a feeling being expressed with the purpose of gaining the attention they need. When the attention is gained...

Matthew: They stop yelling and bawling.

Jez: Right, unless there's some other basic problem causing it, the distress usually passes. If it doesn't, it simply means that there's more stress needing to be expressed.

Matthew: It's amazing how a baby can go from all out distress to a blissful peacefulness in a split second.

Jez: There's an important principle here: When the distress passes quickly it's because the feeling is felt fully. This is because, in Being, we're present to whatever is happening.

Matthew: I think I know what you mean but can you explain a bit more?

Jez: Remember we talked about how, as adults, we lose Choice-less Awareness? We have the ability to choose what we become aware of. We also have the ability to edit what we're feeling, we can suppress and reject feelings, but babies, at least as long as they're in that original state of Being, don't have that option. They simply are whatever life makes them in any given moment. So there's no withdrawal from a feeling, only full expression of, and immersion in it. In this way the feeling, the distress, usually just passes through their system. The stress and tightness that it creates in their bodies is let go of and they return to the more neutral, primal feeling of Joy. Even babies with a difficult start in life caused by birth traumas are able to find rest in their original state of Being in between displays of distress.

Matthew: How does all this relate to Oneness?

Jez: In Being we interact with the play of Duality in the world while remaining located in Oneness. If you imagine the baby represented as a circle, anything can happen on the circumference, but the centre remains absolutely still. The newborn baby develops in all sorts of sophisticated ways as it gets accustomed to being in the world, while remaining energetically located in Oneness.

Now that I've described the Original Relationship to Life and the attributes of Being I want to introduce you to a new phrase: the Natural State. It's an umbrella term combining the Original Relationship to Life with Being. It's a less long-winded way to point to both of them at the same time, because they're so intertwined that you can't have one without the other. The qualities of Being – Stillness, full-Feeling engagement with life, Choice-less Awareness and Joy – all arise out of the Original Relationship to Life, like flowers sprouting from a fertile soil.

THE
WORLD
OF MAN

6

SURVIVORS

We are all survivors of having lost the
Natural State

'To live is the rarest thing in the world.
Most people exist, that is all.' – Oscar Wilde

Matthew: Looking at the world, with the violence, and even the disharmony in my own family, I don't see much evidence of this Natural State.

Jez: You could imagine a world in which the Natural State we came with is not lost, a world in which that Stillness and Joy remains with us as we grow into adults. But that's obviously not what happens; people are not conscious of the Original Relationship to Life. In fact, it would be true to say that we're *survivors* of losing this. It's left everyone with scars and ways of living centred around getting by in this life *without* knowing and living this original experience of Love.

Matthew: But I'd say that most people are trying to Love, trying to do their best.

Jez: Yes, they're *trying*. There's an effort in it; that means it doesn't come naturally. If you think about the Love we feel emanating from a newborn baby, there's no effort involved. The baby is not doing anything; it's just Being what it is.

As adults we've forgotten that we *are* Love. Love has become almost like an altered state, something we only feel when a strong experience jolts us beyond the everyday life of our Personalities back into the wonder and Joy of life.

Matthew: Like if we fall in Love, for example?

Jez: Yes, or we give birth or a loved one recovers from a life-threatening illness. It's as if the experience is so strong that we're momentarily shocked back into a taste of our Natural State. But our ongoing experience is *not* of that Love.

It's important to remember as we talk about this that, from the Absolute point of view, we can't be anything but Love: It is who we are. But our ongoing human condition in the Relative Level is often an estrangement from *feeling* that Love.

Matthew: So we're talking about two apparently opposite things being true at the same time again?

Jez: Exactly. In the Relative world, where Duality runs the show, Love has found an opposite: the apparent absence of Love.

Matthew: You say 'apparent' because on the Absolute Level there's only Love, right?

Jez: Correct, it *appears* that there's an absence of Love in us, and because of that we've lost our Joy and it's been replaced by emotions and the absence of that deep sense of contentment.

Matthew: But we can experience happiness too!

Jez: Yes, but happiness isn't the same as Joy.

Matthew: They're pretty close – what would you say is the difference?

Jez: Unlike Joy, the happiness you're talking about is conditional. If we have some good news... happiness comes; if we get bad news... it leaves.

Matthew: I know what you mean. I was walking down the street yesterday feeling rather happy and then I received a text message from my bank telling me I'm approaching my overdraft limit. It was like a happiness switch had been turned off.

Jez: A whole different mood descends in an instant, and all it takes is a few words of text appearing on your screen. Conditional happiness is transient because it's dependent on certain conditions, and conditions can always change.

Matthew: Just to be clear, you're not suggesting that if we have the understanding you're talking about we can go around ecstatically excited all the time, are you?

Jez: No, of course not. Remember I said that Joy has different modes of expression? It *can* be excited but most of the time it shows as a quiet contentment arising from simply engaging in this life through feeling.

Matthew: 'Chop wood, carry water.'

Jez: Exactly. You can fill in your own experiences of Joy: the feeling of passing soap over the contours of your body in the shower, the subtle flavours smelt and tasted in a sip of fine wine. In Being these kinds of simple pleasures are found in so many daily activities.

Matthew: If Being is part of our Natural State, then why do we lose it?

Jez: That's a good question and the answer is: We don't know.

Matthew: I'm a bit surprised to hear you say that.

Jez: Why?

Matthew: I suppose I thought that when it came to this subject, you'd have all the answers.

Jez: That's one of the myths about finding this: that it provides all the answers. There are some things that you can't know. 'Why do we lose it?' You might as well ask: 'Why do dogs exist?' or 'Why haven't humans evolved wings?' Such questions are irrelevant because the answers are unknowable. Knowledge can take you so far, and then you're left in what I call the Mystery (with a capital 'M'.) The inexplicable, wonder of life.

This reminds me of my favourite cartoon: A visitor stands in the grounds of the Institute of Philosophy in front of a notice board with a map of the buildings on it. On the map is a big arrow, above which is written: 'Why are you here?'

Waking up to this understanding involves finding out what you *can* know, or what you *need* to know in order to rediscover this, not wasting energy mind-f***ing about what you can never know. This is about seeing life as it is, feeling it, and living it. We all lose that original state of Being, that's a clearly perceptible fact. *Why* we lose it is unknowable, *how* we lose it, that's another thing altogether.

*Matthew: So you **can** know how we lose it?*

Jez: Absolutely – in fact understanding the mechanics of *how* we lose it can be helpful in pointing us back to Being. It can be a mirror in which we begin to see the Personality, and once you can see it, you can start to perceive what lies beyond it.

Finding out how we lose the Natural State is a big question though, and we have to do a bit more setting up before we can get into it.

Matthew: So what's next?

Jez: We've discussed the world of the baby, which is informed by the Original Relationship to Life. Now we need to talk about the world the baby enters, which is governed by parents, family and the society in which the family exists. It's the tribe we're born into; another word for it is the Group Personality.

7

THE GROUP PERSONALITY

How our tribe informs the development
of our Personality

*'It is no measure of health to be well adjusted
to a sick society.' – Jiddu Krishnamurti*

Jez: We can make two approaches towards the subject of Personality: the mechanics of *how* it forms in us, and the environment in which it forms. The two are intimately related: How the Personality forms is hugely affected by the environment in which it forms.

Imagine a handful of flower seeds. They all hold the same potential of becoming a flower, but how that flower eventually manifests depends on the environment in which the seed falls. Is it growing in full sun or in the shade? Is it in a windy position? What's the quality of the soil?

To fully understand the Personality you need to look at more than the immediate family environment; you have to go back further and examine the family's history and roots. You need to consider the collective consciousness of all the Personalities that make it up, or what I call Group Personality.

The Group Personality has many levels. On the metalevel it begins with our species. We're not animals, we're not insects, we're Homo Sapiens. The human species differs from others in one crucial way: Thanks to our highly developed brain we have awareness of ourselves. Whereas other species of animals mainly operate on instinct, the 'human animal' operates from the mind, through thought, and this is basically what's behind us having Personalities at all.

Matthew: I guess the next level of our Group Personality would be race?

Jez: Yes, people from a particular ethnic background share some common characteristics; not just physical but also psychological characteristics arising from the history they share. For example, Europeans have a different cultural history from people of African origin; unfortunately, the dynamic of white masters and black slavery is one sordid side of that story.

Matthew: How does that history relate to the discussion of Personality?

Jez: That whole situation originally arose from the arrival of Portuguese visitors to the west coast of Africa in the fifteenth century. There must have been some idea of cultural superiority in these Personalities that led them to think it was acceptable to enslave African natives.

Matthew: You think that was in their Personalities?

Jez: Where else? It certainly wasn't part of their original state of Being when they were born! All such ideas of domination of other people only arise when the Original Relationship to Life has been lost; if you respect and bow down to life, which of course includes your fellow man, the idea of domination of others can't arise.

This initial act of violence by the Personalities of those Portuguese visitors to Africa eventually grew into the Atlantic slave trade and in turn hugely affected the Group Personalities of both the European and African races who lived under its influence. The Europeans who participated in it, by either transporting slaves or by owning them, developed attitudes of superiority, entitlement and racism. The Personalities of the Africans who were victims of it became suffused with hurt, enforced subservience and understandable resentment.

At the time of the slave trade these characteristics were more obvious, but the scars of that history are passed down through the generations; racial tension has not been eradicated. This is just one example of differences in the Group Personalities of races; you could pick any race and find differences, even if they're not so dramatic.

Matthew: The world is such a melting pot now; different races mix together all over the world. This must have an effect on the Group Personalities of those races...

Jez: Definitely. The next level of Group Personality would be Nationality; people of different racial ancestries live together in different countries. And this brings in another influence on Personality on top of race. Different countries have different Personalities; we know this simply by the fact that the word 'Englishness' exists. It obviously evolved to describe certain shared characteristics that have been observed in the English population. We're both English, what characteristics would you use to define Englishness?

Matthew: You might sum it up as stoicism – you know, the English 'stiff upper lip'. Also a politeness – we're known for forming orderly queues, and for our absurdist humour, such as Monty Python.

Jez: Although these are generalisations, if we look around at people we know, and at characters in films, documentaries and dramas produced here, it's easy to recognise them as having some truth. Every country's Group Personality has its own version of this phenomenon. The humour that evolves in each country also clearly demonstrates that these differences exist.

Matthew: What's funny in one country is not necessarily funny in another. It's the same with music; a band that's massive in England can be almost unknown in the American market, and vice versa.

Jez: These national differences can bind populations together and create a sense of identity and belonging that gives a pride in your country. Even if those people are actually from different races, they can be united under the national Group Personality.

Now we've reached the level of nationality, a whole new set of factors comes into effect that in turn produces sub-divisions of Group Personalities. First of all let's look at geography. This can influence a local population in different ways. For example, living in extreme places creates the hardy, strong constitution that's necessary just to survive. But this hardiness also affects temperament; there has to be a robustness of spirit to live where the climate is extreme, be it cold tundra, baking desert, high altitudes, windy plains or humid rainforests. But that's just the climate; the landscape itself leaves its own mark.

Matthew: I imagine living near an active volcano, in an earthquake zone or area of poor soil fertility has a strong influence too.

Jez: Yes, if you live through a natural disaster, or even with the threat of one happening, it will produce a different Personality type from one living in safe, unthreatened areas. To be confronted by a survival situation is certainly going to make you less superficial, and perhaps more pragmatic, more realistic.

But the influence of nature doesn't have to be as dramatic as living where natural disasters occur. I remember visiting Austria once and being told by a local that people who lived in the villages nestling in the valleys of the Alps had a certain mentality that was shaped by their location. He said that being cut off from their neighbours in adjacent valleys by the mountains created a sense of isolation. In order to survive the long hard winters they had to dig in and be self-sufficient. All this bonds the community, as well as toughening it up.

Matthew: Another example would be fishing communities who survive off the sea.

Jez: Yes, there's toughness to them because, as they say, the sea is a harsh mistress. It can provide fish but it can also take lives. It requires courage, and perhaps stoicism in the face of danger, to live such a life. And it's not just the fishermen; the whole family is affected when the men have to go to sea at all hours in unpredictable weather.

Matthew: Of course within that Personality type, there can be all sorts of Personalities. Not all fishermen are the same.

Jez: Absolutely, we're looking at archetypes, but that doesn't mean they don't exist. If you go to these areas you can experience that type, it's in their attitude to life and it seeps into the community.

Matthew: The poverty level must be a factor too. For example, many fishermen are quite poor and this must have an effect.

Jez: Yes, to come from a rich, privileged family in which your needs are freely provided is obviously a very different experience to growing up in poverty. If everything's available to you, you can start to take all those privileges for granted, whereas if you live hand to mouth, every paycheque and every meal is cherished.

Poverty can affect the Personality in different ways. It can make a person feel downtrodden and sluggish, harbouring resentment to people who are born into privilege. On the other hand, it could motivate someone, fire them with ambition and determination to free themselves from poverty's grip.

On the other side of the fence, the classic image of a Personality brought up in wealth or privilege is spoilt, snobby and greedy. All of these can be true of course, but many other outcomes are possible; money can broaden your mind to the possibilities of your life and be a positive influence on creativity. It can even drive someone to find charitable ways to help others who don't have it. So within social strata, different Group Personalities can be engendered; every stereotype has its exceptions.

Matthew: Income is often related to politics, which I imagine is also a factor that informs Group Personalities.

Jez: Yes, low-income earners are naturally interested in the rights of the common man and this can bind them together in a political party. Such political parties are tribes in which all the members have the same goals: to protect their rights and to win power back from the rich elite. To many people whose families have struggled with poverty for generations, being a member of a left-wing party can almost be like being part of a religion. To be anything else would be a betrayal of the lineage of the family and its struggles and ideals.

A rich family can also have its own political ideals to uphold. A belief in capitalism, the right to run businesses as you wish and to protect the wealth that they generate means that right-wing/conservative politics are favoured. Once again there's history involved in this: Businesses and the wealth they create are usually inherited and there's an expectation on descendants to protect and carry them forward.

I'm not arguing the rights and wrongs of any viewpoint or party; from each perspective there are needs to be met. The point is, whichever tribe you're born into exerts an influence on you, a pressure to have certain allegiances and mind-sets.

Matthew: In totalitarian regimes that pressure can be enormous...

Jez: Yes, the strength of a Group Personality is maintained by the solidarity of the individual Personalities making it up, and the people in charge know this. Think about the Chinese Communist party under Mao Tse Tung in the 1950s: Apart from a few brave dissidents, a whole nation was united by having the same goals, thinking the same thoughts, believing the same beliefs and idolising the same dictator. This is the extreme end of the spectrum, where mass brainwashing is involved and the social pressure to conform is so great that some children even report their parents to the authorities if they show any signs of wavering from the party's ideals.

Matthew: What about the devotion to ideals and beliefs we see in religion? That must have a huge influence on a Group Personality.

Jez: It depends on the intensity of the faith; for some people religion is understood to be a personal choice and there's no pressure on family members to make that same choice. But for others, religion is absolutely central to their life and their identity. In these cases the followers are strongly bonded around the tenets of the religion; the more closely they're followed and upheld by the community, the stronger that bond is. Add to that the history of the religion going back generations and you have a very powerful Group Personality.

So the religion in a tribe very obviously shapes the thoughts and beliefs of those within it; it basically informs their whole Personality. Imagine being born into an orthodox family of any religion: A whole doctrine of how life works is handed to you and there's enormous pressure to conform to it, to follow the same rules, marry within the religion, have children and perpetuate the tribe. If you don't follow the rules the consequences can be serious; in the end you have to leave the tribe, because it's bigger and more powerful than you. For a Personality that has found identity in a religious tribe, to leave it is traumatic. It's like a death: You lose your family, your history, even your identity. (This is a good example of how the Group Personality of a religion can be even stronger than that of a family.)

You can see how Group Personalities have a function of self-preservation built into them; threats to their dominance are severely dealt with. We've talked about an internal threat to the Group Personality when people leave it, but there are also external threats in the form of rival groups such as other religions. When religions start fighting each other you can see how defending the Group Personality is even more important than adhering to the beliefs that underpin the religion itself. Most religions at least nod in the direction of the idea of loving your fellow man, but that doesn't stop their members destroying other people with bombs and missiles if they're a threat to their way of life. War is basically the conflict between two tribes holding differing beliefs and defending them.

Matthew: So you're saying that without Group Personalities, wars wouldn't exist?

Jez: That's right. Wars are caused by individual Personalities identifying with their Group Personalities, but wars also have a huge influence in shaping Personalities; they're like a magnifying glass that intensifies the Emotions of the tribe.

Matthew: What do you mean?

Jez: On a basic level, wars engender hatred of the enemy and entrench a sense of us and them. There's also survival fear involved: of losing loved ones and losing security. And all that doesn't stop once the war is over – a soldier scarred by the terrible things he's witnessed on the battlefield may no longer be emotionally equipped to be a good father or a husband and this lack of stability at the top of the family affects the children. Sons can be especially damaged by it, and the damage can then be passed on in their own inability to be loving, stable fathers. Also, enemies are not easily forgotten, scars run deep; hatred for the opposing Group Personality can be passed on through the generations.

Even distant connections to war can have lasting effects on Personalities. My Mother lived through the Second World War and all the rationing and shortages. This affected her deeply; for the rest of her life she had a wartime mentality towards waste, which meant she was not able to enjoy abundance.

Matthew: How did that manifest in your upbringing?

Jez: It was like the opposite of the Jewish mother archetype who always wants to feed you up. When my Mum cooked she always made a limited amount; there was never abundance when it came to second helpings. With regards to money, although she was comfortable financially there was always a certain caution, never an extravagance or indulgence.

So what begins as a practical measure in specific circumstances (like a war) can get engrained in the Group and individual Personality, and become a pattern that's no longer relevant but still has a pervasive influence.

All these factors can be seen as influences that go to make up a particular Group Personality, or they can actually *be* Group Personalities themselves. For example, politics can be an influence in the Group Personality of a town's population; but a political party is also a Group Personality in itself. Religion can be an influence in a family, local or national Group Personality but it can also be a Group Personality itself in the form of a denomination, a sect or a cult.

There's one Group Personality we haven't covered. When it comes to determining an individual Personality's nature it's the most important one, and where we started this conversation: the family.

8

THE FAMILY

Its role in influencing the development of
our Personality

'Parents are the bones on which children cut their teeth.'
– Peter Ustinov

Jez: A lot of people have become interested in their ancestry recently. There are websites helping you to uncover your family history, and programmes showing celebrities doing the same. As well as curiosity, I think the reason for this is because it makes people feel safe to know their lineage: It strengthens their sense of identity. But how does our ancestry actually influence who we are as a person?

Matthew: It definitely affects how we look: My brothers and I all have the same dimple in our chins as my Dad.

Jez: But it's not just facially; I could see my body type in my Dad's body: We had the same musculature, the same arms and shape of chest. Ancestry affects our bodies in terms of health and energy too; we can inherit a predisposition to certain diseases, such as haemophilia, muscular dystrophy and heart conditions, through our parents' genes.

Matthew: My grandmother, mother and I all have similar problems with our digestive systems...

Jez: Ancestry also affects our offspring in all sorts of subtle ways. In Chinese medicine they talk about pre- and post-natal chi (or energy). Post–natal chi refers to the energy we get from the air we breathe and the food we eat while pre-natal chi is the energy given to us on conception from our parents. It's the chi of both the mother and father in the form of the egg and sperm. What this means is that the general health of the parents is thought to help to determine the overall health and strength of the baby.

Matthew: Everyone knows how important it is for an expectant mother to look after her health...

Jez: Age is a factor too. Nowadays mothers often give birth at an older age than they used to, and being born to older parents has a different input into the baby's energy from being born to younger ones, because our energy level generally declines as we age.

Matthew: I recently saw research saying that the children of older fathers have an increased risk of autism, epilepsy and breast cancer.

Jez: Procreating at an older age has an especially strong significance when it comes to the mother of the child. A twenty-year old's body has far more energy available to gestate a baby than a forty-year old's.

As far as the body is concerned, ancestry, both distant and recent, has a huge effect on a baby, but what's pertinent to our discussion is the influence ancestry has on Personality. What influence do you think your ancestry has had on you?

Matthew: Well, I've often thought there was no chance for me to be a traditionalist – there's a line of freethinkers, rebels even, on both sides of my family. For example, my dad's mother was brought up as an Irish Catholic in Liverpool but she became pregnant with my dad by an African American sailor.

Jez: Imagine the stigma of illegitimacy on your grandmother back then; how do you think it affected her?

Matthew: I think her rebellious streak gave her the strength to deal with the stigma of being an unmarried mother with a mixed-race baby at that time. She worked hard to earn money to look after my dad and she worked hard for the rest of her life – I suspect a lot of that came from wanting to prove her worth to people who judged her.

Jez: How do you think being illegitimate and mixed race affected your dad?

Matthew: He had to prove himself too – he's fiercely ambitious, he always worked hard, and he definitely expected my brothers and me to do the same.

Jez: So location (the port of Liverpool), race and being illegitimate are just a few of the influences on your Dad's life. Tell me a bit about your Mum.

Matthew: She's from Belfast. Her parents were Protestant members of the working class and her mother was a bit of a snob. She thought their family was better than their neighbours and kept Mum 'tied to her apron strings' so she wouldn't get into trouble and disgrace herself and the family.

Jez: How did your mother react to that?

Matthew: She was curious and open minded about people from different social groups, and she became quite rebellious when she realised that lots of what her mother had told her wasn't correct. Her parents were particularly upset that she married a mixed-race Roman Catholic.

Jez: So let's put this all together: When your dad met and married your mum, a family unit was created, a small Group Personality. Every family member brings their Personality to the group, and each of them is influenced in turn by their own family and its history, going back through time. It helps to envision this as concentric circles, with the present being in the centre.

Imagine yourself as a newborn baby, in that centre of all those influences. You begin your life in the Natural State, then gradually, under the influence of your family's Group Personality, you develop your *own* Personality.

Each Personality, from the past or the present, brings its influence to bear on you, but of course the conduit of that influence is the last links in the chain: your mother and father. They're closest to you and so it's their Personalities that have the most influence on the development of your Personality.

Matthew: The influence of my parents' rebelliousness and dad's work ethic on my family is obvious: When I was eight they moved my older brother and me from a state school to a private school because my dad felt the state school wasn't pushing us enough. I felt a lot of pressure to perform academically there, like I wasn't up to everyone else's standard. My older brother rebelled against it all – he used to misbehave and get detentions all the time...

Jez: You can see there are certain themes in this story whose origins are obvious. These are just two small examples of how your family history has fed into your own Personality and your brother's; we're just scratching the surface.

Matthew: I can see that if I'd been born to different parents my Personality would be different.

Jez: Absolutely, but your character would be the same. I need to clarify the difference between Personality and character: In general use these words are interchangeable. When *I* use the word

'Character' – let's give it a capital 'C' – I mean the qualities that make you individual: your talents, quirks etcetera. These have nothing to do with your parents; you brought them with you. Your Character is your nature.

By contrast your Personality is the product of nurture. It's grown in the environment of your particular family, and that family's built on the Personalities of your parents, your parent's parents and so on stretching back in time. Understanding this is an important part of this enquiry.

Matthew: Why's that?

Jez: Because we've been conditioned to believe that all that's been handed down to us, and our response to it, *is* what makes us who we are. We believe that it *is* who we are. We think we are our Personality.

Seeing that what we call Personality is built on influences from our family's history can help break your identification with your Personality. For example, had you not had that pressure put on you from your Dad's own need to prove himself, then you wouldn't have felt that stress and inadequacy in yourself. That feeling was not your own originally; it was your father's feeling passed on to you.

Matthew: So you're suggesting that the stress I felt in school is not part of who I really am; it's just a part of my Personality?

Jez: Correct. I'm aware that it's a dangerous suggestion. It's the same as when you look at religion that's been passed down through the history of a family. If you look honestly, you can't help but come to the conclusion that if you're a Christian born in England to a Christian family, your faith is determined simply by the contingency of your place of birth and your family. Had you been born in India you could easily have been a devout Hindu believing in a totally different god – or collection of gods – and a whole other set of beliefs. We're talking about an influence which is handed down; it's not who you are. If it was really who you are, it would not be dependent on where you were born.

In the same way, our whole Personality grows from the environment of our parents and the family we're born to. To understand those influences is to gain insight into our Personalities, and more importantly, to realise that we are so much more than the sum of those influences.

9

GENDER

The influence of gender on Personality

'Love has no gender, compassion has no religion, character has no race.' – Abhijit Naskar

Jez: There's one Group Personality factor that we haven't mentioned yet; your membership of it is determined by your biology.

Matthew: You mean gender?

Jez: Yes. To gain insight into gender Group Personalities we have to look at the history of each group, just as we did with racial Group Personalities. You can see the archetype of each gender by the roles they had when we were living in caves.

Matthew: You mean men were the hunters and women were the homemakers and nurturers?

Jez: Yes. This was dictated by the way nature makes our bodies: being physically stronger, the men went out to hunt the wild animals and the women, having wombs, gave birth, looked after the children and prepared the meat which the men brought back.

As the human race developed we moved out of caves and learned to grow crops, to make houses etcetera. These roles continued to inform what was expected of each gender even though they were no longer totally relevant. In a world where killing a six-tonne woolly mammoth was necessary for the survival of the tribe, it's easy to see how, on a practical level, men were regarded as the more important gender. But this idea of male superiority became ingrained and it cast women as the weaker sex, not just physically, but psychologically too.

Through the centuries this erroneous idea continued to inform women's standing in society. They were expected to be at home, bring up children and leave all the 'important jobs' to do with running the world, such as industry, management and politics, to the men. This had the ongoing effect of robbing the female gender of its power.

It took until the early twentieth century for women to start getting the vote, but of course male dominance didn't end there. To change a Group Personality's belief system is a slow process, especially when those beliefs have predominated for thousands of years. In the Sixties the Women's Liberation movement worked against society's entrenched ideas about women's roles and things moved forward a bit in that it became more acceptable for women to have jobs that were traditionally the domain of men.

The point, as far as this discussion is concerned, is that the history of gender roles has left its mark on each gender's Group Personality – the stereotypes we have of men and women can mostly be traced back to this history of the gender groups. For example, living in a world in which you're regarded as second-class citizens has held back women's freedom to be who they are, to do the job they want to do and to have power and money. Any system that restricts your liberty to be who you are doesn't exactly engender happiness or a sense of freedom and fulfilment. These influences obviously start to inform what it means to be part of the female Group Personality.

In my mother's generation this patronising, limiting attitude to females still had a strong hold, as witnessed by men and women's clearly defined role in marriages. Still informed by the caveman model, it was mostly the husbands who went out to earn money while the housewives did the housekeeping and most of the child rearing.

For many women, whose husbands were locked into these gender stereotypes, marriage became a kind of prison that kept them in these powerless roles. Having been brought up by mothers who had been indoctrinated with the idea that this was the women's lot in life, women like my mother had very little resistance to their situation. There was a belief this was all they could expect from their lives and, until the feminists rose up to disprove it, that belief created their reality.

Matthew: Things have been slanted in favour of the male in the sexual domain too – if a man sleeps around it might be regarded as powerful and virile, if a woman does the same she can be considered a slut.

Jez: Factor that in with the history of violence and rape against women and this has resulted in a strain of anger from the female gender to the male. I remember the early feminists who started speaking up in the sixties when I was a child always appeared angry; when you look at the history of this it's easy to understand why. It's the same as when black rights groups started speaking up; there's a backlog of anger for the repression that's been suffered in the past which comes from a collective pain stored in the Group Personality.

Matthew: So you're saying that this history of the female gender inputs into the family via the mother?

Jez: Yes, it can't help but influence the family because it's a huge factor shaping the mother's Personality. It's particularly influential if they have daughters, because mothers are role models for daughters. A mother represents what it is to be a woman in this world, so her influence over her daughters means that her experience of men and attitude towards them can be passed down.

I have a friend called Julie who told me the story of her love affair with her partner. Everything was wonderful until the day they married. On that day something changed: Julie started arguing with him more; she developed an attitude, an anger that she didn't understand. It was a real problem because it started infecting their relationship and overshadowing the love they had for each other.

It took a few years and some honest introspection for Julie to discover the cause of this unexplained resentment. The clue was in the fact that it began after their wedding day. She realised that her model of what marriage means for a woman came from her mother, and her mother's experience was not positive. Her mother was someone who had a highly developed sense of art and culture and she married a man with simpler interests. While the husband fulfilled his role as the breadwinner, she was expected to bring up the children and give up her aspirations to be an artist, because that was her role as a woman.

Julie's mother was not liberated enough, free of her own conditioning, to leave the marriage and follow her freedom, so she gave up her joy and fulfilled her role, but always harboured a resentment for the husband who had, effectively, taken this freedom away from her. You can imagine the unhappiness this caused, and how that lack of joy affected the children who grew up in that household.

Julie inherited the legacy of all this and one part of it was an unconscious belief that marriage takes away your freedom and your husband is your gaoler. Until she made this belief pattern conscious, she was a victim of what her mother had passed on to her, (which in turn her grandmother had passed on to her mother) and it nearly destroyed her marriage. It's a good example of emotion from the past invading the present.

Matthew: It's been a long time since feminism first flowered and there's still some way to go...

Jez: Yes, there's much more equality, at least in some societies, and this means that a female born now has a different experience of growing up from those in previous generations, and that's thanks to their sisters who came before them and spoke out against oppression. But, as I said, these things take a long time to disappear from the cultural timeline; the effects run deep and can take all sorts of forms.

Matthew: What do you mean?

Jez: For example, things can swing in the other direction: As a reaction to the years of oppression, women can get over identified in the freedom of having a powerful job, of being the breadwinner. Then a conflict can arise between that outgoing part of them and their hormones, which can tell them to be mothers and nurturers. This has been part of the struggle for women: how to 'have it all'. In these cases, daughters get a different message from the mum: Whereas in the past it might have been all about finding a good man and settling down, now the message might be to put your job and your independence first.

Matthew: We haven't mentioned the history of the male gender and how that affects sons and daughters in the family...

Jez: Let's start by looking at the male stereotype: We're good at reading maps, we love cars and sport, we're logical and find it difficult to talk about our feelings.

Matthew: We tick a few of these boxes but I don't think either of us is a stereotypical male...

Jez: No, these factors grouped together actually describe a Personality subgroup, a *type* of man. There are of course many subgroups within any group, and these often disprove the stereotype. But, as with women, there are certain factors that come to bear on all those subgroups, factors which inform any man. And again, a lot of that goes back through history to the caveman.

Matthew: We're talking about being the hunter, the breadwinner, the provider for the family again...

Jez: Yes, imagine the caveman having to go out and risk his life to hunt and kill dangerous beasts. That takes enormous courage. On top of this he knows that if he's not successful his family could starve; that's a lot of pressure to take on his shoulders. The pressure on man to fulfil this role has, in some cases, had a negative effect on the male psyche because it created an imbalance.

Matthew: What do you mean?

Jez: Men are born with the same ability to be tender and sensitive as women but, in order to be the hunter, the cavemen needed courage and toughness so they had to put aside their feeling, nurturing side – attributes which are useless when it comes to hunting. So, just as women became trapped in their nurturing roles, men became trapped in this courageous, dynamic role and it began to define what it means to be a man.

In society through the ages any man who didn't live up to this image of manhood was seen as being inferior and unmanly. This is one reason why homosexuals have often been looked down on by the rest of society. It also explains the stereotype of the man, seen especially in my father's generation, who's emotionally bottled up and out of touch with his feelings. When you're brought up in a world in which real men are tough and don't show their emotions, it's easy to understand how they repressed their nurturing, more sensitive side.

The damage this has done to the male psyche is immense; we talked about how one attribute of Being is feeling. You can see how this pressure on men can cut them off from that interaction with life. If feeling is the medium through which we engage and take in life, then to cut off feelings is to cut oneself off from life itself. This produces a Personality that's unemotional, removed, distant and unhappy. How can you be happy if you're not able to fully take in life? All this then feeds into the Group Personality of the family.

My dad was a typical, unemotional man of his generation. It was frustrating for my mum, who wanted to engage, to talk with him and share feelings. If one person in a relationship is unable or unwilling to do this then the other partner has a choice: Either put up with it or move on.

Matthew: That's what most liberated modern women would do.

Jez: Yes, but women of my mother's generation had been taught that this is how men were, and there was nothing you could do about it. Resigning to this situation and putting up with it was part of their brainwashing and led to female loss of power. So back then most wives suffered in silence, which led them to be unfulfilled in their relationships in terms of their feeling, emotional side, because the breadth of their relationship was diminished.

So the knock-on effect into the family is of an unfulfilled woman, which is obviously not a healthy situation or good example of what marriage is for their children. The impact on sons is equally destructive, because this model of manhood can be passed onto them. If a son was gay, you can imagine that this image of masculinity would not be supportive of his sexuality.

Matthew: My experience is very different; I'm twelve years younger than you and my dad used to tell us he loved us all the time.

Jez: Yes, this change in man's psyche became mainstream in the nineties when a new movement arose: the tribe of the 'New Man.' This was equivalent to feminism trying to put right the imbalance in their own gender stereotypes. So men were no longer just hunters; we were able to be a man and also to feel the pressures of what that role entails, for example sharing responsibility for his family. We were able to feel our nurturing, sensitive sides.

When I was a child, men didn't cry or hug other men; they do now. But to those who grew up with that old model of manhood, the damage has been done and it lives inside them. It's still common for some men of any generation to find it hard to be in touch with their feelings.

Matthew: I still find it hard to cry, having been told 'Boys don't cry' at school and knowing my dad didn't have a lot of time for cry-babies having grown up in the mean streets of Liverpool.

Jez: We rest on the shoulders of the generations before us. In the past, men and women were forced into stereotypical roles but human beings are much more complex than such straightjackets allow; they don't fit the reality. The qualities of power, of being breadwinners, creators, protectors, as well as of nurturance and homemaking can be present in both genders. This obviously varies from person to person, and to be fulfilled involves embracing all sides of what and who you are.

Our parents are the last link in our history and so the impact gender roles and stereotype has had on them has a direct influence on the family and any baby born into it.

Matthew: It's almost like a large part of a baby's destiny is written in the history of the parents.

Jez: I wouldn't call it destiny, because what happens next is down to the interaction between the baby and the parents, and that's unknown. Brothers and sisters don't all have the same Personalities even though they share the same influences from the parents. How we turn out, how all these influences affect us, is determined – to a large extent – by the development of the self. And that's what we're going to talk about next.

CHILDHOOD

10

THE SELF

How the Natural State develops an operating
centre

'No matter where you go, there you are.'

– Confucius

Jez: Now that we've talked about the Group Personality, the family and gender, we can look more closely at what happens when a baby is born and all these influences meet. First, let's remind ourselves of what we covered in our discussion of Duality: From the Absolute Level, Love manifests in the Relative Level (the world) in the form of a body.

Imagine a newborn baby girl: Her body, being physical matter, is immediately tuned to the Relative Level. It has a relationship to it from birth, through breath, and the need to eat and drink. But at this stage our baby is *more* attuned to the Absolute Level from which she has arisen, so there's a meeting of two different realities: the Absolute Level of our baby and the Relative Level of the World.

Through her senses, the baby has awareness of the Separate World. The Relative reality appears to her as light, sound and form. At this stage, she's mostly aware of the form of the parents and family she's been born into. The family is where the Natural State of our baby opens like a flower in the world of man – a place where the Original Relationship to Life has been forgotten and the original state of Being has been lost. As I said, it's the meeting of two different realities.

Matthew: How do the two Realities relate to each other?

Jez: In a sense, they don't, because they don't share the same experience of being human: Our baby, in the Natural State, rests in Stillness and thoughtlessness; the parents are mostly located in the Personality through mind. Our baby has hardly developed one of those yet!

Matthew: But there's some communication...

Jez: Yes. We look at a newborn baby in wonder: It's a human just like us but it hasn't yet learned to *be* like us; babies have qualities we no longer have or understand. This evokes Love in us because we're looking at a state of Being we've once known but have forgotten. So Love creates a bridge between these two realties through which they can communicate. Love, in the broadest sense of the word, is a language babies understand because it doesn't come from the mind, it comes from the heart.

Matthew: I see what you mean about babies being the same species as us but living a very different experience of being human. As you said, it's like two different worlds meeting.

Jez: There's a fundamental reason why these two worlds are so different: Our baby exists only in the present, that's her world. She has no conception of something called 'the past'. The world of the parents, as seen through Personality, is of course hugely informed by their minds: their beliefs, their identity, their history.

Matthew: But our baby may have a genetic condition passed down to her; that's from the past.

Jez: Yes, as we've talked about, the physical body comes from the past, from the union of the ovum and sperm, and that can have consequences in the present, such as genetically inherited conditions. But I'm talking about our baby's state of Being.

   You might notice that all the factors we discussed that inform the Group Personality of the family come from the past, from social history, religion and family history. The Natural State is totally beyond all of that ancestry because it comes only from the present; it's forever fresh and untouched by what has come before. The past comes in through the mind. Our baby has no developed mind yet; she's just a clear mirror to the present moment.

Matthew: What does that actually mean?

Jez: For our baby, the present moment simply involves living the Natural State. So she's simply Being, experiencing Stillness, primal Joy and feeling. Part of this will be expressing her physical needs, which she can make known through crying or agitation.

   As time goes on and she gradually tunes in more to the Relative Level, she starts mirroring back whatever's going on around her. She becomes like a clear lake reflecting the sky above it: If the weather is sunny, or cloudy, that's what will be reflected in the lake.

Matthew: You mean our baby starts to take on attributes or idiosyncrasies the parents and siblings display?

Jez: Yes, and the longer she's is in their world, the more that Group

Personality starts to influence and shape her experience of life. Her primary identification to the Absolute Level gradually lessens and she starts to express her family's energy. She's no longer an outsider: She becomes an insider, a member of the Group Personality.

Matthew: That seems like a big transition. How does it actually happen?

Jez: It happens through the development of the self. (I mean 'self' in the sense of 'being a separate identity' rather than the capitalised Eastern religious use of the word that relates to the 'Atman', to Universal Consciousness.) Before we get into that, let's look at the context for that development: the physical life of our baby *before* the development of the self.

As we've said, energy is 'matter in movement' and in our baby, that movement and change is rapid: Cells are dividing and growing at an incredible rate as her embodiment progresses. On the physical level she interacts with, and explores, the world through her body and its senses. During these explorations her developing mind learns to divide the world into differences of shape, colour, sound, smell and taste. She perceives the softness of the bed, the warmth of the food, the brightness of light, through feeling. You could say that Love (our baby) is exploring itself in other forms, and it's through this exploration that she develops. But the development isn't just physical and mental; on the level of Being there's the development of the self. How does the dictionary define the self?

Matthew: It says here: 'A person's essential being which distinguishes them from others.'

Jez: You can see how the self is very much part of the Relative Level, because it's all about interacting with the separateness of the world. The self is basically a vehicle through which Oneness, in the form of a baby, can interact with the World of Separation.

11

IDENTIFICATION

The appearance of an 'I'

'Adults are just outdated children.' – Dr Seuss

Jez: After a while, this feeling-engagement with life, through the self, changes our relationship to the world. Imagine our baby has been on this planet long enough to learn, through her explorations, that a wooden toy feels and smells different to a woollen blanket. Eventually she realises that these different sensory experiences are in fact separate objects: There's a toy, and there's a blanket.

Matthew: According to what you've laid out so far, they're different manifestations of Love?

Jez: Yes although, of course, as a baby, she has no concept of Love. The world out there is not yet labelled; it's simply lived without thought.

Matthew: But now it's starting to be experienced as a world full of separate forms.

Jez: Yes, and then something happens which changes her experience of being in the world dramatically. So far, we've discussed how she interacts in the world *through* the self. For example, several times a day the self comes into contact with food. Through her senses, she experiences this form of Love as a mushy substance. But one day, during these mealtime explorations of mushiness, she perceives a difference between the pink fingers and the food that they're grabbing. There's a recognition that she seems to be 'in' the fingers in a way that she's not 'in' the food. Something momentous has happened in our baby's development: Just as she's learnt to define objects by their forms, so an awareness of her separateness now defines herself within the limits of her body.

Matthew: She becomes identified as a self.

Jez: Exactly. This is what I meant when I said, 'Feeling changes our relationship to the world', because eventually feeling leads us to see ourselves as *part* of it.

At this stage her identification is rudimentary; it's simply the recognition of being *inside* a body. It's as if, in order for our baby to interact with the physical world, she adopts the perspective of that world. To explore the apparent separateness of the world, she apparently becomes separate herself.

Matthew: You're saying 'apparently' because it only appears that way from the perspective of the Relative Level?

Jez: That's right, the wave *appears* to be separate from the ocean, but if you look at the wider reality, it clearly isn't. So at this stage, there's partial identification with the self; it's a practical outcome of needing to engage in the world more. When not being active in the world, our baby returns to the Stillness of Being. At this stage there's perfect balance between the two, between the inner and outer.

Matthew: OK, so what happens then?

Jez: Through constant interaction with the world, the self continues to get stronger and more sophisticated. For example, our baby gradually becomes aware that, whenever adults talk about or refer to her, they make a sound from their mouth and that sound in some way relates to her. In other words, she's been given a name. Let's call her Lucy.

Matthew: I've heard in some cultures they don't immediately name a baby; they wait a while.

Jez: I've heard that too – they leave a respectful gap before a baby is named, as if it's allowed to reside in the 'everything' for a short while before it's named as a 'something'.

Of course our baby, Lucy, soon learns that she, and her Mummy and Daddy, are not the only things to be given names. Stimulated by her parent's repetition of words, she learns that everything out there in the world is represented by a sound made by the mouth. As her mind and memory develop she learns to name the world out there.

This is an important part of her development: By mapping and naming the world around her, Lucy develops her ability to think and act. Of course, playing is a huge part of her development too. What was your favourite toy as child?

Matthew: I loved Lego – I remember building towers with my bricks at a very young age.

Jez: On the surface it just looked like you were having fun, but as we play we're expanding our capacity for thinking. As all this happens, there's a subtle shift in our energetic centre.

Matthew: What do you mean?

Jez: We've talked about how, in the Natural State, we're responding to life through feeling. Where do you think the energetic centre of feeling is in the body?

Matthew: The heart?

Jez: Yes. When we're in Love, perhaps the biggest feeling we can ever experience, we have a strong feeling in our heart. We say: 'My heart is open,' or 'I give my heart to you.' You see symbols of a heart carved on trees around lovers' names to symbolise this feeling of Love they're sharing. Physically it can feel like the chest is filled up, vibrating with Love that just wants to be shared. That feeling may begin as Love arising towards a lover, but in the end it can't be restricted to a particular person. It's felt by anyone around.

This is why we feel so good around babies in the Natural State; without realising it we're responding to the fact that they're located in their energetic centre of feeling: their hearts. This is where we all began our lives but as we settle in the self and spend more time every day using and expanding the mind, our energetic centre gradually shifts from the feeling centre (the heart) to the thinking centre (the brain). As adults this is taken for granted. If you asked anyone you know to point to where they are in their body, where do you think they'd point?

Matthew: To the head.

Jez: It's where the self identifies itself, if you see what I mean, because thinking is what the self does. Without the capacity for thought, there'd *be* no self. From this point on, thinking becomes central to our lives; it opens up the world to us in so many ways. For example, it introduces us to the concept of time.

Matthew: You mean, because we begin to be able to think about something happening in the past?

Jez: Yes. You could remember playing with Lego yesterday, imagine playing with it again in the future, then find those bricks and bring them into your present experience. So through the mind, the self locates a past, a present and a future; it becomes aware that it exists in something called 'time'.

Matthew: We work out that breakfast happens in the morning and bedtime happens at night.

Jez: Right. So the self is developing and establishing itself through language, play and thinking, and it locates itself in the present through the understanding of the construct of time. But there's another important factor involved in the development of the self: the process of individuation. I think it's time for another definition from the dictionary.

Matthew: It says here: 'How an individual person is held to be distinct from other elements in the world and how a person is distinct from other persons.'

Jez: This happens in all sorts of ways. For example, as Lucy's confidence in operating in the world increases, her self learns that, as a separate being, she has her own unique response to the world. She has likes and dislikes. for example. Furthermore, she finds these preferences do not always align with the experience of life her parents are providing for her. Was there any food you especially disliked as a child?

Matthew: Mushrooms – I hated them...

Jez: And did your parents stop giving you mushrooms to eat?

Matthew: Eventually, after I kicked up a fuss, pulled faces and left them on my plate enough times.

Jez: You became conscious that, through the power of choice, you could sometimes have an influence over what you experienced. You can see how one of the attributes of the original state of Being is starting to change; Choice-less Awareness is slipping away.

The self's ability to have control over its experience through the power of choice becomes the cornerstone of its sense of individuality. Through its likes and dislikes, the self defines and clarifies its identity. It says: 'I like Lego but I don't like mushrooms.'

Matthew: I saw a programme about this stage of a child's development. The first few years are an amazing time of expansion, of neurones forming connections in the brain.

Jez: Yes, physically life is making all these connections, growing our bones and tissues while psychologically we're expanding our consciousness and forming this self, this idea of who we are.

The self develops in other ways too: As well as becoming more skilled at operating in the world, it becomes more individual and distinctive. Particular abilities, talents and quirks begin to show themselves; a unique Character develops. For example, from a very early age I drew constantly; it was something I had a natural affinity for.

Matthew: Apparently the teachers at nursery school realised fairly early on that I was really good at maths and reading.

Jez: These natural talents or quirks don't seem to come from nurture; they're inherent in us and everyone has them.

Matthew: How does all this development of the self and the Character fit in with the Love you said is at the heart of the state of Being?

Jez: It's all an expression of that Love. The Character is simply Love expressing itself in the form of that particular baby. When was the last time you were around a newborn baby?

Matthew: Quite recently: One of my best friends has had a baby boy and some mutual friends and I just visited them.

Jez: How did you all react to him?

Matthew: Everybody went a bit gaga around him; you know how it is.

Jez: People can get a bit besotted with babies; most of us love being around them. It's because they're living in the Natural State and so they show up what we've lost. We feel a sense of wonder, Joy and Love in their presence. In most cases, encountering this Love in the form of their babies, also calls forth the Love in the parents; it's part of an evolutionary cycle.

Matthew: What do you mean?

Jez: Nature gives us the urge to procreate, to propagate the species and it also provides the nurturing spirit in most people to bring up their children. This is all driven and fed by the natural uprising in the parents of Love for their child. This is not the only source of Love for the child; as I mentioned, in the Original Relationship to Life our baby, Lucy, is receiving Love from everything around her: light, air, smells, food, the entire manifest world. Her parents are just one source of the Love that Lucy receives, but a very important source that's part of the evolutionary cycle.

As the self develops it's the parents' job to show their children the rules of how it works to be a human on this planet, to teach them that they need to eat, sleep and not put their hands in fire etcetera. All these practical lessons are about subjects we adults take for granted, so they're easy to teach. But alongside this practical education there's another strand to what's being taught, and that concerns how to 'be' in this world as a self.

Matthew: But you said that babies are in the Natural State so they know how to 'be'.

Jez: This is a really important point: Babies know how to Be – with a capital 'B' – they *are* Being, but they have no experience of being in the world as a self. We have to be shown this, and that job falls to our parents or our guardians. It's this education in how to be as a self that really begins the process of forgetting the Natural State.

12
FORGETTING

How we lose touch with the Natural State

'Man is the only creature that refuses to be what he is.'
– Albert Camus

Jez: We've talked about how, as babies, we develop in all sorts of ways on our periphery through the self, while remaining grounded in Being and Stillness at our centre. As time goes on, baby Lucy is pulled more and more into the self, into that illusion of Separation through simply doing the things babies do: eating, playing, learning to walk and talk etcetera. Through the self she's finding that she can influence the world she's appearing in: Choice-less Awareness is gradually slipping away. She starts to choose what she does more and have attachment to those choices. For example, if she wants to stay up but her parents put her to bed, she may get upset.

Being involved in activity in the world becomes more usual than residing in Stillness. As development continues she become more orientated towards the World out there. The self, through which all these activities happen, becomes denser and more 'real' for her the more it's exercised. Gradually Lucy starts to lose some contact with that Natural State at her centre.

Matthew: You say 'starts' to lose...

Jez: Yes, it can take years and there are levels to losing that connection; how fast or slow it happens depends on a few factors. One would be the Character of the child; some of us seem to have no rush to leave the sacred space of childhood that exists before the world of the self takes over.

Matthew: That makes me think of a friend of mine's son – he still had an imaginary friend when he was six.

Jez: That's a good example of what I mean: The logic of the Mind has not yet taken over. It's as if the world that's perceived has not yet solidified into the rules of reality that we take on from the adults around us; imagination is still as real as 'objective reality'.

Another factor that affects how fast we lose contact with the Natural State is our parents or guardians because, as I said, it's their job to teach us how to 'be' in the world as a self. So their input is enormously influential.

Matthew: Before we go into the influence of the parents in losing that state of Being, can I just get something straight? You're suggesting it's possible to live with the qualities of the Natural State as an adult, is that right?

Jez: Yes, the clue's in the term 'human being'! This is what this whole book is about: the potential in us to live this Being that we are, while operating as an apparently separate self in the world.

Matthew: To be a human BEING.

Jez: Yes, and in order not to lose this connection to Being, we as babies would have to learn this balancing act, but the only agents we have to teach this are people around us: our parents, relatives and teachers.

Matthew: And this is something they don't know...

Jez: Yes, this world is clearly not run on this understanding. Did your parents and teachers know about, and live, the attributes original state of Being? Mine didn't. Have you heard of any parents that did?

Matthew: I can't say I have, but then even the concept of Being, as you've described it, is generally unknown in the world, so how can it be taught if it's not even known?

Jez: You're right; it's impossible. When it comes to Being, parents can only pass on what they know; we can only teach what we ourselves are living. This is what our baby, Lucy, learns from the environment she finds herself in. The child is a seed that grows in the soil of the family.

Matthew: Are you saying that, as babies, we're actually taught to lose that Being which we came as?

Jez: Yes, in a sense you could say that we're taught to forget Being; not intentionally or explicitly, but simply by the example of how our parents are living. It's not wilfully done – no one even knows it's happening, so there's no malice involved. Our parents are simply passing on a way of living in the world that they themselves have been taught. Humans know the 'Human' part of existing as a human being – we know how to eat, to work, to make love etcetera. But we've forgotten the Being part. Because no one has any consciousness of having lost anything, this is all taken as being completely normal.

We've forgotten that we've forgotten!

Matthew: Some people might think something in all this doesn't add up: You said that Love is usually called forth from the parents when in the presence of their baby, so wouldn't that mean the baby experiences nothing but that Love from them?

Jez: With many parents, who are reasonably comfortable in their lives, that Love felt around the baby will predominate. However sooner or later the everyday life of the parents is going to come in and disturb the calling forth of that Love.

Matthew: By everyday life, you mean...?

Jez: The normal ups and downs of the Personality's emotional life. Perhaps Lucy's mother is feeling unfulfilled in her creative life or her father is fearful about his job security. Maybe their relationship is going through a difficult time, all the normal stuff of human life. These emotions temporarily block the Love Lucy receives from her parents.

Matthew: So you're saying that when we're angry, or depressed, we aren't expressing Love to our loved ones?

Jez: Yes, it doesn't mean that we don't love them, it just means we're not *expressing* our love for them in that moment. Naturally most parents try to keep their emotions away from their children but, however hard they try, they can't always succeed.

Matthew: Why is that?

Jez: Because babies are supremely sensitive. Remember, in the Natural State they have no sense of separation between themselves and their environment.

Matthew: So Lucy feels it all...

Jez: If she's still rooted in the Natural State she's not yet learned how to cut off from feeling. Whatever's around her, whether it's happiness, tension, anger or sadness, she feels it as if it were her own.

Matthew: That must be awful for her.

Jez: Not really, at least not at first, because the feeling is felt fully so it doesn't get stuck, it just passes through her system. Negative emotions are just a different experience for her, like feeling cold water after feeling warm. Remember, in the Natural State there's Choice-less Awareness, so all experiences are felt; there's no mind to judge one as good or bad, pleasurable or unpleasant.

In a way you could say that the Natural State protects her because, although she requires her parents as providers of her needs in the world, as far as Love goes, at least at the very beginning of her life, she is self-sufficient. In Being, Lucy is already whole, already complete because she's in touch with the Love that she is.

Matthew: So, if our Natural State protects us, how is our parents' lack of it passed on to us?

Jez: It happens as an outcome of the process of identifying with the world out there. The more we do that, the more we lose the Natural State and become attuned to living as all adults do. At first we can rub up against all sorts of things in the world and remain essentially unaffected by it, but as we identify more and more as the self, that immunity is lost. As we spend more time engaged in life as this self, Oneness, the source from which the self has arisen, is gradually forgotten.

Matthew: It's like the self takes over; it takes control.

Jez: Exactly. What once had simply been a device with which to operate in the world now becomes something in its own right; the self is fully adopted as Lucy's identity. Her consciousness, which had previously been unlimited, is now confined to this finite idea of who she is. She becomes locked into the belief of being an 'I'.

In this narrowing down of her Original Relationship to Life she loses the experience of herself as Love and takes on the belief that the core of who she is, is the thing that appears to operate her self – her mind. The self is of course a vital part of her development as a human being, but in becoming *identified* as it, she starts to lose her connection to Being and joins the Group Personality of her family.

Matthew: I can understand all this logically, but this transition from Being to identification as the self is a difficult one to get hold of.

Jez: I know. As long as you think you are only that self, then it doesn't compute. How can the self conceive of the absence of itself? As we know, it helps to see things from different angles and to hear them said in different ways, so I've come up with a story to illustrate this:

The Story of Finn the Fish – Part One

A fish called Finn lives in a Great Sea close to the shore. He's gloriously happy just swimming about in the water, darting through the weeds and rocks, doing all the things that fish do. Finn has lived his whole life in the Great Sea; he's so used to this wonderful watery world that he feels like it's a part of him and he's a part of it.

One day, while swimming around exploring the sea near the beach Finn pokes his head above the water and notices something very strange: a place beyond the shore where the sea ends – a place that isn't the sea! It's a strange world out there, with different colours, shapes and sounds. He swims through the shallow water, right up to the shore to have a closer look; that's when he notices that the world out there beyond the sea isn't wet. It's dry. He flips around and swims back to his home – the Great Sea, this place of delicious, never-ending wetness.

***

The summer brings scorching high temperatures. Finn notices that the land on the shore is baked dry by the searing sun; but he just carries on happily darting and diving around in his own safe world. The raging heat doesn't affect him at all because the water in the Great Sea is so deep and wide it remains nice and cool.

When the autumn arrives, dark skies appear, the winds

pick up and a hurricane blasts its tumultuous breath over the Great Sea. Finn watches the grass quivering and the trees shaking and bending on the shore. The water all around starts to rise and fall in choppy waves, tossing and turning him until he becomes dizzy. Before he has a chance to dive deep and take refuge at the bottom of the sea, the rampaging wind plucks Finn from the water and sucks him up into the dark tempestuous sky.

Finn doesn't remember what happens next. Buffeted about by howling winds way up in the clouds, he passes out in shock. When he wakes up, the hurricane has passed, the air is still, but he's stranded in the world out there, on a sandy bit of ground on the other side of the shore.

Finn is in a state of shock; he's seen dryness from the sea but this is the first time he's actually experienced it. Before long his scales become scratchy and itchy, his throat is parched. Finn has to do something before he dries out altogether. He needs water, he can't live without it, so he decides to try to find the Great Sea.

By hauling himself forward on his front fins and flipping his tail behind him, Finn finds he can move very slowly across the dry dusty land. He flips, flaps and flops but there's no sign of any familiar trees or rocks. He can't find his way back to the Great Sea.

Exhausted, Finn lies down in some mud. That's when, just behind him, he sees a little muddy pond. It looks just like the sea, only smaller. He slips down the bank into the delicious cool water. It feels just like the sea. Finally he feels safe again.

The little muddy pond quickly becomes Finn's new home; he spends his days swimming happily in water again. After a while, he starts to get used to this small pond and realises that in his old life he'd made a mistake: He thought he was a part of the Great Sea, but he isn't, he's separate from it. Because he has a body, with fins and a tail, he can swim anywhere there's water. Gradually Finn forgets about being outside the Great Sea; it doesn't matter any more. In the pond he's the king in his own kingdom and he likes it.

13

THE WOUND

The moment we first experience estrangement from Love

'Nothing has a stronger influence psychologically on their environment and especially on their children than the unlived life of the parent.'

– Carl Jung

Jez: When we lose the Natural State by becoming identified as the self, we also forfeit the experience of Love that was central to that way of Being. Love is a need as vital for our healthy development as the physical requirements of air, food and water. Now that it's no longer our ongoing experience, we have to rely on another way of receiving that Love.

Matthew: You mean from our parents or guardians?

Jez: Primarily, but also from other family members or whoever's around. As soon as we're born, we enter the Relative Level of a human being; part of that is needing to receive Love and nurturance from parents. This arises alongside our innate connection to Love that's part of the Natural State.

Matthew: You mean beyond human, personal love.

Jez: Yes, this Love is who we are. But as time goes on, the balance shifts: That innate connection to Love in all things diminishes and our need to receive personal love increases. It's like a substitute for what we've lost. It's not the same as living 'as' Love but it's the best we can get.

Matthew: But our parents or guardians aren't aware that we've lost anything, are they?

Jez: Not at all, because they aren't aware that *they've* lost their own Natural State. No one knows any other possibility, so this is just the way things are. Our experience of Love shifts from the universal to the personal and in that shift our parents, or whoever serves as our primary guardians, become the centre of our universe. When we lose our Original Relationship to Life, the Group Personality becomes our strength and our comfort.

Matthew: Because we need that personal love now?

Jez: Yes, and that need places us in a vulnerable position because, like happiness, love in the world of man can be conditional.

Matthew: This sounds like a big subject.

Jez: You're right, and to help us explore it I'm going to pick up with our story about Finn the fish.

The Story of Finn the Fish – Part Two

Finn is happy in his new home, the little muddy pond. Winter turns to spring; spring turns to summer and the temperature starts to rise. But Finn isn't worried; why should he be? His experience in the Great Sea has taught him that he can keep swimming around in the cool water; the heat won't affect him at all.

But as each sweltering day passes, Finn notices that the water in the pond is starting to get warmer, and worse, there's less of it. Inch by inch the level of water drops lower and lower down the dry muddy bank. Swimming up and down in ten inches of water that remain, he starts to become stressed; worrying about what he's going to do.

Eventually he's lying in a small puddle only two inches deep, just trying to survive. Finn feels terrible; he has no control over what's happening. He's lost in a new world he doesn't understand.

We'll pause the story there for a moment. Finn put his trust in a water source that was not dependable, but what else could he do? He had no choice. He had no clue where the Great Sea was, or how to find it and get back to it. This pond was the best he could get.

Like Finn, we had no choice, we were no longer self-sufficient when it came to our need of Love; we had to get it from somewhere.

Matthew: So let me get this straight: We become dependent on others to give Love to us. Our parent's Love becomes our main source of Love and this makes us vulnerable because they don't exist in the Natural State.

Jez: Yes, as we discussed last time, the Love from our parents, despite all their good intentions, can be conditional.

Matthew: I'm reminded of that line from the Philip Larkin poem:

They f**k you up your Mum and Dad

Jez: It's a line that most people know because it's so widely recognised to be true. It's brutal but you can't argue with it, because anyone can see that, at some point during childhood, we lose the Natural State we come with and it's our environment that facilitates that loss.

The pond is not the same as the sea; there's a limited supply of water and its presence is conditional on the state of the weather. Most of the time Love may be there, but because our parents have lost the Natural State, sometimes it *won't* be. Their Love is conditional on their emotional state.

Matthew: So if they're depressed or angry, for example, their ability to perceive and express love is lost, or at least compromised?

Jez: Yes, and it's the same for any emotion: resentment, jealousy, grief etcetera. You can observe this in yourself – whenever you're emotional, see if you're in contact with Love.

Matthew: I can see it clearly the other way round: Whenever I'm feeling loving, I'm not emotional.

Jez: As adults the constancy of our Natural State is replaced by the changeability of our emotional life. In some Personalities this is pronounced, such as the angry temperament of a violent alcoholic, but it can also be very low key and less dramatic. Whether it's a chronic ongoing emotional state like depression or a passing moment of sadness, the fact remains that, as children, at some point we come into contact with the absence of Love in human life.

Think back to baby Lucy. As I've explained, while she's still rooted in the Natural State she's protected from the full impact of that experience. However, once fully identified as the self, she loses that protection, because she's no longer in the embrace of her own connection to Love. Now she's vulnerable, because she needs the Love from outside sources.

I call that moment, when we need that Love from outside ourselves and it's not there, the Wound. It's the initiation into a life lived outside the 'sea' of Love. When Finn realises that the water in the pond is not stable, that's his Wound.

Matthew: I remember, when I was very young, drawing on a wall with an orange crayon and being confused because my mum, who was usually a peaceful earth-mother type, became furious. It was as if a terrifying, angry monster had replaced my mother.

Jez: As this moment stuck in your memory so well, it's possible that this may have been your Wound, or at least it was the first time you became conscious of it. Don't forget, you may have experienced anger previously from your mum, but if it was before you became identified as a self, it wouldn't have registered in your memory.

Matthew: Just clarify why for me again.

Jez: Going back to our story of Finn the fish, there had been droughts before where the pond had evaporated, but safe in his Great Sea, Finn was unaffected by it. Now he's outside of the sea, in the pond, it's a different story altogether. Now the drought affects him personally.

    Once we identify as the self, we're no longer self-sufficient when it comes to Love. We're no longer unaffected when, for whatever reason, our supply of Love from the world is interrupted.

Matthew: You mean we don't just feel it and return back to the Love of the Natural State any more?

Jez: We can't: Our ongoing connection to that has been cut. Finn can't find his way back to the sea; the hurricane dropped him far away from it. It's as if we've come too far into the world of man, into the World of Separation, to turn back. Now, when we experience the absence of personal love, we confront the full implications of being identified with this self. We encounter our estrangement from the Love that we are; we feel for the first time the existential pain of being in the world yet outside of Love's embrace. That is the Wound.

Matthew. I was so scared when my mum shouted at me; it almost felt as if my life was being threatened.

Jez: It feels that bad because our connection to Love is a vital part of our connection to life. If you saw that moment on a film now it probably wouldn't look so terrible from the outside. It's normal to see mums or dads getting frustrated with their kids; being a parent is a stressful job. All it takes is one moment of emotion, but that moment can be devastating for the child.

Matthew: Do you think the Wound happens at roughly the same time in everyone's development?

Jez: Depending on our parents, it can happen early on or quite late in childhood. For me it happened very early: As my Mother was post-natally depressed, I experienced that absence of Love from the start of my life. As a baby in the Natural State I still had protection from it but, as soon as I identified as the self that Wound impacted on me.

My wife's experience was different. She managed to protect herself from her family's emotional dysfunction until she was three because she spent her first years sleeping a lot – it was like a form of meditation. In sleep, something in her had found a way of keeping her connection to the Natural State intact, but that could only last so long. As all the normal demands of operating in the world kicked in, that connection through extended sleep slipped away.

Matthew: From what you've said before, I'm guessing that the Wound happens to everyone – no one escapes it.

Jez: Do you know any adults who appear to be living in the knowledge that they are Love? Let me put it another way: Do you know anyone who doesn't exhibit any form of behaviour indicating the loss of that Love?

Matthew: What sort of behaviour?

Jez: Emotions such as anger, fear or grief running their life, worry, extreme busyness, addiction of any sort, egomania, lack of self-esteem, insecurity etcetera.

Matthew: When you put it like that... I can't think of a single person.

Jez: There are endless ways that the Wound can manifest as the self continues to develop, but one thing's for sure: After the Wound, our lives are changed forever.

14

THE LOSS OF INNOCENCE

How we learn that, in the world of man, love is conditional

'A man cannot be comfortable without his own approval.'
– Mark Twain

Let's pick up with our story:

The Story of Finn the Fish – Part Three

Is this where things end for Finn, stranded in a little muddy puddle under the blazing summer sun? No – he hears the plop and splash of water falling all around; his scales moisten: It's raining. The water level slowly rises, the puddle turns back into a pond and Finn starts swimming again.

Before long, everything starts to look and feel just as it did before the drought. But it's not. After all that's happened, Finn is not the same as he was before. Something's changed: He's become aware of the world out there; he's seen what it can do and he's learned from his experience. In the Great Sea there was so much water it could never run out, but now he knows that the water in the little muddy pond is not as abundant as the water in the sea. It can dry out; it can disappear. This water is untrustworthy.

Finn tries to carry on as if nothing's happened; he swims around all day long, just like he used to. But deep inside he can't forget the terrible day that the water ran out and the pond disappeared. He can't help remembering how dry, washed up and powerless he felt. And then he has another, even more terrible thought: 'The water disappeared once – it could disappear again.'

Matthew: So Finn's first response to what happened is to try to understand it?

Jez: Yes. He re-evaluates his circumstances, he examines what's happened and tries to learn from it.

Matthew: And that's what we do?

Jez: Yes, the self responds to the Wound as it has learned to do with any new experience: It observes and then pieces together the information it acquires in an effort to understand the world in which it operates.

Matthew: So, just as Finn realises that the water in the pond isn't as abundant as the water in the sea...

Jez: ...Some part of us becomes conscious of the fact that Love in the world is an unstable commodity. We learn that when this 'personal' love is absent we experience traumatic feelings of being cast adrift in the World of Separation without the security of being anchored in Oneness. It's the first time we experience feeling hurt by life.

Matthew: You make it sound terrible...

Jez: Well it is. Think of your worst nightmare, what you're most scared of in this life – all of that comes from this central root, the Wound. It's the feeling of disconnection from Love and a loss of trust in it.

    The self doesn't want to feel this terror, so it continues to analyse what's happened in order to understand more so that it won't be hurt by it. Lucy trusted her parents to protect her in the world – why shouldn't she? That's the way it's always been for her, but now the self recognises it's her parents who have apparently denied her their love and caused her this hurt. So for the first time she experiences a loss of trust in them.

Matthew: This is all happening unconsciously, I presume.

Jez: It's all instinct; it's not like she's thinking: 'I don't trust you any more.' When the Wound happens she's too young to put complex psychological feelings into words, but inside, her trust in that personal love has been lost and there are far-reaching outcomes to this in her life.

Matthew: Such as?

Jez: You have to remember that the self is still trying to make sense of this world and how it works; the Wound is a momentous event in terms of understanding it. Love has always been present, this is what she's come to expect, but now, as far as personal love goes, she has an experience of it *not* being there. The self tries to make sense of all this by asking the question: 'Why did the Love go?' and it's easy for her come to the conclusion that it's something to do with her.

Matthew: Why would she come to that conclusion?

Jez: By this point in her development the self has understood some basic concepts about humans and their behaviour. She's been taught that how she acts produces different responses in her parents: She knows there's something called 'being good' and when she's 'good' it produces a positive response. If she finishes the food on her plate Mummy's pleased with her. She feels it like a warm ray of love and that makes her feel good.

She's also learned that there's an opposite to 'being good' – 'being bad' – and that produces a different response from her parents. If she throws her plate on the floor, Mummy's *not* pleased with her and she feels her displeasure, as if that ray of love has been turned off.

Matthew: That's what I felt with my Mum after I'd drawn on the wall with that crayon.

Jez: Before you'd become identified as a self, your Mum's angry reaction wouldn't have bothered you. In the Natural State you didn't need her love because you were already 'in' Love; you had no need of her approval.

Matthew: I see what you mean: Love doesn't need approval, Love just is.

Jez: Exactly, but by that point you'd obviously been drawn into the self enough to have forgotten that you *are* Love. You'd taken on the construct of your behaviour being bad and, when you felt your Mum's displeasure, it took on a different significance. Because you *needed* her love, her displeasure became a sign, a threat to you, of losing that love.

Matthew: But as a parent you have to teach your child that some things are unacceptable. Surely that's part of the job?

Jez: Definitely, it is, but you can do that with Love. Doing that with anger, with the implicit threat of the withdrawal of Love, is a whole different thing.

Matthew: I think my Mother's anger on that occasion really affected my self-image. I didn't like feeling I was bad. It's like I took it personally, as if there was something wrong with me.

Jez: One of the things that can occur as an outcome of the Wound is that the concept of *'behaving* badly' can be conflated with the idea of *'being* bad'. The thought that we can, in some way, be fundamentally 'wrong' is a radical new concept for us and we can take on the idea that it's this imagined imperfection which has made us unworthy of our parents' love. This is where the belief that we're not loveable grows from; it's the root of all self-esteem problems.

I saw an article in a magazine yesterday about a really famous model, someone who millions of women and men look up to as an example of female perfection in their beautiful face and body. It's funny how each culture has its own ideas of what constitutes beauty: In India larger bodies are perceived to be the most beautiful, but this model is western so she's a classic, ultra-thin, honey-skinned blonde. The great and tragic irony is that, in the article, she talked about how she always hated her body! Can you believe it? Half the world is drooling over your beautiful curves and long limbs but that means nothing to you, because you believe you're ugly. And as long as you believe it, as far as you're concerned it's true.

This is not natural – life gives you an amazing body and you turn against it, you start hating it! All of this Suffering comes from the Wound and the belief that you have some imagined imperfection.

Matthew: I don't have any memory of deciding I have an 'imagined imperfection'.

Jez: No, of course not – as a baby this is all pre-conscious. The operating system, which is the self, is growing and making all sorts of deductions about this life, but there's no overview that's conscious of what it's doing. Of course, like the model in the magazine, you may become aware of it later in your life, but by then it's taken root and become ingrained.

Matthew: I mainly regard myself as having healthy self-esteem, but when I look back, I remember feeling inadequate when my parents moved me from state school to private school. Everyone was ahead of me academically – and seemed posher...

Jez: My point is, in the Natural State, the very idea that we are in some way wrong, or not good enough, is impossible. So that feeling you had at the private school, as far as I'm concerned, can only have come from the Wound. That situation would not have affected you so strongly if, somewhere inside, you didn't have some sort of belief about 'not being good enough.' To quote Jung:

No one can make you feel inferior without your consent.

Most people have some form of this. I'm not saying everyone goes round self-flagellating all the time, but the belief that we're somehow not good enough can be embedded deep in the subconscious and have all sorts of knock-on effects, especially with regard to our emotional life. Let me ask you, how did you feel in that situation at the new school?

Matthew: Confused, scared; I wanted to hide. I didn't think I'd ever make it academically or fit in socially.

Jez. I'd suggest that all those feelings had their roots in the Wound. This primal belief that we are, in some unknown way, unlovable creates in us one of our first 'negative' feelings: the feeling of sadness. It's the primal Joy of the original state of Being turned on its head.

Matthew: What about the fear I felt?

Jez: Before the Wound impacted on our life, the past was only called to memory for functional reasons: remembering places, names and objects from our past enabled us to operate more effectively and control our environment in the present. But because the memory of the Wound is traumatic, it's continually activated in our consciousness. Not for any practical use in the present, but simply because the experience was so strong its imprint has become 'stuck'.

Having become familiar with the concept of time, our mind instinctively takes this memory and projects it into the future: If Love is unreliable, and I'm found to be unlovable again, then Love could be withdrawn from me once more. It's like Finn, our fish; he's aware that the drought could come again, the awful feeling of being without water could return. He may be splashing about in the pond full of water now, but somewhere deep inside he can't forget

134

what's happened in the past, and what could happen again in the future. That trauma is etched into his memory; he knows that the drought might come again. This is how we're introduced to our first experience of existential fear.

Matthew: What do you mean by 'existential fear'?

Jez: If a lion approaches us, fear releases adrenaline into our body which increases our alertness and strength, enabling us to get away from there as quick as we can. Once we're out of danger, the fear response passes too. That's survival fear.

Existential fear is a different sort of fear – it arises after the Wound and is a response to the threat of losing our 'lifeline' of Love. It's a threat to our psychological, rather than physical, wellbeing. Because this threat of Love going is always there, and we're powerless to do anything about it, the fear doesn't just go away. I'm not saying it's constantly turned up to maximum, but it remains latent within us. This fear affects our behaviour. We understand, for example, that if we can avoid displeasing our parents we won't feel their disapproval of us, and in turn we won't feel the withdrawal of that Love.

Matthew: I wouldn't have dared write on the wall again!

Jez: You started to become self-conscious about your behaviour; you chose how to act in a way that didn't displease your parents. You learned how to 'please' to gain positive attention from them. But I'm sure you also felt angry with them at times as well.

Matthew: Because they seemed to withdraw their love, you mean?

Jez: Yes. We place trust in our parents as our protectors and teachers, and suddenly they're telling us we're bad and they're withdrawing the Love they'd previously given. It's like a betrayal of our trust.

Matthew: I remember feeling really confused after that crayon incident.

Jez: I was going to say that in the Original Relationship to Life we know what we are: We're Love. But that statement is incorrect, because there is no 'I' there to know that we are Love, there's just

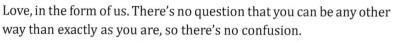

Love, in the form of us. There's no question that you can be any other way than exactly as you are, so there's no confusion.

When we become identified as a self we lose that knowledge of ourselves as Love, we lose that Original Relationship to Life. Already this is a confusing situation: We're cast adrift in a world we don't know or understand, a world of confusing feelings where we're sometimes told we're bad. Then we realise that we can adapt our behaviour to try to be good in order to please our parents. And all this is underpinned by the threat that Love could be withdrawn at any time.

Is it any wonder we become confused? Like Finn the fish, we have woken up in a strange place, with different rules that we don't understand.

Matthew: Does Finn make it back to the Great Sea?

Jez: That's what this book is all about! Can the fish make it back to the Great Sea and stay there? First of all he has to remember that there *is* a Great Sea, and then discover how to find it again.

15

CONTRACTION

How we learn to contract from love to protect
ourselves from being hurt

'Living is easy with eyes closed.'

– John Lennon

Jez: The Wound is a momentous, formative event in our early lives. It changes everything. Part of the reason for that is our response to it: We don't just lie down and take it; the self is proactive in response to it.

Matthew: In what way?

Jez: First let's look at the initial effect the Wound has on Lucy, our baby. Consider the existential pain she feels at finding herself, for the first time in her life, outside of Love's embrace.

Since its formation the self has been adding to its experience, extending its knowledge of how the world is and how it operates. The more familiar the world becomes, the more the self feels safe operating within it. With the event of the Wound, this process of increasing familiarity and security is undermined. The Wound does not make Lucy feel safe – on the contrary, that existential pain of the lack of love makes her feel abandoned and insecure. She loses trust in the world as a safe place to be.

This insecurity is added to by the fact that she can now think and project into the future; she needs love from a world in which love is unstable, in which it could disappear again. The simple order of life lived in Oneness is replaced by a sense of chaos. The self's short existence has been cut in two: There's the safe version of life it experienced and remembers from before the Wound and the unstable, frightening experience that came after it.

Matthew: What does the self do?

Jez: The self responds as it's done with every challenge it's faced: It uses the information it has and tries to master the world in which it's operating. When it comes to the Wound, it tries to neutralise its negative effects by performing a great disappearance trick. In an attempt to return to the peaceful, safe life it remembers from *before* the Wound, the self tries to deny that the Wound has happened at all.

Matthew: You mean it lies to itself?

Jez: In a sense, yes. The self pretends it never became conscious of the event of the Wound, or the disturbing feeling of being outside of Love's embrace.

*Matthew: But the Wound **did** happen; Lucy did feel that existential pain.*

Jez: Yes, and strong feelings aren't just wiped out once the event causing them has passed; if they were, there'd be no such thing as post-traumatic stress disorder. Lucy can't actually make those feelings disappear. But she can make it *seem* as if they have.

Matthew: You mean by repressing them?

Jez: Exactly. Her mind effectively divides in two and creates a place within itself in which it confines all that it chooses not to be conscious of. In the world of Duality her conscious mind gives birth to its opposite: the subconscious mind.

I use the word 'choose' loosely – she's not actually choosing to do anything; all of this happens instinctively. Just as the self is programmed to explore, to learn, to take on the idea of itself as a separate entity, so it's programmed to protect itself in this way. It's a survival strategy.

Matthew: It makes me think of soldiers who manage to put aside all the horrific scenes they're witnessing in a war zone so they can keep on doing their job of fighting the enemy.

Jez: It's a good analogy. Just like the soldier, the self has a job to do. It has to get on with living in the world and expanding its development. If it became overburdened by the chaos and emotional fallout of the Wound, it wouldn't be able to carry out that job; it would collapse and Lucy's development and growth would be derailed.

This type of repression is something humans are programmed to do as a coping mechanism for dealing with extremely stressful events. We put aside the impact of the event in order to remain operational in the moment. The event of the Wound is the first time in our lives that this function kicks in.

Matthew: The self is kind of editing the experience of our life... Choice-less Awareness isn't operating any more, is it?

Jez: No, the self is choosing to believe its own version of events, rather than an objective record of what's happened. We believe our edited version of reality, the one without the Wound, because it makes us feel safer.

Matthew: Like when I decided as a toddler that I didn't like mushrooms: Through the power of choice I kind of edited them out of my life by letting it be known I wouldn't eat them.

Jez: Yes, except that the choice I'm talking about here is much more radical and far reaching. You, or rather instinct, decided you didn't like mushrooms, so something in you refused to eat them. You effectively edited mushrooms out of your diet but not totally out of your life; you still saw them on other people's plates.

Matthew: I see what you mean: Mushrooms still existed; they just didn't show up on my plate any more.

Jez: Right. The self's editing is more radical than that. The self rejects the whole event of the Wound and tries to banish it from its experience as if it had never happened. Effectively it chooses the memory of how life was before the Wound and rejects those painful feelings of the absence of love that arose in the chaotic life that came after it.

Matthew: It's like the self is playing God.

Jez: Yes, but there are outcomes to this strategy that arise from the fact that repressed feelings can't just disappear. When soldiers return from war, all the terrifying experiences they've repressed can start surfacing in post-traumatic stress syndrome. We'll discuss repressed feelings in the next talk, for now I want to focus on another outcome of our repression of the Wound: the effect it has on our relationship to Love.

Remember how I said that in the Natural State we live from the heart centre? This is where we feel and express Love. It's because we're absolutely open in our hearts that the experience of the absence of Love hits us so strongly and feels so painful. In that moment we have no protection from the experience, which is why it hits us so hard. And this pain brings with it a powerful lesson: It teaches us that personal love is dangerous, because when it's withdrawn, it can hurt us.

Matthew: Personal love can hurt us by its absence.

Jez: Right, and the trouble is, now we know love comes laced with the possibility of its withdrawal; we become conscious of the fact that it can go at any moment. We learn that personal love is unreliable.

Matthew: So what can the self do about that?

Jez: In order to regain its sense of control the self tries to protect us from the dangers of being hurt again; it changes our relationship to love from one of openness and trust to closedness and mistrust.

Matthew: What does this mean in practice?

Jez: It means that, when Lucy is with a love source like her parents, she may adopt a protective strategy: before love can be withdrawn and she can be hurt again, she pulls back from it in a protective flinch. It's a contraction from love. In order to not feel the existential pain of the absence of love she has to contract. It's a closing down of her full-feeling engagement with life.

Matthew: So that's another attribute of the Natural State she's losing.

Jez: She doesn't stop feeling completely – that would be impossible – but she closes down her *openness* to feeling; she become wary of it. It's like Finn the fish: He's learned that the water in the pond is unreliable and this starts to inform his viewpoint about water in general; he becomes cautious and wary of it.

Matthew: You mean he starts to distrust any water source?

Jez: Yes, not just the water in the pond. If he could get to any other pond he would apply the same caution, because he now believes that *all* water is untrustworthy; it could go at any moment and leave him stranded.

This thought has a very specific outcome in terms of Finn's happiness because as long as he's worrying that the water could start disappearing at any moment he's not experiencing the Joy of being a fish swimming around in the delicious cool water.

Matthew: So Joy is also starting to be eroded?

Jez: Yes, like Finn, Lucy starts thinking more than feeling. The Contraction

141

– I give it a capital 'C' to distinguish it from other kinds of contraction –
is a subtle closing down of her heart, a further move away from the full
feeling of the heart centre and into the thinking of the mind. Personal
love is dangerous; it's much safer to think than to feel.

*Matthew: When I was about seven, some family friends had a toddler
who was so happy, open and easy to please, it was as if the light used
to shine out of her. But one day I noticed something had changed.
She became difficult, stroppy even. It was as if she was a completely
different kid.*

Jez: Now you know what happened; it shows in different ways, but the
Wound happens to all of us. There's a photo of me from my childhood
and I can see the after-effect of the Wound; the openness in my face
and the light in my eyes has been replaced by a subtle look of mistrust.

Matthew: It's like the loss of innocence.

Jez: It *is* the loss of innocence. To use a biblical reference, it's the end
of being in the Garden of Eden. You can try looking at early photos
of yourself and spotting whether they were taken before or after the
Wound.

By contracting, the self is using the skills it's learnt in the
world not just to experience life, but also to control it, to shape our
perception of it and our relationship to it.

Matthew: And all this happens instinctively?

Jez: Yes, the Contraction, this spontaneous reflex action of self-
protection, operates without our conscious participation.

*Matthew: Even though you've said that the self has an awareness to
examine and evaluate the world around us?*

Jez: There is a growing awareness of the physical world out there,
but our minds are not yet developed enough to turn that spotlight of
awareness on the self. It's like a blind spot. Without self-awareness,
there's no part of us that's able to decide consciously how to act
beyond these instinctive protective patterns. Through the choices
it apparently makes, the self controls our relationship to the world
and we experience the outcome of those choices.

16

REPRESSION

How the Personality consigns unwanted feelings
to the subconscious

'Humankind cannot bear very much reality.'

– T.S. Eliot

Jez: Yesterday I saw a toddler running on the beach. His face was so lit up by Joy, he looked as if he was going to burst. All his senses were alive to the sensations of the crashing waves, the fresh salty air and the warm sun on his skin. Everything was stimulating his senses; there was nothing in him that was blocking or limiting that absorption of it all. Do you remember being like that?

Matthew: Yes, I remember many moments like that from my childhood, for example the sheer exhilaration of playing Hide and Seek in the park, running barefoot with the grass under my feet and smell of the summer air in my nostrils.

Jez: When we talked about the original state of Being I said that one of its attributes was feeling. We spoke about how, as babies, we're present to whatever's happening – whether it's Joy, frustration or sadness, we totally engage with whatever feeling is arising. Even when experiencing distress, we express it fully; the stress and tightness it creates in our body is let go of and we return to the more neutral feeling of primal Joy.

Matthew: So you're saying, until the Wound, that's our experience of life.

Jez: Yes, a full engagement with wherever we are, whatever is arising, through feeling.

Matthew: And after the Wound... You're saying we're somehow pulled back from being fully engaged in the world?

Jez: We interact with the world through feeling so, if there's a Contraction, a pulling back from feeling, then there's a pulling back from full engagement with the world. Think of Lucy: After the Wound, she lost trust. She learned that the world is potentially an unsafe place to be. Feelings are dangerous because she can be let down, she can be hurt, she can be pulled back to those painful feelings of the Wound which she's consigned to her subconscious.

Matthew: I don't understand how she can be 'pulled back' to those original feelings if they're locked away?

Jez: Most of the time her repressed feelings are inactive; as long as they're not disturbed, they remain latent and she gets on with her life as if they aren't there. Because remember, as far as she's concerned, they don't even exist. They've been banished to her subconscious, so she's not conscious of them. If you notice, I didn't say: '*She* has banished them,' I said: '*they've* been banished'. It was that self-protective instinct which banished them to her subconscious; it happened without any conscious participation on Lucy's part.

Matthew: OK, so you're saying we instinctively protect ourselves from those painful feelings of the Wound by editing them out of our experience.

Jez: Yes, by now Choice-less Awareness has broken down; the self has started to pick and choose what comes into our consciousness. But this strategy of denial and repression to stave off unwanted feelings is not totally successful.

Matthew: It's well known that feelings can't just be silenced, that repression doesn't work forever.

Jez: Yes, but *why* doesn't it work? Why can't feelings just be locked away? We're talking about psychology but the answer is actually very scientific. Albert Einstein said:

Energy cannot be created or destroyed.

I thought about this last night when I watched a nature documentary about beavers building dams in Yellowstone Park. The energy of the river wants to flow and the dams are working against that flow, trying to stop it. In spring, these beautifully engineered structures are really tested because the ice melts higher in the mountains, releasing phenomenal amounts of water into the river, increasing its flow. As this torrent reaches the dam there are two possibilities: Either the dam breaches, and the spring flood breaks through, or it holds fast. If it holds fast the water starts to back up and eventually it overflows, bursts the banks of the river and finds another path across the land.

Energy cannot be destroyed: The river doesn't want to be stopped; it wants to move. To put it poetically, you could say that life wants to express itself.

Matthew: A river wants to flow...

Jez: Yes, that's what a river does, and this principle applies to all areas of life, including feelings because feelings are energy just as water is energy. All psychotherapists know that repressing feelings doesn't have the required effect of making them disappear; they remain stored in the body and mind in a latent form. This means they can be activated at any time. If a strong feeling in the present resonates with a feeling that's been locked away in the past, it can wake up and activate that original feeling.

Imagine Lucy, now three years old, becomes separated from her mum in a supermarket. In the Original Relationship to Life she would have been happy being looked after by strangers until she was reunited with her mother. She's not yet focussed on her mother as being her primary source of Love so there'd be no threat, no separation trauma. She's already receiving Love from life in all its forms: the colours of the food on the shelves, people walking down the aisles, the light coming through the window. But after the Wound, being separated from the primary love source of her parents causes Lucy to be totally distraught because her repressed feelings of abandonment and extreme fear from the Wound are being activated.

Getting lost in a supermarket is a chance happening, usually a one-off mistake, but less dramatic, everyday events can also trigger such repressed feelings. For example, when Lucy goes to school and is the last to be picked for a netball team, that rejection can also activate those latent feelings of abandonment. Or maybe her best friend at school finds another friend who they like more than her. When these triggers catch her unawares, and the painful feelings are brought up, what does she do? She can deal with this just as she did with the original feelings from the Wound, by pulling back from feeling, so she doesn't feel that pain. This is what the Contraction is for. This is its function.

*Matthew: If I've got this right, you're saying that originally the Contraction closes us off from the painful feelings of the Wound. That's from the past, but the Contraction **also** protects us from feelings rooted in the past that are happening in the present.*

Jez: Yes, it's a partial closing down of our openness to feeling; it takes the edge off life because we're not submitted to the traumatic feelings that can come up. The Personality buries them deep in a box of concrete so they won't bother you. You could argue that this strategy works to an extent. If you look at most people, they're able to get on with their lives, they're adapted; their functioning is not compromised by being pulled into their deepest pain. This is the group mind's idea of health: It's all about getting on, being productive. Looking at one's pain is seen as being self-obsessed.

But like I said, this strategy is not wholly successful for two reasons. Firstly because, as Einstein said, energy can't be destroyed. By repressing the feeling, it builds, gets stronger and is always seeking ways to release itself.

The second reason why this strategy isn't successful is down to a fundamental law which applies to feelings; you can't isolate one feeling and repress it. We want to close down to *traumatic* feelings and keep open to 'good', happy feelings, but you can't close down to 'negative' feelings without closing down to *all* feelings. The extent to which you close down to undesirable feelings is the extent to which you also close down to desirable feelings.

Matthew: This reminds me of a time I took anti–depressants... The switch was turned down on feeling the depression but I ended up feeling like a zombie, de-sensitised.

Jez: Life may be easier in some respects, but at what cost? Think of it like an aperture on a camera – the more you close it down the less light is let in. After the Contraction we're closing down from taking in the full richness of life, and interacting with life through feeling is a central part of our Joy in the Natural State. So by contracting we're diminishing our capacity for Joy.

Matthew: But we still feel things...

Jez: Yes of course, but our openness to feeling is reduced, our capacity to feel is diminished. There's a heart-breaking story about a young girl who'd obviously not lost her primal Joy yet – let's imagine it's Lucy. She's dancing in front of her aged grandmother who's sitting hunched up in a chair watching her. Lucy stops dancing, looks over at her and says: 'Granny, did you use to dance when you were alive?'

Matthew: That's painfully poignant...

Jez: It's excruciating. But why? Because it points to a truth about all of us: Being less vibrant and full of life is taken for granted as we get older. We believe it's an unavoidable outcome of the aging process. In fact, so much of that deadening and stiffening, both mental and physical, comes from the Contraction and the closing down of full feeling. We'll go into this more when we talk about health.

Matthew: But these days there's a whole anti-aging culture.

Jez: Yes, and much of that is the *pretence* of being young, and the hiding of the aging process through cosmetic surgery. But that's just a mask, literally. What's being hidden is the outcome of losing that *natural* vibrancy and passion. Have you seen an older person who's still alive and open in their heart? That aliveness shines from their skin, from their eyes. It's not forced or faked. You can't manufacture that with cosmetics; like the river, it's energy in flow.

To feel is to be alive. To put it brutally, a corpse is a person who's stopped feeling. Technically, as long as your heart is beating you're alive but within that definition there are degrees of energetic aliveness that show as vibrancy and engagement with life. You could make an argument that there's a correlation between how alive you are and how much you feel. The more you feel, the more fully alive you are.

So you see the Contraction and repression of feelings has major consequences to the life that we live, not just because of this loss of aliveness but also because the repressed feelings become emotions, and emotions have their own consequences.

17

EMOTION

The difference between an Emotion and a feeling

'You are the sky, everything else is just weather.'
– Pema Chodran

Matthew: People usually use the words 'feelings' and 'emotions' interchangeably but you seem to make a distinction between them.

Jez: Apparently the word 'emotion' was originally used to describe a '*strong* feeling' but gradually it came to mean 'any feeling'. I think the original definition is more correct; it's certainly more accurate and useful when trying to describe what happens to unfelt, repressed feelings.

Matthew: So you're saying, the way you use the word, emotions are what feelings become if they're repressed?

Jez: Yes, the second line of the quote from Einstein sheds some light on this:

> *Energy cannot be created or destroyed,*
> *It can only change from one form to another.*

As we've said, these rejected feelings can't just disappear; they have a momentum that keeps them active. The more the self pushes feelings down into the subconscious, the more they want to rise up to gain our attention, and in their effort to be heard they become exaggerated and distorted.

Matthew: Like our family friends' little girl I told you about who suddenly turned from being full of Joy to an ongoing state of stroppiness.

Jez: I'd say that was a *feeling* of anger that had been repressed and turned into an *Emotion* of anger. Let's give it a capital 'E' to distinguish this definition. The energy had simply changed from one form to another, from feeling to an Emotion.

Matthew: So you're saying that, if that initial feeling of anger had been heard, and been allowed to be expressed, then it wouldn't have built up into an Emotion?

Jez: You could say the energy of that feeling would have gone through its full cycle and not been interrupted. It would have resolved itself; there would've been no emotional residue left in the girl's psychology. The energy would have returned to her default setting of Joy, which you had previously experienced around her.

The thing to remember about feelings is they just want to be heard. Imagine having an argument with someone, being really angry with them and expressing that feeling to them? You expect them to contradict you, to fight you but instead they say: 'Yes, you're absolutely right, I made a mistake. It was my fault and I apologise.' What would happen to that build-up of energy in the form of anger and indignation inside you?

Matthew: I think it would dissolve.

Jez: It's like the wind has been taken out of its sails because it's been heard, it's been allowed to come to its conclusion. So it would dissolve as anger yes, and the energy would be freed up.

Matthew: According to Einstein it can't just disappear; it can only change form.

Jez: I'd say the energy of anger is turned back into the source of energy from which it arose, which is Love.

Matthew: This links up with what you were saying earlier, about how when there is Emotion, Love is obscured.

Jez: Yes, all is made of Love, but in the Relative Level, Love can be obscured, and that has consequences. For example, if you don't express anger, it grows inside you; it becomes more intense, volatile and turns into an Emotion. In the end it will affect your ongoing mood, it will look for any excuse in your life to let off some of its accumulated energy. You could become an angry person rather than a person who's capable of getting angry and then dropping it. That is what an Emotion can do: It can take over your psychological landscape and block feeling and perception of life in the present.

Living from Emotions like this is far removed from the primal Joy of the Natural State. That Joy came from a full-feeling engagement with life. Feeling is the bridge between the Love that we are and the Love manifested in the world. In feeling we're in relationship to whatever we experience, we're present to the Love manifested in this moment. In Emotion, we're disconnected from feeling, so we're disconnected from engaging with life fully. From what you've told me, it seems that the girl you spoke about became stuck in an Emotion of grumpiness.

Matthew: I've been wondering, are you suggesting that the girl's parents were responsible because they didn't hear the child properly and fully?

Jez: No, unless you're talking about cases of child abuse, no one is at fault here. There are so many factors: Parents are busy, other siblings demand attention, the parents have stresses that occupy them from their own lives... To complete the Larkin quote from earlier:

> *They f**ck you up your mum and dad,*
> *They may not mean to, but they do.*

The Wound happens and the child's delicate operating system (the self) deals with it in any way it can – and that's by the Contraction from full feeling. It's so easy for the mind to think in terms of blame and fault but when it comes to this enquiry, all of that becomes irrelevant. The only point is to see what *is*, to understand the forces of feeling and Emotion at work in us. To comprehend what happened back then, yes, but only as a step to seeing what behavioural patterns are operating and limiting our aliveness *now.*

Matthew: So some people end up with predominant Emotions of anger like that little girl, but there must be other responses to the Wound.

Jez: Yes, some children become withdrawn, frightened and timid, others become confused or sad. These are all natural, feeling responses to the Wound. After all, before it happened we were living in our very own Garden of Eden. The Wound is a rude awakening out of that into the ways of the world – specifically, the fact that in the world of man and woman, Love is not always unconditional.

It's not surprising that we have strong feeling responses to such an earth-shattering experience, but what starts as a healthy feeling response to the Wound can crystallise, through the Contraction and the repression of feelings, into an ongoing Emotional state.

Matthew: I remember erupting in a rage of frustration when playing with Lego as a kid and I couldn't get it to stay stuck together. I can still feel the heat of that anger – it was out of all proportion to what was going on...

Jez: Emotion is like a charge; it wants to be released and any excuse in our daily lives can act as a trigger. For example, when as kids we ask for ice cream and are met with a 'no' from our parents we may become aggressive, moody and have tantrums. Or fear may arise for no apparent reason, projecting itself onto what had previously been benign situations like being alone or falling asleep in the dark. We may enter melancholic moods simply because the darker nights of winter are drawing in.

We're no longer responding to life through feeling but *reacting* to it with the Emotions our original feelings have turned into.

Matthew: Last week my other half and I walked up to a bus stop and an elderly woman randomly accused my partner of intending to push in to the queue in front of her. Without thinking I leapt in and told her that was an unfair accusation. The funny thing was, even though I knew I had right on my side, I found myself shaken and even slightly upset afterwards...

Jez: We don't know what was actually going on with her, but let's say she was holding annoyance from people cutting in on her in the past. When you showed up at the bus stop that scenario was triggered in her and its Emotional charge was released, unfairly, onto your partner. That's the woman's side of the story. What often happens with Emotions, because they're powerful, is they can set off latent Emotions in those around.

Matthew: You mean me?

Jez: Yes, otherwise you wouldn't have felt upset and shaken afterwards. Her Emotion of anger set off your Emotion of anger or indignation.

Matthew: I felt protective of my partner; it felt unjust. So yes, I did feel angry.

Jez: So you reacted to her Emotion from your own Emotion. There are consequences to that: Firstly, when Emotion hits up against

Emotion, there's no clarity brought to the situation because no one is seeing things from Choice-less Awareness. It's simply one person's reality hitting up against another's. Neither is viewing the scenario objectively, so there's no chance of any real resolution of the situation. The Emotional charge in each of you has been released a bit, so the body might feel a little energised, shaken up, but there's no real resolution.

The other thing to remember is that to engage with a situation from Emotion means that you're coming from a position of weakness. As soon as you engage with the Emotion you've given your power away, because you've lost your awareness.

Matthew: So what should I have done?

Jez: There's no 'should' in it. We're not talking about self-help here, we're using this example to examine the subject of Emotion and shed some light on it.

Matthew: I didn't feel good after; I was upset by my own loss of control as much as by her reaction.

Jez: While possessed by these Emotional states we may be aware that we don't feel good but, due to their momentum, we're usually unable to stop them. We're victims of these moods just as much as those around us on whom they're inflicted.

Without Emotion we're able to *respond* to a situation; that means we can act with awareness. When you respond rather than react, your actions are so much more effective: You bring your awareness and clarity to the situation. In the light of your awareness the other person's Emotion is shown up clearly. Even in this small incident at the bus stop you can see how pervasive and powerful Emotions are in our daily life.

18

GAINING ATTENTION

What we substitute for Love

'Most people are other people. Their thoughts are someone else's opinions, their lives a mimicry, their passions a quotation.'

– Oscar Wilde

Matthew: The way you've described things it sounds like, as children after the Wound, we must all have been Emotional wrecks walking around stuck in states of heightened Emotion, but most kids I've known haven't appeared like that.

Jez: In order to discuss how we lose the Natural State, we've had to focus on the negative aspects: the Emotions, the things no one wants to talk about. But as you rightly point out, this is rarely the only narrative that's going on in our childhoods; it's just the one that's usually pushed aside as if it wasn't happening.

As we grow up, most of us experience many times when the 'negative' fallout from the Wound is forgotten. Notice I'm not saying it isn't there; just that it's not active. This is partly because there can be a lot of positive, wonderful things happening in our lives at this stage. For example, as our Character unfolds we enjoy the exercising of our talents and the growing mental ability to express ourselves, to be creative, share friendships etcetera.

As a boy my great loves were football and drawing. On schooldays I could be found out on the pitch kicking a ball around with friends at every opportunity between lessons. The rest of my free time was spent drawing: copying cartoons from comics, trying to capture likenesses of my family and sketching the world around me. There seemed to be no limit to how much pleasure playing football and drawing brought me; these activities were an expression of my Joy. This isn't to say that I hadn't lost the Natural State; it's just that, at those moments of engaging in the activities that I loved, I wasn't focussed on the Wound or its fallout. I was distracted from it.

We've used your family friends' daughter as an example of how the Wound can manifest in a life because her Emotional transformation was extreme, so it illustrates the point I'm trying to make. She's a good example of Joy being replaced after the Wound by an ongoing mood of grumpiness.

Many Wounds don't totally stagnate into one Emotion like this; they flow between a range of Emotions. Unhappiness might not seem to be a problem but that's because it is, to some degree, stored away in the subconscious. There's so much going on in our young lives, and a lot of it is positive, but it's important to understand that successfully distracting ourselves from unhappiness is not the same as being in the Natural State. The question to ask yourself is:

After the Wound, were you in the same Joy and freedom that you experienced before the Wound?

Matthew: No, I was no longer completely carefree, I don't think I knew why. I felt like Finn the fish – even when he's in water, he knows the water can run dry. I can still remember the panic I had every time Mum dropped me off at playschool. In the end they moved me into my older brother's class; that was the only way I felt safe.

Jez: Some might put this down to a child learning how 'real' life is: You have to go to school, separate from your Mum etcetera. That's all true, we have to learn and adapt as a child to new situations and challenges. But, to use your story as an example, what I'm saying is it's not normal to have such an extreme, fearful response to going to school. This sort of response, and that girl's extreme grumpiness, are not the normal outcomes of a child adapting to new challenges; they can't be explained by the life circumstances that are attributed to them. I'm suggesting there's a deeper reason for them, and that's the Wound.

In this society the sort of Suffering that arises from the Wound is normalised. These talks are all about another possibility. We're asking the question: Is it possible, as an adult, to live the freedom, Stillness and Joy that we came into the world with or is it just human nature that we slough it off in the process of growing into an adult?

Matthew: I know what I'd like to believe.

Jez: Of course you want to believe that a background sense of latent unhappiness doesn't have to be the normal state of the adult. But this isn't about belief. Belief doesn't get you anywhere when it comes to this enquiry, because belief is the absence of questioning. It's the *absence* of enquiry. If you believe something's true, you're basically making the statement that you're unwilling to *find out* if it's true. This is about finding out what's true; at least, it's about finding out what it's *possible* to find out.

Matthew: How do you do that?

Jez: By honestly looking at our own experience and examining how life is, without in anyway influencing our enquiry with how we'd *like* things to be. I'm leading you, step by step, into what is for you at the moment a *'possible* truth'; it's nothing more than a story at this point. All you have to do at this stage is be open to the fact that this 'story' *could* be true, and continually measure it against your experience, your own honest enquiry. You have to ask yourself: 'Do you remember that way of being in the world when you were still 'connected', still in that primal Joy, and do you remember that sense of unhappiness in you as a child when you lost that Joy?

Matthew: Yes... I knew something was wrong, or at least it wasn't as 'right' as it used to be...

Jez: But the tell-tale signs of unhappiness weren't there all the time, were they?

Matthew: No. Like you said, there were things I loved to do, like building Lego models and playing games like 'Hide and Seek'. When I was doing that... Maybe they distracted me from the unhappiness.

Jez: This theme of distraction is important. The self finds that, by being occupied in activities that we like, we can distract ourselves from unhappiness. We'll give this particular form of Distraction – to avoid Suffering – a capital 'D'.

Matthew: It doesn't work all the time though, does it? When I was really upset, no amount of Lego could have made me feel better.

Jez: When we're possessed by Emotional patterns we don't feel good, life is scary, the unhappiness feels bad and we can't escape it. At times like that, as children, we need the security of our parents' love even more. The trouble is, our ability to *take in* love and be healed by it had been compromised by the Contraction. And even if we could take it in, when we're in Emotional states such as temper tantrums, we're not at our most loveable. So we wouldn't be attracting much Love in our direction anyway.

Matthew: I remember our family friends getting fed up with their daughter's moodiness and tantrums.

Jez: In such cases our parents may tell us we're 'being bad'. This disapproval of our behaviour can have the effect of entrenching the primal belief that we're somehow 'wrong' and unlovable. This in turn can feed the unhappiness that caused the tantrum in the first place.

Matthew: So having a tantrum doesn't really do anything positive for a child does it? Some people think it's a way of gaining attention but it doesn't usually work, it doesn't elicit a response of love...

Jez: I'd suggest that it does work in one way, because at this stage it's not really love the child is after – it's attention. By now, a child has learned that love is dangerous because it can be withdrawn and so it can hurt us. Attention, by comparison, is much easier to elicit. For example, when Lucy starts having a tantrum, her whining and crying are designed to get attention, and it usually works.

Matthew: Are you saying that attention becomes a kind of substitute for love?

Jez: Yes, a safe substitute.

Matthew: Even if her angry parents become tired of her tantrums and start getting angry with her?

Jez: It doesn't matter; even negative attention is preferable to no attention at all.

*Matthew: Why **is** that?*

Jez: Because no-attention reminds her of the Wound, and that's something she doesn't want to be taken back to. She wants those feelings to be safely packed away, undisturbed in her subconscious.

You can see how Lucy's relationship to Emotions is changing; because of the attention they're able to provoke, her Emotions now become her allies. Using her memory of how Emotions feel and look, she can act them out in order to provoke attention whenever she needs it, for example turning on the waterworks to get sympathetic attention.

Matthew: You've said that there are many possible responses to the Wound: If Lucy had become sad and withdrawn this would naturally have elicited sympathy and compassion from her parents. Are you saying that this too, would not be able to help her feel loved?

Jez: Not necessarily. Even if we're given the love we so badly need, we're often unable to receive and be soothed by it because of the Contraction. The love we receive is never enough; we can't be filled up by it. It's like trying to pour water into a pot that has a lid on.

Matthew: The lid is the Contraction?

Jez: Yes. In protecting us from love's possible withdrawal in the future, the Contraction also cuts us off from Love in the present. So even when love *is* there, to us it may feel like it's not. This is an important lesson about beliefs: When we project our beliefs about how the world is out into life, they affect and shape our experience – life starts to conform to the beliefs and so confirm them. If we believe we're unlovable then our experience of life, whether in our parents' disapproval of our moods or our inability to feel their concern and love for us, seems to confirm our conviction.

Matthew: So it sounds like we're just stuck with our unhappiness whatever we do!

Jez: In a sense, yes, but this is where gaining attention comes in. The self learns that it can feed off the attention it gets and also be Distracted by it. Remember I said that as a child, by doing things that we like, we're able to Distract ourselves from our unhappiness? The self finds that attention can *also* momentarily distract us from our unhappiness. The self has learned that love is painful; it can bring out memories of the Wound, whereas attention is safe. It's like a dummy to suck that distracts us from the legacy of the Wound, from our estrangement from Love. When we receive attention, the unhappiness inside us transforms into its opposite: happiness.

Matthew: It's amazing how children become expert at gaining attention, isn't it?

Jez: We learn the art of manipulation. We've all seen a child turn on Emotions to gain a response from the parent. So when Lucy wants an ice cream and her mother says 'No!', she goes into a sulk. If her mum relents and buys the ice cream then her petulant mood can disappear just as quickly as it arose.

Matthew: Lucy discovers that she can control her parents.

Jez: Yes, even though as adults her parents are ultimately in control, Lucy learns that, if she plays her cards right, she has a certain power over them. Then a power struggle can arise: 'Give me what I want or I'm going to make your life hell!'

Matthew: Playing the role of the bad or naughty child doesn't always work though. If Lucy's parents refuse to be manipulated they might just ignore her Emotional displays and withdraw their attention altogether. They might banish her to her room with no supper.

Jez: Yes, they could punish Lucy's 'bad' behaviour by withdrawing all their attention, both positive and negative. This is the worst scenario for the self because it echoes the absence of Love Lucy experienced in the Wound.

Matthew: So what can the self do then?

Jez: It tries to win back the attention with a new strategy. Seeing that her 'bad' behaviour is displeasing her parents, the self reasons that, if it can please them by demonstrating 'good' behaviour, it can win their approval and so regain their attention. Becoming a pleaser is just another acting strategy in the self's bag of tricks.

Matthew: Guilty! I loved the feeling of being considered a nice boy, a good boy... For example, I used to be the 'helpful' one out of the three brothers in my family; it was the role I adopted. If my brothers and I got in trouble, I knew I would be looked on more favourably because I had good behaviour and helpfulness in the bank, so to speak.

Jez: You can see how clever and crafty we become; the self turns into an actor. It learns to change roles constantly, playing out whatever is the best means of winning attention in the situation it finds itself in. The more the self feels in control of the source of attention, the safer it feels in the world. We soon become so used to acting out Emotions, or versions of ourselves which please our parents, we forget we're even doing it.

Matthew: Being helpful and nice just became something I did; I didn't question it...

Jez: These patterns become unconscious habits, and so we drift further and further away from the knowledge of who we are, from the Natural State, without even knowing it. Feelings become counterfeit. We don't know what's real feeling any more and what's fake.

Remember how I said you can see the Wound manifesting in childhood photos? You can also spot this 'pleasing' technique when a certain smile appears on children's faces. You know the one: 'Smile for the camera, Johnny.' You see people doing it all the time now in selfies. It's that false smile, designed to put on a show, and it can change into a scowl at any time. A real smile comes from the heart, not the mouth.

Matthew: Just like a fake smile, the Distraction from unhappiness that comes from acting out these roles to gain attention doesn't last, does it?

Jez: I heard a story from a colleague of mine who's friends with someone called Kate; she's the partner of a famous actor. (I'll call him Tom.) To get away from the stresses and strains of fame, the couple went on holiday and stayed in an exclusive hotel, nice and quiet, far from the prying eyes of the public.

After a few days of this reclusive tranquillity Kate noticed that Tom didn't seem to be enjoying himself, so she asked him what was wrong. Tom said he found the hotel a bit dull; there was no atmosphere in the place. Kate was a bit surprised, but she was determined to give him the holiday he wanted, so she arranged for them to move from the peaceful, luxury hotel to a busier, cheaper establishment nearer the local town.

After a few days in the new hotel, Kate noticed that, despite it being much shabbier than the first one, Tom seemed happier. She asked him if he liked the new hotel. 'It's alright,' Tom replied, 'but it's a bit tiresome that fans keep coming up for autographs all the time.'

Unlike primal Joy, which is a natural and unconditional expression of our Natural State, happiness is caused by certain conditions; in this case, the attention being received from Tom's fans. When those conditions change, if the attention is withdrawn, we're no longer distracted from our unhappiness. In effect, the happiness changes back into its opposite – unhappiness. Attention is much more desirable than a posh hotel.

PERSONALITY

19

PERSONALITY

The self grows in relation to the Wound
and crystallises into our Personality

'My dear Sir, you are quite mistaken about yourself.
You are not the person you take yourself to be.'
– Nisargadatta Maharj

Matthew: So at last we're ready to pin down what you mean by Personality.

Jez: Yes, let's start with the dictionary definition.

Matthew: It says here the Personality is: 'a set of individual differences that are affected by the development of an individual: values, attitudes, personal memories, social relationships, habits, and skills.'

Jez: Just to be clear, I'm not making up my own definition, it's just that I'm approaching the 'development of individual differences' from a specific angle, which is the angle of our own particular version of losing the Natural State.

Through the years the self became habituated to an experience of life that formed in our childhood. That experience began, and grew, out of the Wound. The nature of our own particular Wound is primarily dependent on the Personality of our parents or guardians.

Matthew: So theoretically, without the Wound, the self could have developed in a totally different way?

Jez: Theoretically, yes. The Wound is our initiation into the world of man, where Love is conditional, where the immersion in our Original Relationship to Life has been lost. In an alternate reality, in which people lived as adults in the Natural State, there'd be no Wound to pass on, and the Natural State that the child comes into this world with could continue into adulthood.

Matthew: It's a beautiful thought.

Jez: (Laughs.) Beautiful, and to go any further with it would be a total waste of time.

Matthew: Why? What's wrong with beautiful thoughts?

Jez: Nothing as such, but what we're doing here is about seeing life as it is, not hoping or dreaming about how we might like it to be. The fact is, if you gain any insight into what I mean by the Natural State, you'll start to see that our adult selves have been built on a reaction to losing that, a reaction to losing the perception of Love. What I'm saying is, the self grows in relation to the Wound and gradually transforms and crystallises into our adult Personality.

Matthew: So finally we have your definition of Personality!

Jez: Yes. It's taken a long time to get to because it's built of many components and I had to explain them before I could pull them all together. To summarise, as far as this enquiry is concerned, the Personality is what the self becomes in its unique response to the Wound. The Personality is built on the building blocks of the Contraction, Emotion, primal beliefs about oneself (such as 'I am unlovable') and the search for attention.

Matthew: What happened to Character?

Jez: Good point. The Character, the specific inborn traits and talents that make you unique, wants to keep growing and expanding in the same way that feelings want to be expressed and a river wants to flow. Expressing and sharing our talents brings fulfilment; it's a function of Joy and part of what survives of the Natural State.

Matthew: It doesn't always function though, does it? Sometimes my writing, which I consider to be an expression of my Character, goes well and I feel so fulfilled by it. At other times I just get stuck and frustrated. Why is that?

Jez: I can answer that in one word: Emotion. Creativity comes from the heart, and Emotions block the heart. If you look honestly, whenever you feel stuck, you can always trace the cause back to Emotion. If you imagine the Character as a beautiful, unique plant, Emotions are like weeds that grow around it and try to take it over.

Matthew: So it's like an epic battle between your Character and your Personality?

Jez: I suppose you *could* say that. In the story I'm telling, the more your Character gets the upper hand, the more fulfilment you'll have in your life. But the Character is often compromised by Personality, which strangles and suffocates it.

Matthew: So it's not a case of either/or? That is, either the Personality wins and is lived, or the Character is the dominant force?

Jez: No, as your example when writing confirms, both are operating at the same time.

Matthew: But people can exhibit amazing levels of talent and creativity, like some musical superstars, for example.

Jez: Yes but that doesn't mean that they're free of the legacy of the Wound. It's not a case of: 'The more Character you live, the more the Personality's influence fades away'. That would be another one of those beautiful, but ultimately useless, thoughts. If you look at what *is*, you can see that isn't the case.

Take an extreme example like John Lennon: Estranged from his mother, he was brought up by his aunt. When he was seventeen, his mother, with whom he'd recently been reconciled, was killed by a passing car. Despite this unhappy childhood his Character expressed enormous talent. He knew that 'All you need is Love,' but from what we know, despite therapy, his Personality could be depressive and angry. His fame and talent in no way made him immune to the Suffering of Personality. So, although we think of Lennon as being an enormously gifted artist who expressed great ideals about Love and peace for us all, in the nitty-gritty of his life he wasn't exactly living the peace of the Natural State.

The point is, unless you see through, and break free from the Wound in your past, it's always going to have an influence on and input into your life. And the main outcome of that will be unhappiness.

Matthew: You're not talking about a passing sort of unhappiness? The type you feel when, say, your cat dies?

Jez: No, I mean the sense of unhappiness that Suffering of the Personality brings into a person's psychology. At its root is the estrangement from Love. This book is all about seeing the truth of this, and also proposing the idea that, despite the fact there's little evidence for this around us, it *is* possible to become free of Personality and its Suffering.

Matthew: I'm intrigued to know how that's possible.

Jez: The mind wants a neat little formula, doesn't it? A philosophy, one more thing it can possess and use to make it feel more secure.

Matthew: Who wouldn't want that?

Jez: The thing is, that would just be strengthening the Personality. In the end, only deep understanding, beyond concepts and formulas, can make any real difference. At the moment, it's enough to engage in this exploration of what Personality is. This is what's happening now and, if you're open, it could perhaps start a journey towards that understanding.

Matthew: OK, I'll take your word for that...

Jez: How this is found is such a big topic, and naturally it's going to keep coming up. I'll address it in detail later but for now, it's best if we stay on the subject of Personalities.

Matthew: It seems a bit odd talking about the Personality in this way, like it's not us, as if it's some separate entity with its own volition.

Jez: I know, but that's only because you've taken your Personality to be 'you'. It's not you; it's just what you think you are.

The Story of 'You'

20

PERSONALITY IN THE WORLD

How the Personality interprets the world according to its beliefs

'The emotions of man are stirred more quickly than man's intelligence.' – Oscar Wilde

Jez: Tell me something you've observed about Personalities.

Matthew: OK... Some are obvious, aren't they? Big Personalities are easy to spot... They can be loud, energetic and self-confident...

Jez: Yes, some Personalities are extreme, while others are mild and easy-going. You can measure this by the strength of reaction people have to them: Extreme Personalities provoke strong reactions in others. You could say that all dictators and many religious or political leaders fall into this category: Some people admire them and want to follow their every word, while others just want to keep far away from them. Mild Personalities are more transparent, producing little reaction in others. They're easier to get along with. A greater proportion of people fall into this category.

Matthew: Within this general distinction, there must be hundreds of different Personality types.

Jez: Yes, from the basic building blocks of the Contraction – Emotions, the lack of self-love and the search for attention – the self can develop in countless different forms, each one taking on specific characteristics.

I'm not trying to build a catch-all system of identification here, but out of interest you could make a basic category division based on the primary Emotions. Through the years Emotions can become entrenched; one in particular may become more pronounced and this can determine our Personality type. These dominant Emotions are based on our original reaction to the Wound. If Lucy's response is mostly fear based, she might become an insecure type: timid, shy, indecisive, unsure of her own capabilities and her place in the world.

If anger predominates, she could become an aggressive type with much pent-up energy and self-confidence that could seek to dominate and control others. If grief was her main reaction to the Wound, Lucy could become a withdrawn Personality, lacking physical energy or drive and possibly prone to negativity or depression.

So any of these emotional categories, if the Emotions are strong and intense enough, can produce strong Personalities. For example, in a fearful type, the fear can be so overwhelming that it becomes oppressive to those around; the same applies to grief. And nobody likes being around extremely angry types either – the whole life of the person is shaped by that abrasive Emotion. But whatever takes precedence on the top level, beneath will be layers of all the other Emotions – a record of the whole history of the self.

Matthew: As modern psychology has pointed out, we're all walking round carrying baggage with us from our pasts.

Jez: Yes, and the beliefs that the past has created from that baggage are part of the problem too.

Matthew: What do you mean?

Jez: Each Personality builds a set of beliefs about how the world is, based on its particular response to the Wound. The angry type sees the world as an aggressive, violent place, as somewhere that you have to dominate to survive. The fear type believes it is a place to be feared and the grief type believes it to be a place of sorrow. When these beliefs, or worldviews, are projected into our lives we attract people and events that mirror back our convictions, and disregard anything that conflicts with them.

For example, say a terrorist bomb goes off in a high street. An angry Personality type may respond with anger and hatred to the perpetrators. This might lead them to want to exact revenge. A fear type may feel unsafe and nervous going out into the street again. A grief type could feel sad at the state of the world, at how terrible it is that people could do such a thing to each other.

The event is a mirror in which the Emotion is reflected. Of course you can have a mixture of all three responses, but in general it's true to say that an angry Personality type finds much to hate in the world, the fear type much to fear and the grief type much to mourn. But every Personality attracts life experiences as a result of the Emotion it's projecting.

Matthew: One of the other building blocks of Personality you mentioned is the primal belief that we are unlovable. How does this feed into the makeup of Personality?

Jez: At the root of all Personality types lies the unfulfilled promise of our Original Relationship to Life in which Love is lived, received and given. One response to this, which let's say Lucy has, is to take on the belief that she's unlovable. She feels somehow wrong or not good enough, and this gives her a sense of emptiness that grows with the passing of time. Having lost her intrinsic sense of self-worth, she feels the need to *prove* that she is deserving of love. Sometimes this proving can actually look like self-confidence.

Matthew: Like someone who's always talking about themselves and their achievements. You start suspecting they're trying to convince themselves of their own worth...

Jez: This is the classic definition of being egocentric, isn't it? A sort of 'big headedness.' After a while you realise: 'Hang on a minute, they're not asking *me* any questions; the conversation's all about them and how great they are.'

Matthew: It's like that joke: 'That's enough about me, let's talk about you. What do you think about me?' (Both laugh.) But most people like that have no idea they're doing it.

Jez: Not at all, the Personality's not interested in becoming aware of itself, because then the whole edifice would start to fall apart. We crave attention just as we did when we were children, but now the attention that we sought from our parents is sought in the world.

Matthew: You mean from authority figures, like teachers, bosses and role models?

Jez: Yes, looking up to role models, and getting encouragement and approval from them, is a natural part of growing up too, but in many Personalities this childish need for approval survives into adulthood.

But it's not just from individuals; we seek the approval of the Group Personality in which we grow, as well. As the Group Personality is a projection of the individual Personalities of which it's made, all the basic characteristics of the individual Personality are manifested in it. So an individual's fear of being unlovable, of being a 'nobody' in the eyes of others, is held collectively in the belief system of society. The tribe looks up to people who, either through their achievements or just the circumstances of their birth, have risen above this 'nobody-ness' to become 'special', to become a 'somebody', because these people represent what most Personalities aspire to be. Everyone wants to be a 'someone.'

Matthew: Which explains the cult of celebrity worship.

Jez: Yes, but let's clarify things here: As I said, there's nothing intrinsically wrong with having a hero; as children it can be a way we explore the world and ourselves. The hero can represent a quality we aspire to. As a child I was really into football, and at that time there was one Irish footballer whose skills surpassed everyone else's. Even his name – George Best – seemed to announce his supreme talent. He was, literally, the best. Football has been referred to as the beautiful game, and whenever I hear that phrase I think about George Best effortlessly weaving through his opponents' defence. It was just magical; he turned football into a kind of physical poetry.

People talk about that kind of talent as being 'God given', meaning he was born with it. He didn't train harder than any other footballers; he was just blessed with this innate talent. As we've discussed, talents like this are part of the Character, they exist independently of whatever's going on in the Personality. In George Best's case, his Personality was troubled by addiction. He was an alcoholic and sadly it killed him in the end. But at this stage of his life, when I was a boy, he was a symbol for me of a kind of beauty and quality that I found in the game of football. So George Best was a hero to me, because I found his skills inspiring; they encouraged me to train harder, to get better myself, and this is the positive side of having a hero. However, when Personality comes into the picture, following a hero can become just another way of dramatising your Suffering.

Matthew: What do you mean?

Jez: For example, having taken on the belief that she's in some way unlovable, Lucy has a self-esteem pattern; she has low self-confidence and feels her life has little worth. Like many other teenagers, she idolises a Pop star, a beautiful, idealised version of girlhood who she looks up to. The pop singer is a 'somebody' in her eyes, and in the eyes of the tribe. Just associating with this pop idol, listening to her music, following her on social media, looking at her photo and hanging out with other fans, makes Lucy feel better. It's as if, through these distant connections with her idol, some of that 'specialness' is somehow passed on to her.

Matthew: It's a two-way deal, isn't it? The Pop star needs their fans as much as the fans need her.

Jez: Yes, this is the contract. The Pop star makes Lucy feel special, and in return Lucy, and all the other fans, make the pop star feel special. They buy her music, go to her concerts and in so doing promote their idol's brand. The brand is the badge of their identity.

To win the acceptance and approval of her tribe, Lucy wants to become a 'somebody'. I don't mean that she wants to necessarily become a famous pop star, but in her own life, in her own way, she seeks acceptance from those around her.

Matthew: Isn't this what you wanted to do by having George Best as a hero? You wanted to become a better player, so that when you played, your skills would make you stand out on the pitch, so you'd be a 'somebody'.

Jez: No, there's a difference, and it's to do with the intention behind the hero worship. Like everyone else, I had Personality problems, Emotions and insecurities, but that wasn't what was being played out in my love of George Best. Yes, I wanted to play better, that was my intention, but it was motivated simply by the love of the game and the desire to develop whatever talent I had. So for me it was a part of my Joy; the incredible talent of George Best was simply a beacon of quality and beauty that I could look up to. Engaging with him as a hero in this way brought out that Joy.

When hero worship is governed by Personality, it becomes something very different. The intention behind it is to develop and strengthen the identity, to become more of a somebody. Why? Because safety, the feeling of being accepted and loved, is linked with having a strong identity. Lucy's identity is built on the choices she makes (she loves this pop star and not that one), her beliefs (she's unlovable) and her history. I'm not talking about her family history now; I'm referring to her own history, the story of her life. For example, the more exams Lucy's passed, the more places she's been to, people she's met, money she has, the more her Personality's identity is strengthened and established. All of these aspects make her feel stronger and safer, because in the world of Personality, having a strong identity is seen as a mark of success. So she actively collects and pursues attributes that strengthen her identity. Most people will go to great lengths to look good in the eyes of their tribe.

Matthew: It makes me think of the fashion industry – it wouldn't exist if this need wasn't in us, would it?

Jez: You're right. All advertising and the following of fashion feeds off this trait, this need to conform to the tribe's current classification of what's hip and fashionable. If you think about it, it's crazy: In a design studio in Italy, somebody decides that a certain style of coat is what's 'in'. Then it's promoted in magazines that girls like Lucy read, and suddenly, all over the world, people want that coat. For a while that design has great value in the fashion market because everybody wants to wear it. Why? Why does Lucy go out and buy that coat? Because she believes the message that if she buys this coat she'll somehow be more loved and accepted by her social group.

Matthew: And that's good for business!

Jez: And then suddenly, once the money's rolled in, guess what?

Matthew: The fashion writers and magazines tell the tribe that this style of coat is 'last season' and now a new style is 'in'...

Jez: No one questions this mass hypnosis; they simply follow what's being dictated to them like sheep. How is it they can they be controlled like this? Simply because of that need to be accepted, to gain attention from the tribe. It's this need that makes us susceptible to manipulation. If Lucy had *no* need for the tribe to tell her that she's OK, she couldn't be controlled. She would never buy a coat that someone else says is 'in', she'd buy one that suits her. Even if it happened to be what the fashion magazines deemed to be last year's style.

Matthew: So everyone's looking to build this sense of identity... I guess social media's a great tool to do that.

Jez: Yes. Everyone gets to be their own PR person, and by continually retelling our stories we assert our identities to the world and to ourselves. Even if Lucy has no great story to tell from her past, her Personality can build its identity through projecting into the future.

Matthew: What do you mean?

Jez: By striving to possess the highest goal of the tribe, the one thing that confirms that we've become a 'somebody', and that is success. We may not have it now, but we can work towards it.

In our thirst for success, our need for recognition and attention is projected onto adult pursuits in the world, such as money, power, fame, wisdom, health and marriage. Whatever defines our Personality's particular idea of success becomes the object of our desire. We believe that, in some imagined time in the future when we achieve our desires, when we get rich, famous, powerful, thin, healthy, wise enough, or when we meet that one person who'll love us, *then* we will be happy and feel whole again. This is what I call the 'When I get this I'll be happy' syndrome.

This search for our idea of success gives meaning and a sense of purpose to our lives. To the world we act out a version of ourselves, how we would like to be seen, but underneath this mask resides the whole history of the self. Despite our belief that we are free individuals, it's this history, and the thought patterns it's produced, that largely inform our behaviour and govern our lives.

Matthew: So you're saying we're not free?

Jez: We may be lucky enough to live in a democracy – so there can be that level of freedom – but personally, we're enslaved to a repressed, unhappy way of living that's founded on separation rather than Love. We're not free to fully be the Character that we are, we're tyrannised by our Personalities. And the joke is, most people are not even aware of it. They walk round with the idea they are free, but they wonder why they're not happy.

21

PERSONALITY AWARENESS

How Personality edits our experience of life

'We don't see things as they are; we see them as we are.'
– Anaïs Nin

Jez: When describing Being, I talked about Choice-less Awareness. I've also mentioned another kind of awareness, which comes from the Personality.

Matthew: Apart from where they're coming from, can you remind me of the differences between them?

Jez: The tell–tale sign that characterises Personality Awareness is the fact that it can be turned on and off. In other words, Personality appears to choose what we become aware of and what we don't.

Matthew: You talked about Personality doing this when we discussed the Contraction.

Jez: You're right, this editing of our life experience goes all the way back to the Wound. Personality took the painful event of the Wound, hid it away in the subconscious, and pretended it never happened. This was the first time the Personality learned it had control over what it became aware of. Living like this, editing what you see and how you view it, is one of the main factors determining what sort of life your Personality is creating.

That same functioning is going on in adults: Personality does all it can to stop you becoming aware of itself and the life experience it's creating; anything which shows up its functioning is seen as a threat to its position of control. So Personality is quite happy to see patterns of behaviour in others, but when life confronts you with any of your own Emotions, beliefs, addictions and Distractions it usually refuses to become aware of them. The Personality manages this through one of two reactions. The first is to look the other way and pretend that we're actually not experiencing it, that we're not aware of it.

Matthew: I recognise that one: I do that every time I get tobacco out of the pack to roll a cigarette. You know they have images on them to dissuade you from smoking, horrible shots of scars on a torso after lung surgery, or the black tar that accumulates in a lung? When pulling the tobacco out, I subconsciously block myself from taking in those images.

Jez: Otherwise, you might just have to confront the message they're giving...

Matthew: I guess I'm not ready to give up smoking yet...

Jez: Right, and by having you ignore it, Personality Awareness allows you to stay in that state. Here's another more shocking example. I watched a documentary about a British celebrity who was posthumously exposed as a serial sexual abuser. They interviewed one old lady who worked as his assistant for decades. She'd obviously been totally taken in by his front of being a kind and honourable man, as witnessed by all his charity work. Despite claims of abuse through the years, this woman simply looked the other way, preferring instead to hang on to her own version of reality. Even now, after literally hundreds of revelations, she still clings to her fantasy of how she wants to remember her former employer.

Matthew: It's a bit like what happens when someone suffers from anorexia.

Jez: Yes. Something in them has chosen to create an alternate reality in which they're fat, despite what the mirror shows them.

Some people use an 'Ad Hominem' approach to justify a denial, extinguishing the threat of the story being told by calling into question the character and/or reliability of the person it's coming from. The serial sex offender's assistant brushed away accusations against her boss by saying the victims just wanted attention and or money, and the papers will print anything to sell copies...

Personality Awareness happens a lot when someone talks about the subject of going beyond Personality. The threat of that message can be neutralised by all sorts of slurs against the person who's daring to talk about it. They may be called mad, deluded or accused of being motivated by ego...

Matthew: Which, of course, can be the case...

Jez: Absolutely. Sometimes self-aggrandisement *is* what's happening, but that doesn't mean it's *always* the case. Sometimes that accusation is just a way that the Group Personality tries to discredit anyone who's posing a threat to the status quo.

Matthew: I'm sure this is the origin of the 'Tall Poppy Syndrome' – grow too far above the rest and you'll be cut down first.

Jez: Yes. Imagine a caterpillar with an inferiority complex: Seeing a butterfly with its beautiful wings hurts, because it *brings out* that inferiority. So in order not to feel the pain of that feeling, the caterpillar chooses not to look at the beautiful wings. Instead it starts criticizing, saying: 'That butterfly's big headed. It thinks it's better than the rest of us.'

*Matthew: But as I said before, it **could** be true. The butterfly might be egotistical.*

Jez: If we're using the butterfly as a symbol of someone who's *really* living beyond Personality, then it couldn't be true.

Matthew: Why not?

Jez: If you're no longer identified as Personality, you're no longer governed by any patterns of low self-esteem that could give you the need to put yourself up or put anyone else down.

The butterfly doesn't feel superior; all the butterfly is doing is being what it is. Its colourful wings may bring up all sorts of judgements and insecurities in other creatures but that's none of its business. Is the butterfly meant to hide itself away so its wings don't bring up the inferiority in the caterpillar that sees it?

Matthew: That would be a denial of what the butterfly is.

Jez: Exactly, and he hasn't come all that way, gone through the transformation in the chrysalis, only to come out and hide his beautiful wings. His only motivation is to Be, and fully enjoy being, a butterfly.

Matthew: You said that, when the Personality is threatened, it has two possible defensive reactions. If denial is the first, what's the second?

Jez: The second reaction is to rise up and fight off the threat with all its might. I remember showing my dad an early version of a book about this enquiry. Reading it provoked an extremely angry reaction in him that manifested as a verbal onslaught telling me how ridiculous and badly written my book was. I was amazed by the furious reaction it incited in him – normally he was a measured, logical man who'd calmly explain his reasons if he wasn't fond of any creative work I showed him. That day I witnessed a side of him I'd never seen before; my writing prompted a strong fighting reaction from his Personality because it felt threatened.

Matthew: How can you be so sure that's the reason? Maybe he just didn't like it!

Jez: As I said earlier, strong Emotional reactions like this are always tell-tale signs of the Personality's defence system being activated. You can have a negative opinion about something, but that doesn't mean it has to be expressed with anger or outrage. You can very calmly give a response, explaining why you think something's not very good.

Matthew: So, just to be clear, you're not suggesting your dad should have blindly accepted the material in your book?

Jez: Not at all, he should apply his discrimination, his own response from where he stands. But if that judgement is coming from a bias, an agenda, that's something else: That's simply the Personality throwing out its defensive Emotions.

This reminds me of something that happened at my local train station recently. A woman came up to me saying she'd lost her credit cards and needed money to get a ticket back to Scotland. She asked for my address and promised, if I lent her some money, she'd send it back to me with extra cash as a thank you for my trouble. I asked her a few questions and, from the holes in her story, it soon became clear she was trying to con me.

So you can see the difference: I used rational discrimination, which means there's no Emotional, reactive response in it. I just asked some questions and found the truth of what was going on.

As soon as reactivity comes in, that sort of clarity goes out the window. Imagine someone had used this con trick recently on a well-meaning and financially stretched friend of mine, and it had fleeced them of a hundred pounds. Before I discovered life beyond Personality, I may have reacted with anger if I'd encountered a person who seemed to be trying the same con trick on me. That anger would have clouded my rational discernment. Even if the person had *genuinely* lost their credit cards, I wouldn't have been mentally clear enough to determine that fact.

This is an example of where what you encounter is not much threat to your Personality; it's just a mild threat to your sense of justice. But when what you encounter poses more of a threat, such as when it challenges the Personality's belief system, then these self-protective mechanisms kick in by turning off the switch of Awareness.

The Personality works under the cover of your unconsciousness – that's how it keeps in control, by neutralising any threat to its sovereignty. So it operates in a self-protecting, self-regulating circuit. If it wasn't the cause of such Suffering, you could say it's almost quite beautiful, it functions so well. It carries out its job of keeping you Distracted, unaware of its workings so perfectly. The function of belief is a vital part of the way this is carried out; we're going to discuss that next.

22

BELIEF

The foundation of Personality

'A casual stroll through the lunatic asylum shows that faith does not prove anything.' – Nietzsche

Jez: Beliefs form the foundations of Personality. We have beliefs about who we are, such as: 'I am unlovable', 'I'm not good enough', 'I have to prove myself to be worthy' or 'I'm the best'. Then we have beliefs about others, such as: 'I have to dominate others to feel safe' or 'People are out to get me'. As we discussed in our talk about the Group Personality, beliefs about politics, society and religion can also be handed down through the family line. Donald Trump's father instilled in his family the belief that Trumps are high achievers or, as he put it: 'killers and kings.'

Having amalgamated into this identity, with its history and collection of beliefs, the Personality now has the job of maintaining and protecting itself.

Matthew: Protecting itself from what?

Jez: From any threat to its integrity. The most common form of threat comes through encounters with other people. Although all Personalities are constructed from the same building blocks born of the Wound, they also of course have different configurations, different Emotions, beliefs, identifications and needs. So you have one Personality here, feeling safe with its worldview, its beliefs. Then it meets another Personality doing the exact same thing, hanging on to *its* beliefs, but those beliefs happen to be different. *So* different in fact that they actually oppose the beliefs of the first Personality and therefore pose a threat to their sense of security.

Matthew: How?

Jez: If your identity and feeling of security is linked to your beliefs, any opposing beliefs become a threat to your feeling of security because they could disprove your beliefs, they could take away what keeps you feeling safe.

Imagine someone points out to Lucy that the Pop star she loves so much has been accused of behaving like a diva and mistreating her female staff, which is out of alignment with her feminist public image – and Lucy's beliefs about what is acceptable behaviour. She's invested so much love in her idol that this news threatens the security she's gained from being a fan and having her as a heroine.

But it's not just opposing beliefs that can be a threat; different types of Personality can challenge our sense of safety. Let's fast forward in Lucy's life: Imagine she's left college and is now employed by a successful company. She's been working there a year and she's doing well in her role; she's using her skills and is appreciated by her boss. Then a new employee joins the department: a younger girl who's more efficient and has better ideas. If Lucy's sense of security is attached to her status in the office, that new employee might become a threat to her.

Let's be clear, we're not talking about confrontations with bully Personalities, people who are wilfully saying nasty things with the intent to hurt. (That's a specific Personality type in itself, which needs to dominate others in order to make itself feel stronger and safe). We're talking about the everyday occurrence of different Personalities rubbing up against each other.

Matthew: When I was at school I had a best friend called Stephen who became very friendly with another boy. It really got to me that I wasn't his only close friend any more; it hurt me and, I guess, it also made me feel angry.

Jez: Basically, anyone could be a threat to a Personality's sense of wellbeing, by challenging its beliefs about itself and the world. If you're dependent on a friend's love and attention to make you feel a sense of worth, you're in a precarious position. From the point of view of Personality, interacting in the world is dangerous.

Matthew: OK, we've established that Personalities need to protect themselves from various threats to their sense of security, but how do they do this?

Jez: One obvious way is by grouping together with other Personalities of the same type, who share the same beliefs.

Matthew: Safety in numbers, you mean?

Jez: Yes. Lucy feels safe when she's with all the fellow fans at her idol's concert because she's surrounded by people who hold the same belief as her; the belief that their idol is the most glamorous, most talented in the world. These fans form Group Personalities that even have their own names.

The same dynamic can be seen at football matches: Supporters identify with their team, and this allegiance can become a strong part of their identity. The supporters become a Group Personality, a collection of Personalities who share the same beliefs and ideals. Even if it's just as simple as 'I believe this team is the best and I want them to win', having others around you who want the same thing makes you feel stronger and safer. If your team wins, you feel happy together, so the euphoria is magnified; if your team loses you feel unhappy together. But then, even in that shared experience of disappointment, there's a kind of bonding which strengthens the group.

Matthew: You're not saying that kind of bonding is a bad thing, are you? Isn't that just people feeling good by coming together, sharing feelings? It doesn't hurt anyone does it?

Jez: Unless you happen to be a supporter of an opposing team! The fights that can occur at matches just go to show how strongly people hold on to these beliefs and how willing they are to defend them. Just the colour of a rival fan's shirt can be enough of a threat to make them risk their physical health. To a non-football fan they're just different teams, from different towns, with different colour shirts, but to a fan it becomes a way of life. It's a defence of your hometown, your background, of your very identity.

Don't get me wrong, enjoying a collective experience like watching a football match can be a wonderful example of sharing; it might even give you a feeling of Oneness with your fellow fans. But, in order to illustrate my point, I'm focussing on the violent aspect of that scenario which *can* occur. We're examining the nature and function of belief.

When you apply the same modes of behaviour around beliefs – the sense of threat and defensiveness – to areas other than football, the trouble that can arise can get more serious.

Matthew: You mean areas like religion or nationalism?

Jez: Precisely. It all comes from the same set up of ownership and identity: 'I was born in this country, with a belief in this God and I follow this holy book.' Seems innocent enough; people should be free to believe whatever they want. What's the problem?

But thousands of miles away another child is born in a different country and inculcated with a belief in a *different* God and holy book. The sense of purpose and security the belief brings to each child means that some are willing to fight or even die for their beliefs, and then you have the whole mess we see going on in the world. It's in the name of religion, but underneath it's all the theatre of Personality. If you didn't feel unsafe, then what would it matter to you that other people hold different beliefs to your own?

Matthew: But not everyone has extreme or fundamentalist beliefs like that...

Jez: No, and we've strayed into different territory here. My main point is not to discuss how fundamentalist beliefs lead to violence; we're looking at the building blocks of Personality. By seeing the extreme we can observe the mechanics of what goes on when we hold beliefs about who we are. The beliefs can be less extreme, but those principles are the same. It's all to do with what makes *your* Personality feel safe. For example, an educated liberal type will be able to intellectually entertain the idea that others can have different beliefs from their own. Nothing's threatened, nothing much is challenged because it's all entertained on a mental level. But when things get personal, when feeling is involved, it's a different story.

Matthew: I consider myself 'an educated liberal type' and yet recently I found myself overreacting when I thought a friend was sympathising with a far-right politician.

Jez: You mean you became Emotional?

Matthew: Yes, I got really agitated and defensive, and couldn't hear the point they were making, which wasn't actually sympathising with the far right at all. Looking at it now, I can see my reaction came because I feel threatened and scared by the growth of the far right, and that stopped me hearing the point that was being made.

Jez: You can see it's all to do with what makes your Personality feel safe. If you believe you're a strong person and someone shows up a weakness in you, if you believe you're clever and someone shows up the limits of your knowledge, all these beliefs can make you feel bad if they're what you use to make yourself feel secure and something undermines them. When our beliefs are threatened in this way we often react; it may not need to get to the point where we fight to defend them, but we do defend them in subtler, less violent ways.

Matthew: Such as?

Jez: First of all by avoiding those people who challenge our Personalities. This is the opposite of the 'safety in numbers' idea.

Matthew: Safety in isolation from opposing beliefs?

Jez: Yes. Of course, like the football supporters, we like people who strengthen our Personality and dislike those who threaten it by exposing it or showing it up in any way. This is a natural law: Like attracts like. You choose to hang out with people you get along with and avoid those who you don't.

Matthew: What about if we can't avoid them? For example, the boy who became friends with my friend Stephen was in the same class as us. I was confronted with this painful situation everyday...

Jez: You had a belief that Stephen was your exclusive friend; the other boy exposed that belief to be untrue. The Personality doesn't want to change; it doesn't want to take on that information. When Lucy was confronted with the negative information about her idol, it posed a real threat to the feeling of safety she got from identifying with the idol and her fellow fans. So she didn't want to hear the news; it felt like a personal attack and she may even have reacted aggressively.

Matthew: I've heard of fans of certain young stars sending death threats to anyone who makes even the slightest criticisms of their idols...

Jez: The Personality doesn't want to broaden its view, to see itself in the mirror of the other person. It wants to stay as it is, safe within the walls of its own beliefs. The most common response to being confronted with what we don't want to see is to look the other way. This is Personality Awareness in action.

Matthew: I certainly didn't want to see Stephen and his new friend together, because then I'd have to admit I wasn't his best friend and feel how much their friendship upset me.

Jez: Yes, you'd have to *feel* something, and remember, to the Personality, feelings can be dangerous. They can make you feel unsafe by stirring up painful repressed memories of the Wound. Did you tell your friend Stephen how you felt hurt? Did you share that painful feeling with someone who could hear and support you?

Matthew: No: I didn't want to admit that I was hurt – that would have made me look weak. I remember feeling really angry though.

Jez: The Personality sometimes likes the feeling of anger; it's not so threatening as feeling hurt. Instead of facing our vulnerability, the Personality can pump itself up with anger and make itself feel stronger.

Matthew: I disliked my rival intensely and ridiculed him to other classmates, even trying to turn them against him by spreading my negative attitude about him.

Jez: I admire your honesty. In these situations a Personality will seek to discredit the offending person by undermining their status. This kind of violence, in the form of thought and word, starts in the playground and continues in adult life. It can be seen in the phenomenon of online trolling – the anonymity offered by chat rooms has exposed this vicious streak that many Personalities have latent inside them.

Then there are the magazines dedicated to gossiping and bitching about celebrities; this is simply the flip side of putting them up on a pedestal. By revelling in their misfortune, their marriage falling apart or even their gaining weight, the readers feel better about themselves.

Matthew: Why does bringing others down, or seeing them brought down, make people feel better?

Paul: It's the paradoxical nature of psychology. Personalities put heroes on a pedestal but deep inside they resent them because they have what they want. Just as that boy had the level of friendship with Stephen you wanted exclusively, on the subconscious level the pop star's success hurts Lucy's Personality, because it shows up her own lack of 'success'.

Matthew: Sometimes an attack on our Personality can be more direct and personal, for example a criticism of our work from a colleague. How would you say the Personality defends itself then?

Jez: The Personality uses logic and reasoning to counter the attack, to explain why it's wrong or unfair. It will construct a case that disproves the accusation.

The Personality sees what it wants to see and rejects through denial what it doesn't want to see. Our minds become so skilled at justifying our viewpoint, our beliefs, that we even convince ourselves of our arguments and so further strengthen the identity we're defending. All these defence mechanisms are seen most clearly in strong Personalities, but it's something that *all* Personalities do to some extent.

Matthew: I can imagine a confidant Personality defending strongly like this, but what about a timid, shy type?

Jez: They may not argue or express strong opinions, but that timid type is a very strongly held Personality stance in itself that has no more intention of changing its viewpoint than a strong extrovert type has of changing theirs. Shyness is a defence in itself, like being in a shell where nothing can reach you; all it needs to do is stay in that shell and maintain it.

The point is, we're locked into these Personality types and, whether we're aware of it or not, we're constantly defending them with various strategies. There's another possible response to criticism and that would be to listen to it and possibly learn from it. If what's being proposed is found to be correct, then the other person has given you a gift. If it's not, it will simply be recognised as being untrue and will be ignored. But such a response would require you to go beyond an Emotional reaction; it would need you to go beyond the domain of Personality. At this point we're examining how *Personality* reacts in such situations, and that is always through some form of defence.

Matthew: But isn't it good that we're defending ourselves? Doesn't that show that we're robust, powerful even? And isn't having a strong ego just how we have to be in order to survive in this world?

Jez: Well if your only motive is to keep your Personality intact then yes, defending your Personality at all cost, in any way you can is the way to go about it. But there's a lot more to life than just surviving: Anybody can do that. This book is about questioning if we can live with the Joy and Love we entered this world with. And that involves actually examining this thing called Personality and the Dream that it creates.

Matthew: What do you mean by the Dream it creates?

Jez: That's our next subject.

23

THE DREAM

How our beliefs create the Dream
of the Personality

'The world has fallen in love with a dream.' – *Kabir*

Matthew: Will you explain what you mean by the 'Dream' the Personality creates?

Jez: We've talked about the building blocks of Personality: desires, beliefs, Emotions. All of these combine to produce a version of life you inhabit. That version of life seems real to the Personality, and in a sense it *is* real because it *is* being experienced. But the point is: It's only real to that particular Personality – it's subjective. No one else is experiencing that version of life, only the Personality that's creating it. So in that sense, it *is* a Dream.

Matthew: Can you unpack that a bit more?

Jez: OK, here's an example of what I mean: Earlier, we imagined that Lucy suffered from anorexia. Despite all physical proof to the contrary, such as her reflection in the mirror, Lucy believes she's grossly overweight. Within the worldview of her Personality, this has become a fact. If you believe something is true, then it's true for you.

Those around Lucy, her family and friends, don't share this belief – they can see objectively she isn't fat at all. The problem appears within Lucy's mind, within the psychology of her Personality. It's subjective, it's part of the Dream it creates.

Matthew: I see what you mean, but this is an extreme example. Surely it doesn't relate to most people?

Jez: I'm suggesting it does; I'm saying that everyone is walking round within their own Personality's Dream. It may not be as extreme or apparent as Lucy's anorexic Dream, but it's definitely there. All Dreams are different because they arise from each individual Personality's history, Emotions and beliefs. Lucy's childhood experience has led her to believe she's unlovable, so her Dream can involve a lot of rejection and sadness: She rejects her body, and in so doing rejects herself. All this has all been created by the belief that she's unlovable.

This idea, that your beliefs create your reality, isn't some mystical, esoteric myth; it's actually very practical and obvious once you see the mechanism by which it works. For example, if you believe you're unlovable, then your ability to create, to live the talents in your Character, can be overridden by that belief. By not reaching out in the world and sharing your talents, naturally you attract less attention, recognition and love from other people.

Matthew: That makes sense; it's like that aphorism: 'What you give is what you get.'

Jez: Exactly. Remember we talked about the talents we have that are part of our Character? Let's say Lucy is gifted with a wonderful singing voice and she shares her talent by singing once a week in a bar. During and after her performance she receives the attention and approval of her audience.

But this cycle of 'What you give is what you get' works both ways. If Lucy's anorexia and low self-confidence is so acute that it stops her reaching out and sharing her talents by singing in the bar, she'll obviously have less human connection in her life. All of this can then be interpreted by her Personality as proof of her belief that she is 'unlovable'. You see how the belief is creating the Dream-life of her Personality? This is what all Personalities are doing.

Matthew: What about if someone's successful? Can that also contribute to the Personality's Dream?

Jez: Yes, you just get a different kind of Dream. I mentioned earlier how Donald Trump's father had instilled in him and his siblings the belief: 'You are kings, you are killers.' On the surface this might look like the diametric opposite of a low self-esteem pattern, but in fact it has its roots in the same belief.

Matthew: How do you work that out?

Jez: Where do you think the need to prove yourself to be a 'killer' or a 'king' comes from? Imagine a king sitting on a throne in his palace, surrounded by subjects and advisors. Do you think he needs to keep saying to himself: 'I am a king, I am a king?' If you feel like a king you don't need to prove you *are* one, to yourself or anyone else.

Donald Trump has lived his life putting out this belief, and it creates his particular Personality's Dream in which he is a 'killer and a king'. Within the Dream, it takes on a kind of reality, because he believes it and, from his perspective, it's real. So, if he feels he's a king, he'll see himself as superior to others, and this will lead to him feeling he has the right to dominate others. All these things are maybe good for his ability to make 'killer' deals in business, but they're not going to endear him to most people. That kind of business success might attract a certain kind of respect in the world, but it's unlikely to attract a lot of love.

In the Relative Level, everything has consequences; every nuance of your Personality has outcomes in the Dream it creates. This is especially true of Emotions. For example, if you have a lot of repressed anger, that's going to influence your experience of the world in a very direct way. I remember a time when my Personality was releasing a lot of built up anger. I was out shopping and, as I walked through town, I noticed people were looking at me differently from usual. I saw distrust, fear, and also anger in them. I hadn't acted violently in any way, I hadn't said a word, but I realised they were all responding to the anger I was emitting. It was a strong lesson to see how my Emotion was instantly affecting my experience of life.

In that example I was just releasing a pocket of anger – it soon passed – but as we've discussed, a whole Personality can be built around the repressed Emotion of anger so the whole Dream can be continually informed by it.

Matthew: We've all met people like that; I know a guy who's habitually grumpy, like he's always looking for an argument.

Jez: How do you feel when you're around him?

Matthew: I try not to be, but when I have to see him it makes me tense because I know that his anger might start being directed at me, and also angry, because he's acting so horribly to everyone.

Jez: You see how Emotions go round and round, provoking more Emotion in those nearby? But that's another subject, what we're talking about here is how this guy's beliefs are creating his experience of the world – i.e. that he's not liked.

Matthew: What sort of beliefs might be behind his angry Personality?

Jez: Let's get an angle on that by thinking about a positive, more happy Personality. What sort of beliefs about the world do you think they have?

Matthew: That it's a loving, happy place?

Jez: Yes. So an angry Personality will have had experiences and reacted to them in such a way to create the belief that the world is an unfriendly, threatening place. Your understandable response of wanting to get away from your angry acquaintance would only serve to entrench that viewpoint; and you can be sure that you're not the only one who feels like that around him. As I said, Personality creates the Dream from its beliefs, which then attracts events and experiences that confirm those beliefs.

Matthew: So the moral is: Be careful what you believe.

Jez: Absolutely, the whole practice of making positive affirmations has been built on this understanding.

Matthew: So to summarise, you're saying that as long as you're identified as Personality, you're living inside the Dream its beliefs and Emotions are creating?

Jez: Yes, both in a long-term way, such as in deeply held beliefs of inferiority or superiority, or in a short-term way like when an Emotion of anger passes through you for a few hours or even five seconds. A momentary flash of anger could cause a car accident, a fight in a pub, or maybe a marriage breakup.

Through its Emotions and beliefs every Personality is constantly creating its Dream; there are as many Dreams as there are Personalities. Most people are fully identified with the Personality so what they live is the Dream it creates.

*Matthew: But you're saying that it doesn't **have** to be that way.*

Jez: Yes, it's possible to wake up from that Dream. Then our lives are no longer obscured and limited by beliefs; we start living what we are, to our full potential. If you look at animals, this is how they live. Their minds don't hold beliefs, their bodies don't store up old Emotions, so they have nothing to stop them reaching their full potential. You don't find eagles that are too scared to fly; an eagle simply lives its eagle-ness.

It's odd that man has the gift of consciousness, and yet it's this very gift that gives us the ability to get stuck in Emotion, to worry about the future, to be laden with the past, to have a Personality and all that involves.

Matthew: So you're saying that being identified as Personality, and its Dream, stops us realising our potential as humans.

Jez: Yes. If you want to look at it from a human potential point of view, this is really good news because it's a failsafe path to living your potential. However, reaching your potential is an outcome of this enquiry; it's *not* the goal.

Matthew: What do you mean?

Jez: I mean that if you approach this with the goal of reaching your full potential you're going about it the wrong way; you're turning this into self-development and you'll miss out on both counts: Your self won't develop and you probably won't get free of the Dream you're creating. This understanding cannot be reduced to pursuits of Personality because the operation of Personality is the very thing that's seen through in order for the understanding to happen.

Matthew: OK, but you're saying that, potentially, anyone could get free of their Personality's Dream?

Jez: Yes. However, although this understanding is available to anyone, as far as the general public is concerned it's unknown, it's a secret. But, as the old books say so poetically: It's an open secret. No one is hiding it from you but yourself. Your eyes are wide shut!

Matthew: That kind of blows my mind: I'm hiding it from myself, but I don't even know that I'm doing it! What am I meant to do with that?

Jez: *Find out* if you're hiding it from yourself!

Matthew: How?

Jez: By doing exactly what you're doing now: by listening to the suggestion that you *are* hiding it from yourself. That's a start, but of course, listening isn't enough: If you have a longing to find out, you'll *engage* with this suggestion and find out in your own experience if it's true. Asking questions about how this works will be a matter of life and death to you, because you know that nothing in your life could ever be as important as finding the answer. Someone once said: 'You've got to want this like a drowning man wants air.'

Matthew: I don't know why, but I'm starting to feel frustrated.

Jez: This is absolutely frustrating to the mind, but how can it be any other way? It's about something that's beyond mind, so the mind can never understand this. The strangest part of all this, from where I'm looking, is how we become so divorced from this understanding that it becomes confusing to us. How can you be confused by what you are? The baby's not confused by what it is; the eagle isn't confused by its eagle-ness. We're only confused because we have a mind and we take ourselves to be that mind, rather than the Natural State in which that mind arises.

24

MIND

How we identify the mind as the centre
of who we are

'Oh, the thinks you can think.' – *Dr Seuss*

Jez: When we identified with the self, we took on the mind as the centre of who we are. Right from the start, in the development of the self, it appeared like this was the case. Our abilities to think, to choose, to do what we take to be activities that make us human, all come from the mind. To even process these words, to turn the sounds I'm making into language, you have to use the mind. The mind is central to our operating in this world, to our beliefs, our thoughts, our idea of who we are.

*Matthew: And yet it seems that you're saying the mind **isn't** the centre of who we are?*

Jez: I'm saying that it is as far as the Personality's concerned. If there were no mind there'd *be* no Personality. It's like imagining a computer without a central processing unit: without it, all the software, and the rest of the hardware, are unusable. Without the 'mind' of the computer, you can't really call it a computer; it's just a group of components linked together. It can't do anything.

Matthew: It's the same with people: Without a mind, there's just a body that's unable to function.

Jez: Yes, of course, but there's a big difference: We're not just computers. We're not robots. We have a whole other dimension to our existence: We have Being and the perception of Love.

Matthew: Is this anything to do with the soul?

Jez: No. How does the dictionary define 'soul'?

Matthew: It's the 'essence of a human being that is regarded as immortal'.

Jez: Immortality is a belief that usually has a religious root to it. In religion there's recognition that we're more than just a person living this life, that there's something greater than us. Wonder and a call to surrender to that which is 'greater than us' are part of our Original Relationship to Life, so what I'm talking about is completely in accordance with that. However, it's what's done with that wonder and call to surrender which separates religion from this enquiry. In religion that natural sense of wonder and awe is taken by the mind and applied to all sorts of thought abstractions: gods, goddesses, gurus, angels, devils, sin and redemption. All of that is the domain of belief and, as you may have noticed, the one thing I keep saying is this has nothing to do with belief. In fact, in this enquiry, belief is an obstruction; belief is what has to be removed to perceive this. Nietzsche has a good quote on this:

Faith: Not wanting to know what the truth is.

There's no belief required with regards to Being; babies are pure Being but they have no mind yet to even hold a belief. If this enquiry takes root in you it's very likely that you'll start to perceive Being in yourself. It's the perception of and living of what we are, which is Love, in all its forms and expressions.

Matthew: And one of those forms is the mind?

Jez: Exactly. The mind is such a beautiful, wonderful expression of Love. The fact that matter, cells, water and electricity can hold thoughts, memories, language and even consciousness is one of the greatest natural wonders of all. The mind is one manifestation of the life force being expressed as a human but it's not who we are, any more than the central processing unit is the computer.

Matthew: This isn't generally known, is it?

Jez: No, because we're conditioned to forget this; we're trained by our families and tribe to believe that we *are* the mind. We've lived our whole life with this belief and it's not surprising really because, once we've lost connection with Being and the Original Relationship to Life, it seems to be true.

Matthew: Can you explain that?

Jez: In the Natural State, Being is lived as the centre of human life. When that Original Relationship to Life is lost, as children we're not conscious of what's happened.

Matthew: Because we have no self-awareness.

Jez: Yes, and anyway, we're too undeveloped to be able to think or speak. Imagine if, as a baby, Lucy did have these faculties, she might have said to her parents: 'Hey, I'm fresh from heaven (Laughs.) I know that we're all One; I know that we're all different expressions of Love. You may not remember what Being is, but I do. You're changing my nappy and spooning food into my mouth, you're caring for my body but you're missing something. You're not recognising Being. It looks like you don't know that it is who I am.'

Matthew: How are her parents not doing that?

Jez: By relating to Lucy as if her centre is her mind, as if her mind is all she is. Don't get me wrong, of course it's a parent's job to develop their child's mind, but I'm saying that doesn't have to happen at the expense of the child losing contact with Being.

Matthew: But that's what happens.

Jez: As I've said before, you can only pass on as much as you yourself know, so if the parents have taken on the existential belief that they *are* the mind, then that's what's passed onto the child. In that set up, in those circumstances, there's nothing else that could happen. So identification with the mind is hardwired into the tribe of man.

*Matthew: Out of interest, if a baby **was** born to parents who had rediscovered this, who were living as that Being...*

Jez: Ah, another one of your 'Wouldn't the world be wonderful if...' thoughts! It's a good question actually because, although this enquiry is concerned with 'What is', sometimes looking at 'What isn't' can help give a clear perspective on that.

In the next collection of discussions, we'll talk about what it means practically to rediscover and live the Natural State as an adult; at its very root is the seeing through of this mistaken identification with Personality and the mind. Practically this means that while you perceive the different forms of the world, you recognise them all to be manifestation of Oneness. So when relating to a baby, an awake parent would recognise that Being or Love that the child is, just as they would with anyone. The difference with the baby is: Being is not hidden or obscured as it is with most people, because the Personality, which obstructs it, has not yet formed.

When it came to the mind, there would of course be development of the baby's mental faculties just as with any parents, but there would still be the recognition of Being as the centre of who the baby is.

So, and now we get to the point, this diversion demonstrates what we *didn't* grow up with. We *were* taught that the mind is the centre of who we are, and having lost our connection to Being, as time went on, those lessons that we are the mind fell on fertile ground. There was nothing to refute them; we took on that belief without any question because we had no ability to fight it. The part of us that could have fought it is the part that was trained out of us.

Matthew: I can understand this logically, but the idea that I'm not my mind still feels alien to me because, in my everyday life, this is who I think I am; this seems to be who lives this life.

Jez: I totally understand. Everything we do in this life, thinking, choosing, acting, believing, seems to confirm it to be true. It's my mind that's able to express this point, and your mind that's able to hear it and think about it, so it seems madness to even suggest that we're not our minds. But that doesn't mean it's not true, that just means we've got so used to the idea that we *are* the mind that the suggestion we are more than it seems ridiculous.

But it's only from the viewpoint of Personality that it seems ridiculous. If you have an experience *beyond* Personality, then you have a glimpse of the fact that there's another dimension to life that exists before the mind. We've adopted an inaccurate perception of how life works; we've put things in the wrong order of importance.

Let's jump sideways for a moment and think about a camera as an example of this, it's perhaps a closer analogy than a computer. If you think about it, a camera is an amazingly clever, almost magical device: It can capture the forms and light which appear before it, remember that information, and then pass it on so it can be reproduced as photographs. So just like a mind, the camera can memorise and interpret life that appears in front of it. But you wouldn't say that the camera itself or the images it stores and produces *are* life itself; they're interpretations, reflections of life created by a camera, which is itself appearing *within* life. Life is the context in which the camera appears, but what I'm saying is that we fall into the mistake of identifying *as* the camera rather than the context in which it appears.

To take ourselves to be the mind is an outcome of forgetting where we come from; it is, in the bigger picture, a misconception. And apart from those who've remembered or rediscovered the original state of Being, the world of man lives with this misconception as truth.

There are many outcomes to taking the mind to be who we are, but perhaps the most important is that identifying as the mind takes us away from our spiritual centre. I'm wary of using the word 'spiritual' because, like 'love', it's been debased through misuse. In popular culture it's become linked with angels, crystals and all sorts of esoteric beliefs, which is the very opposite of what I mean by it.

Matthew: I've just looked up the word 'spiritual'. When referring to a person, it means: 'Not concerned with material values or pursuits. In general, it seems to point to a connection to something bigger than ourselves'.

Jez: You see, in its original meaning, the word points to what we talked about earlier when we discussed 'soul'. It has nothing to do with wacky, New Age beliefs. When I use the word 'Spiritual', with a capital 'S', I mean 'connected to something bigger than ourselves' because when we do that, we see beyond Personality. Only then do we rediscover our innate connection, as human beings, to Oneness, to Love.

The centre of this connection in the body is the heart. We've shifted the emphasis from our Spiritual centre (our hearts) to our thinking centre (our minds). We've shrunk down from a connection to 'something bigger than ourselves' to the self. In this identification we lose contact with the most fundamental part of who we are; we lose the knowledge of ourselves as Oneness, as Love.

Matthew: And, as you said in our first talk, that's why it feels good to be around newborn babies.

Jez: Yes, because they're still centred in the heart and they remind us of our beginnings. They remind us of our Spiritual roots, of where we come from. But as we grow up and become identified as Personality, we become estranged from the heart.

Matthew: I think many people hearing this would say: 'What do you mean estranged from the heart? The heart is an organ with a function of pumping blood around our bodies and as long as you're alive it's doing its job.'

Jez: Pumping blood is the physical level of what a heart does, but the heart is so much more than just a pump. (I say 'just' a pump, but that pump contracts about seventy-two times every minute of our lives and is of course a miracle in itself!) So, with the greatest respect to the miracle that is the physical functioning of the heart, I'm saying that the heart has another vital function in human life. In the physical body the heart is the portal to the Absolute Level, to Oneness, to Love.

The heart is the first organ that grows in the human embryo. It's central to our lives, yes, because without it we wouldn't be kept physically alive, but also without it we wouldn't be Spiritually alive. Science can replicate minds to some degree by building computers, but as every science fiction writer knows, it can't build a robot that feels Love. It's this aspect of the heart that we can become estranged from.

This estrangement principally happens at the time of the Contraction. We learned that feelings are dangerous, and the feeling centre is the heart. So contracting from the painful feelings of the Wound is a pulling away from the heart centre.

Matthew: OK, so having convinced me that we become identified with our minds at the expense of becoming estranged from our hearts, can you go into more detail about the consequences of that identification?

Jez: Firstly, becoming estranged from our hearts is what's behind the unhappiness and Suffering in human life. The extent to which you're compromised in feeling Love is the extent to which you can't feel Joy, contentment or fulfilment. Psychologically this can manifest as ongoing sadness and depression.

Matthew: Most people would put those symptoms down to disturbances of the mind.

Jez: There's a great interconnectedness between the heart and the mind. In ancient Chinese calligraphy the symbol for the mind and the heart are the same. Let me put it like this: Have you ever been in love?

Matthew: Yes.

Jez: When we fall in love it's a gift from life, a reminder of our Natural State because falling in Love causes a spontaneous opening of our hearts. If you remember the feeling, especially when it was new, how did you feel?

Matthew: Full of Joy, bursting with life, positive, happy…

Jez: I used to have a picture of me around the time I met my wife. You can see in my face that I've just fallen in love; I remember everyone telling me that I looked radiant. Do you remember feeling any sadness when you fell in love?

Matthew: Of course not. I see what you're saying: Falling in love gives an insight into the experience of the heart being open, which is the opposite of estrangement from the heart.

Jez: Exactly. Depression of course manifests in the mind, in negative thoughts, but I'm suggesting it *begins* in the estrangement from heart. If the heart centre is open, you're feeling life and connecting with it. Depression has its roots in being cut off, estranged from life and feeling.

That's the psychological side of things, but there are physical consequences too. The medical profession is starting to recognise that excessive sadness and depression lowers the body's immunity to disease. So there's an increased likelihood of diseases coming from *outside* the body, but then there's the effect depression and a heavy, closed heart has on the body from the inside. We're unable to relax; we find that our busy minds start to disrupt our sleep. This increases the stress we're already feeling and puts us in a vicious cycle. Over the long term this can lead to high blood pressure, and of course when all of this is prolonged, strokes and heart attacks become increasingly likely.

Matthew: I can see this relocation of our centre of living has serious consequences.

Jez: All those side effects are not always so obvious in daily life because they're internal things; you don't usually know if someone's heart is in poor shape, and unhappiness can of course be masked when in public. But there's one symptom of this which can be seen everywhere in daily life, even though no one is really aware of it, and that is mankind's addiction to thought. That's the subject of our next talk.

25

THOUGHT

How we become addicted to thinking as a way to avoid feeling

'We are what we think.
All that we are arises with our thoughts.
With our thoughts we make the world.' – Buddha

Matthew: When we use the word 'addicted' we normally think of addiction to substances such as alcohol or tobacco, but you use the phrase 'addiction to thought'. What do you mean by that?

Jez: Many activities require us to use the mind: When at work, we might have to process data, go to meetings, use computers, communicate with other companies etcetera. Then we leave work and use our minds for entertainment. If you watch yourself, how many moments from your whole day are spent resting your mind?

Matthew: (Pauses.) Not many.

Jez: We've learned to keep our minds almost permanently engaged, whether it's in the pursuit of our desires, in business, or just for entertainment. I'll give you an example: Every time I see you walking up my garden path you're staring at your phone.

Matthew: What's wrong with that? I like checking what's happening in the news and on social media.

Jez: There's nothing wrong with it as such – if you'd just received a call or needed to look something up urgently, that's what mobile phones are for. But if constantly going online becomes a compulsion then I'd say that's an expression of being addicted to thought.

Matthew: But surely it's a good thing to interact with the world we're in and to stimulate the mind?

Jez: Yes, but there's a difference between interacting with the world simply through Joy and interacting with it through a *need*, a compulsion to be busy, to be constantly stimulated. One is a natural sharing, an overflow of energy; the other is a habit, a habit which the progress of technology facilitates perfectly. There are moments when calling someone while you're on the street is helpful, for example when you need to tell the person you're meeting you'll be late. But that's not what's happening. All over the world, on every street right now, people are walking around while interacting with people or websites in distant locations. We're connected all over the world in a way that we've never been before, but when it comes to the Original Relationship to Life, we're essentially disconnected. We're not present.

Matthew: What does that mean practically?

Jez: We have amazing minds that can multitask; we can walk and talk and look at websites all at the same time. But when you're dividing your energy in this way, each subject of your attention gets less energy. This means that when you're staring at the screen as you walk, you're not 'in' your feet which are doing the walking.

Matthew: I have to admit, the other day I was walking along reading something on the screen and I actually bumped into a lamppost. (Laughs.)

Jez: Suddenly you were brought back into your body, and your senses, right?

Matthew: Very suddenly – I could feel my head throbbing!

Jez: Japanese Zen masters use a Zen stick to hit students on the head to jolt them into awareness of the moment. With you, life has very compassionately used a lamppost instead! It's a wake-up call: How many times will you need to collide with a lamppost before you get the message? (Laughs.)

Matthew: Getting the lesson from you is a lot less painful!

Jez: Is it? Maybe I'm going too easy on you! (Both laugh.) The point is, your attention is on the screen and the information coming from it; you're isolated in the mind and you're not interacting and feeling life that's going on around you... until it hits you on the head!

Matthew: But can't you be in the mind at the same time as being in the moment?

Jez: Of course. This moment can include the mind and its activities, so that busyness becomes your experience of the moment. But that busyness of mind creates a moment which is not exactly full of Stillness and fulfilment. If mental busyness becomes an ongoing state, I'd suggest that's a phenomenal narrowing down of experience.

Matthew: Why do you say that?

Jez: Because, as we talked about last time, we're not just our minds.

Our Original Relationship to Life *includes* the mind and thinking, but it's built upon feeling, which happens through our senses in the present moment. It's in the step your foot is taking on the pavement.

I'm reminded of another story about a student who visited a Zen master one rainy day. He's eager to get inside the temple and hear what words of wisdom the Master is going to impart to him. The first thing the Master says is: 'On which side of the entrance did you leave your umbrella?'

Being habitually located in the mind all through the day becomes an exclusion of feeling and awareness of the present moment.

Matthew: So why do you think we're like that?

Jez: To be present is to feel, to take in life. But the Personality links feeling only with what it sees as *dangerous* feelings; that means painful feelings which can lead back to the Wound. The Personality's job is to protect you from those disturbing feelings. So, as far as the Personality's concerned, anything that distracts us from feeling is good. However, like I said when we discussed the Contraction, you can't just shut off from 'dangerous' feelings: If the aperture of the heart is closed down you're cut off from all feeling, i.e. 'positive' as well as 'negative' feelings. I'm not saying this is a conscious plan; for most people the Personality's activities go on without their awareness of them. If you asked yourself why you keep yourself so mentally busy, what would you say?

Matthew: I don't know why; I'm certainly not choosing to do it. It's like a compulsion: I'm aware of it from time to time, because you've pointed it out to me, but it seems to be a default setting, a habit.

Jez: What do you think you get out of it? What's the payoff?

Matthew: I suspect sometimes I do it so I don't have to think about things that make me feel bad, such as being behind in work, things I said I'd do that I haven't done yet, things I have to do that I don't want to do...

Jez: It's a programme that's running in your system and it can all be traced back to the Wound.

Matthew: Really? It started so far back?

Jez: Yes. After the Wound we were confused: We had all these painful feelings, we felt out of control and we *were*, because we couldn't control the love source that we were dependent on. So, along with pushing away those painful feelings from the past in the Contraction, we found another way of dealing with them in the present. As I said when we were talking about attention, we found we could distract ourselves from them by being busy.

When you were playing with your Lego as a child, your focus shifted to those bricks, and the fun you were having with them. But as our capacity for thinking develops we find that thinking can distract us too.

Matthew: I remember when my Mum told us we'd soon be going on a trip to the zoo: Even when bad things happened, it made me feel better to know that a good thing was coming in the future.

Jez: Escaping to the future by thinking about an upcoming event is another Distraction technique to avoid the present. You can see how we learned to use the mind to control our experience: We felt out of control and the mind did everything it could to rein back some sense of control.

As we've discussed, we learned this after the Wound. It had hurt us, so we analysed what happened and started Contracting in order to protect against being hurt again. We learned that analysing what was going on made us feel safer; it was the opposite of being caught off guard. But this sort of over-analysing things has a downside too: Fuelled by fear, it can turn into worry about what *could* happen in the future.

Matthew: I arrived here today having just received news about an exciting business possibility. After the initial buzz, I started worrying about how I was going to make the most of the opportunity, and after a while I ended up feeling a bit stressed.

Jez: You can't control what's going to happen, but the mind starts doing all it can to try to. *Over*-thinking is not *clear* thinking, because it comes laced with stress, and that means there's less clarity in it. It's not the case that the more thinking we do, the better we get at it, the clearer it becomes – mostly the opposite is the case.

Thoughts can be powerful: Used with intent and focus they can change your experience of life, but over-thinking and worry don't give you access to thought which can serve you in this way. In fact they're a barrier to it.

Matthew: What happens to thinking when you live beyond Personality?

Jez: There's thinking that comes from the Wound: This is the internal dialogue which has stress in it, which is obsessive and never stops. Then there's thinking that doesn't come from the Wound, it's just the mind doing what it's evolved to do. The difference is, this thinking is not obsessive, there's no stress in it, and it can stop. Beyond Personality the mind returns to a natural balance in which thinking happens when it's needed, and when it isn't, there's a return to a more neutral, quiet mental state.

Matthew: I know what that state feels like, I just don't have it often.

Jez: Nature has built our body organs and parts to do certain jobs and they need healthy conditions to do those jobs effectively. For example, they need to be fed by blood and oxygen, but most importantly they need periods of inactivity where they rest and recover. If they're overused, they can wear out and start functioning less well. For example, if you overuse your knee joints by jogging too much it can lead to arthritis; if you strain your eye muscles by staring at computer screens too long the damage can be permanent.

Matthew: What about the heart? That's constantly pumping blood; it never stops.

Jez: The heart is created with the job of beating for a whole lifetime, but it has different rates of beating: It has restful, slower rhythms and faster active rhythms when more blood needs to be pumped around the body. If the heart is constantly stimulated to beat at a fast rate, by stress for example, it can lead to problems such as enlargement.

This principle, that organs and body parts require periods of rest to function well, applies just as much to the brain. Anyone who's experienced meditation knows how turning off thoughts, even for a few minutes, rejuvenates the brain and our ability to think clearly.

Incessant thinking without resting the brain is not natural for our systems. I've heard a theory that it's behind the rise in frequency of Alzheimer's disease, as if overuse of the brain is putting too much strain on its functioning and wearing it out. I have no idea if this is true, but it would make sense.

Matthew: So you're suggesting that we should think less?

Jez: I'm not suggesting that we *should* think less; 'shoulds' don't have any place in this enquiry. I'm just pointing out something which isn't recognised in society: That it's become normal to think constantly. If you're at all interested in finding out why you're Suffering, then becoming aware of this addiction to thought is a vital part of becoming aware of the functioning of the Personality.

Our minds have a certain configuration built upon our experience of the Wound and what beliefs we've taken on from our parents and tribe. These beliefs are thought formations which have becomes stuck; they've solidified into knots. So you may believe that you're not good enough, you're not loveable, that you're superior, that you're weak, ugly, or that life's out to get you. Whatever your particular configuration is, all these beliefs are built of negative thoughts which have become trapped. What you end up with is a voice in your head that's forever spouting the opinions of those beliefs: criticising you, telling you what you did is wrong, what you could have done better, or that this person is out to get you or that person is inferior to you. This mental cacophony is not freedom; it's hell.

Matthew: I was recently working with a guy who I've always thought of as being very strong and positive, and he made a little mistake. What shocked me was that he exclaimed: 'You idiot!' It was so violent and condemnatory; I was surprised to hear him speak about himself in that way,

Jez: That voice inside your head can be vicious! There's no kindness in it – it can be like having a sadistic drill instructor shouting in your ear. But it can also be a quietly undermining influence, whispering negative thoughts into your day.

If you look at cases of mental illness, in which people hear voices and their minds are manic and out of control, it's just a little further along the road of a mental state that's taken for granted in the general population. In those cases, at least the madness of being controlled by the mind's beliefs and negative thoughts is on the surface. The incessant internal dialogue has become external, that's the difference; in most people it's internal, hidden away. It's not talked about much because it's taken to be normal. It's normal in the sense that it's common in the world but in relation to the Natural State it's not, because there's no Stillness in it. It's not where we come from; it's only how we've been trained to be in a world where addiction to thought is the default setting of Personality.

26

THE MASK

What we wear to hide the parts of ourselves
that we don't want to be seen

'Man is least himself when he talks in his own person.
Give him a mask, and he will tell you the truth.' – Oscar Wilde

Jez: You can learn so much about the Natural State from animals because, unlike humans, they don't lose it in their early years; they live *in* it, and *as* it throughout their lives. However, it's not a direct comparison because, as we talked about before, animals differ from humans in that they have no self-consciousness. They don't have the capacity for self-reflection and therefore, unlike us, they have no thoughts about how they appear to other animals. This means there's no idea of being anything other than what they are; they don't pretend.

Matthew: I'm trying to imagine a dog pretending to be loving to its owner.

Jez: It's impossible to imagine isn't it? Dogs don't know how to *pretend* to be loving because they *are* loving. (Or not loving, other expressions of life in dogs are possible!) Dogs may have smaller brains than us but, like all animals, they have one important thing over us humans: They know how to be exactly what they are without the thought of being any other way. A dog is simply and fully whatever it is in any given moment. If it's aggressive, it's aggressive; it doesn't pretend to be nice. If it's hungry, it's hungry; it doesn't pretend it's not.

Matthew: Just the thought of being like that makes me feel relaxed and happy.

Jez: I know, because here in the world of man, where there's self-consciousness and self-reflection, things are different. That self-consciousness manifests as a constant commentary from the mind, and a lot of our internal dialogue is about how we appear in the world. It says: 'Do this, don't do that', 'Don't say this, she might not like it', 'Don't think that, it's not very kind.'

There's this constant censuring of our behaviour because we humans have learned the skill of pretending. We can make a *presentation* of what we are by putting on a mask to present a particular version of ourselves and hide facets that we don't want to be seen. Let's give this specific use of the word Mask a capital 'M' to differentiate it from other uses of the word.

Matthew: Why do I keep thinking of politicians?

Jez: They're the most obvious example of what we're talking about.

In fact, in many circles the word 'politician' has become a byword for lying, for untrustworthiness. What politicians generally present to the world is not their truth but a spin, a presentation of whatever's the most expedient to their needs – or those of their party. In other words, what's presented often bears little relation to the truth of that moment – it's fabricated and so it's untrustworthy.

But let's not be too hard on the politicians; I'd argue this template is just an exaggerated, public version of what's going on in every Personality. All Personalities have a public image, a front, a Mask of how they'd like to be seen. And behind this lurks a different reality.

*Matthew: Politicians have incentives to present an image to the public that's going to cast them in a favourable light so they get more votes, but why do you think **we** wear a Mask and hide parts of ourselves? To hide our socially unacceptable thoughts and feelings?*

Jez: Yes, when you boil it all down, it's pretty much the same reason: the need to be liked, the need to be loved. We touched on this when we talked about gaining attention earlier. As children we learn to please our parents to gain attention, for example by being good, by hiding aspects of ourselves that could make us unlovable. We may not be aware of it, but this strategy of pleasing doesn't stop after childhood; it goes on to a greater or lesser extent throughout the life of a Personality,

Matthew: I've noticed in conflict situations I find myself defaulting to the role of the peacemaker; I want everyone to be happy.

Jez: Why do you think you'd want to take on that role?

Matthew: I prefer peace to conflict – I like the idea of everyone getting along.

Jez: Of course, everyone wants world peace! (Laughs.) But I think there might be another reason. I wonder what your Personality gets out of it?

Matthew: I guess I hope everyone will like the peacemaker!

Jez: Right, because from a moral point of view, it's an admirable stance to take. Of course taking that role can come from a purely altruistic position, but we're not talking about that. We're discussing the Masks that the Personality wears in order to gain acceptance and love. And when it appears as a strategy like that, some people might see through it and may actually *dislike* you for manipulating the situation for your purposes. You think you're being loving but actually you're exploiting the conflict for your own needs.

Matthew: That might explain the negative reactions I sometimes get when I think I'm doing a good deed...

Jez: The point is, whether we're aware of it or not, all Personalities, to a greater or lesser extent, are acting, pretending, wearing Masks.

Matthew: Perhaps we're only real, we only take the Mask off, when we're with close friends.

Jez: Maybe, but even then, are you really who you are with your friends? Are you really authentically who you are with me?

Matthew: Now you're put me on the spot!

Jez: No mercy here! I don't mean that I expect you to tell me all your secrets – what you reveal about yourself can be an aware choice. Of course, to an extent we all present a version of ourselves, simply by choosing what we say and what we don't say, and that can be done knowingly. So we're not talking about that. We're discussing being under the continual directives from Personality telling you how to be, what to say in order to manipulate other people's opinion of you – usually to make them like you. The acting and Mask wearing are unconscious.

Matthew: If I'm honest, I...

Jez: Sorry to interrupt but, it's interesting that you use that phrase: 'If I'm honest'. It's become so commonplace. The very existence of that phrase surely points to the fact that we're habitually *not* honest. But, honest is the very thing I'm asking you to be with your answer because otherwise, you'd be wearing the Mask that presents a spin on the truth.

Matthew: OK, so... If I'm honest, I'd say I try to be authentic with you but I'm probably not always successful.

Jez: Ah, but you were then. Thank you, for your honesty. It's interesting how, when you're brutally honest with me, a different dynamic arises between us. Did you feel it?

Matthew: Yes, it becomes more... intimate. I feel closer to you in some way.

Jez: When you're honest, you're going beyond the Mask, which is the surface of you. In a way you're being intimate with yourself, with who you really are, underneath the Mask. But also, by removing your Mask in this way, you're honouring me by trusting me with your truth, trusting me enough to go beyond the image your Personality wants to project.

This level of honesty and self-awareness is of course the basic requirement to engage in this enquiry. Otherwise it will remain just an intellectual pursuit, which may stimulate the mind and please the Personality in its cleverness but won't reveal the truth of what's being pointed to here.

Matthew: I'm quite surprised with my answer about how authentic I am with you. It's making me question how much I wear a Mask in all my relationships.

Jez: I'd say most of the time, because if Personality's running the show then all its strategies to get attention, to be liked, to present a good image etcetera. are being played out. For most people, the programming of Personality is running continuously without them even knowing about it.

Matthew: Then maybe most people are only being authentically themselves, without any censure, when they're on their own.

Jez: Some of the time, but then there's the possibility you're not being absolutely honest with *yourself*. The Personality can even fool you into thinking you're something that you're not. There's the famous case of the American socialite and amateur soprano Florence Foster Jenkins who history remembers as the world's worst opera singer. The fact that she couldn't hold a tune didn't stop her filling concert halls, and even though the sneers and laughter from her audiences provided ample evidence that she couldn't sing, she still managed to maintain the self-conceit that she was almost on a par with the great sopranos.

You can observe this kind of self-deception going on all the time when you're with others. Have you ever been with someone and the surface layer, the front they're putting out, seems to be really friendly but for some reason you don't trust that friendliness? Most of us have a sensor that can detect disparity between what someone is projecting and what we're picking up. A lot of entertainment TV shows are built on our ability to pick up on the games that Personalities play in terms of manipulating and lying to each other.

Matthew: Especially reality-type shows, like Big Brother...

Jez: Yes. That show's based on a psychological experiment that was originally about observing human behaviour. It's an ingenious format because the constant scrutiny of the cameras, the incarceration with other people and lack of personal space creates a pressure cooker environment that's designed to bring out Personality in all its manipulative glory! So you can sit back and watch the contestant's strategies playing out: the shape shifting, the allegiances made for safety or for gain. The whole game of Personality is exposed for our entertainment. It's a circus of all the Masks the contestants are displaying.

Matthew: They have the Diary Room, where they speak to Big Brother, don't they? I suppose the idea is this is where they take their Mask off so the viewer gets to see what's behind it.

Jez: That's the pretension, but of course what the contestants show Big Brother via the camera in the Diary Room is still only a version of the truth, just another Mask designed to get the viewers to vote for them.

The success of the format worldwide proves it can be great entertainment and it's all based on the fact that, from the comfort of our sofas, we love to see through the Masks of other Personalities. And it's easy to do, because we have this bullshit detector. But it's not so easy to see the workings of your *own* Personality. That requires Choice-less Awareness, and that's something that most people have lost.

27

THE SHADOW

The hidden side of the Personality

*'Until you make the unconscious conscious,
it will direct your life and you will call it fate.' – Carl Jung*

Matthew: We've talked about how we present a good image of ourselves with the Mask because we want to be liked, but you only have to look at the news to see that 'goodness', be it real or affected, isn't exactly predominant in the world. So I'm wondering: How does hatred and violence fit into all of this?

Jez: With the help of the Mask, most people are able to present what's acceptable to society. The other side of this equation is keeping everything that might *not* be acceptable *behind* the Mask. For example, you're basically a kind and loving person, but when your school friend Stephen made another good friend you showed a different, more malicious side, a side you'd normally keep behind the Mask.

Earlier we discussed how Personality Awareness chooses what we become aware of; when this is applied to ourselves, everything we don't want to confront is consigned to the subconscious. Carl Jung called this the Shadow. (We'll capitalise this use of the word.) It's because we have Personality Awareness that the Shadow exists. It's important to note that the Shadow can contain both positive and negative aspects.

Matthew: Positive aspects?

Jez: Yes, for example one's sexuality. If it's not acceptable to the family or society we live in, it can be confined to the subconscious and so form part of the Shadow.

Thankfully, the Group Personality can evolve and gradually extend parameters of what it considers acceptable. Some things that once had to be kept behind the Mask can now be shown openly.

Matthew: It's amazing to think that, in your lifetime, it was illegal in the UK for gay men to express themselves sexually.

Jez: Yes. More recently society's becoming more understanding and accepting of transgender people. Unfortunately, it's not like that everywhere; across the world the group mind of each society evolves at different rates.

Matthew: But at least there are some signs of change, harbingers of what's possible in society...

Jez: It takes individual pockets of society to change before that change spreads and transforms the whole. It takes individuals to act as agents of change, to stand up and confront the prevailing view of what's acceptable in the collective consciousness. People like Emmeline Pankhurst, Martin Luther King and Nelson Mandela were incredibly brave because they had to face the hostility of the prevailing view from Personalities around them. Nelson Mandela paid the price for this with his freedom, Martin Luther King with his life.

Matthew: So effectively, through this process of people challenging the status quo, the collective Shadow of the Group Personality is shrinking?

Jez: I think that's true in some areas. The general direction seems to move gradually towards more personal freedom: A hundred years ago few women anywhere had the vote; gradually we've reached a point where almost all women have the vote now. So this might make you feel positive, right? We're all going in the right direction and peace and Love will prevail on the planet.

Matthew: You know I'm quite idealistic about this sort of thing so yes, I'd like to think that's true.

Jez: Unfortunately, seeing what *is* true is different to seeing what one would *like* to be true.

Matthew: This is becoming a bit of a theme!

Jez: We're forgetting one vital factor, which is that what's hidden behind the Mask can be both positive and negative. So far we've mostly touched on the positive aspects, but to answer your question about hatred in the world, we need to focus on the negative aspects of the Shadow. These are relative terms I know, but I use them in relation to the human, relative world, so in that sense I think they're appropriate. The negative aspects we're specifically referring to are hatred and violence.

Matthew: I don't think you're going too far out on a limb calling hatred negative...

Jez: Violence is one part of the Shadow that, in most progressive societies at least, is never going to be acceptable because violence works against society's stability. Society develops moral codes to control such antisocial aspects of human behaviour and to prevent chaos, but of course moral codes don't always stop people being violent.

Matthew: I think it might be useful to look up a definition of 'violence'. Here's one: 'The intentional use of physical force or power, threatened or actual, against oneself, another person, or against a group or community,'

Jez: You'll notice that definition includes the idea of violence against oneself – it's important to understand that self-hurt is also a form of violence. The most extreme example of this would be suicide, another level would be self-harming, and at the lower end of the scale there's self-criticism. But whether you look at violence against oneself or others, to go deeper into the subject we have to examine where violence begins.

Matthew: If you look at nature documentaries it seems there's violence in most animals. The poet Tennyson wrote: 'Nature, red in tooth and claw.'

Jez: This is the violence that arises from an innate will to survive, whether it's killing for food or self-protection. That accounts for some of the violence in mankind too: Even a peace-loving man like the Beatles' George Harrison fought for his life when a schizophrenic intruder attacked him in his own home.

But the violence that arises from the 'kill or be killed' instinct in all of us only explains a small percentage of violence that occurs in the world. So where does the rest come from?

Matthew: I'd say it comes from hatred.

Jez: Right, and hatred is an Emotion; it's an original feeling of anger that's been allowed to fester and contract into an ongoing, intense resentment of a person, a race, a sexual orientation or whatever. So my contention is that violence which isn't survival based originates from the Personality. Physical violence is an outcome of mental violence; it's mental violence that's reached the physical level of manifestation.

So to understand violence you have to look at the mind, at the psychology of the Personality: specifically Emotion and thought. Violence has many appearances, from the ultimate level of taking someone's life to a less extreme level like gossiping and bitching about someone. As I always say, to see the bigger picture it sometimes helps to examine a microcosm, so let's talk about gossip.

Matthew: You'd call gossip and bitching a form of violence?

Jez: Yes, because it all comes from the same root: the intention to hurt someone. Your negative thoughts about the boy who became close with your friend Stephen turned into a bitchy tirade against him to everyone else. The intention behind it was to hurt him, so although you may not have been aware of it yourself, you were being violent to him.

It's very easy to see the violence in other people, but it's pretty obvious the seed from which the violence arises is in all of us – it's just that in some Personalities it's more active and becomes physical. We may despair at the street violence reported in the media while remaining unaware of the 'normal' violence hiding inside ourselves.

Matthew: You can see this sort of thing on a bigger scale in the nastiness that appears on the Internet.

Jez: In the Regency period gossip was whispered behind fans at high society balls; now it's broadcast round the world on social media. It's all violence, and it's in most Personalities. I read that Charles Dickens once said he was aware of two sides to his Personality: One was the 'good' side, from which he tried to live his life. This explains his philanthropic works for the poor and it's the wellspring from which he created his benign, loveable characters such as Mr Micawber in David Copperfield. But Dickens was also aware of another aspect of his Personality, his 'bad' side, from which he wrote all his malevolent characters such as Uriah Heep.

Recognition of the hidden, dark side of our Personalities can also be found in Robert Louis Stevenson's novel *'The Strange Case of Dr Jekyll and Mr Hyde'.* I suspect the enduring success of that story is down to the fact that we all recognise this Shadow side within us.

Matthew: There have been times in my life when I think my Shadow side really came forward for a while; certain people have brought it out.

Jez: I'm intrigued...

Matthew: Everything seemed perfect in my life until just before my fifth birthday when my younger brother was born. I didn't appreciate my place as the youngest in the family until I lost it to him. I'm not exactly proud of this, but I used to give poor Daniel a terrible time and was always undermining him. I remember once, when I was about eleven, telling him: 'You'll never beat me. I'll always be stronger and smarter than you.'

Jez: You can see how vicious the intent is behind that.

Matthew: I guess, but I always had a good reason for going after him, he'd always done something to provoke me, like...

Jez: Like being born? (Both laugh.)

Matthew: In my teens, friends would say to me: 'Matthew, you're usually such a nice guy. Why are you so horrible to your little brother?' It wasn't until many years later that I saw I was punishing him for having taken my place in the family, and for taking my Mum's attention. It's only now that I'm recognising the anger behind it.

Jez: You've led us perfectly back to the subject of Emotion, which takes us to your original question: *'Where does the violence in us come from?'* To answer this we're going to have to delve into the roots of the Personality, and the Wound. Let's use your example with your brother as a template: Had the Wound not happened, if you'd still been in your Natural State, there wouldn't have been any negative reaction to your brother's arrival into your life.

Matthew: I think I know what you mean but can you clarify that?

Jez: It's actually very logical: In the Natural State we exist as Love. If we exist as Love, there's no lack of Love, so no Emotion can arise from the lack of it.

Matthew: So what you're saying is, if I hadn't lost my perception of that unconditional Love...

Jez: Yes, it's all your fault – you screwed up! (Laughs.)

Matthew: I'm glad I know you well enough to realise that's a joke!

Jez: I'm being ironic to make the point that there's no suggestion that you – or any of us – could have done things any other way. We were not even conscious, so we were simply running on instinct. What happened is what happened; the point is to understand the *outcome* of what happened.

Matthew: OK, but what you're saying is, if I hadn't lost my perception of that unconditional Love, this Emotion of jealousy and hatred wouldn't have arisen when my brother was born.

Jez: Exactly. We're examining our response to the love not being there, or being there less, and the outcome of that. In your case it was your Emotions of jealousy and hate.

This response may start out as a survival instinct in the same way that cuckoos push rivals for the surrogate mother's food supply out of the nest so they survive. Nature is brutal; the will to survive at any cost is encoded into animals, including human animals. But in man, where we have a mind, this instinct can become negativity, hatred and violence.

Matthew: What about the self-violence you mentioned earlier?

Jez: The violence which arises from the lack of Love being received can be turned outwards to others or inwards as self-hatred. It then appears in the form of negative thoughts about oneself such as: 'I'm worthless', 'I'm ugly' or 'I don't deserve to live', which can manifest physically as self-harm, anorexia and, in extreme cases, suicide.

*Matthew: So there's a propensity for hate, whether turned inwards or outwards, in all Personalities. But is the hate that exists in us a given? Does it **have** to be like that?*

Jez: I don't think so. If you're filled with Love, there's no hate. That's a reasonable statement to make isn't it? Do you feel there's any hate in babies?

Matthew: I think most people would agree that there isn't. It's like saying 'Where there's light, no dark can exist.'

Jez: So it's reasonable to conclude that all hate grows out of the loss of the state of Love which we entered this world with. Once we've lost that, we can start to have the perception that there's less personal love to go round, which can lead to competition, jealousy and hatred. In most Personalities these aspects of the Shadow are not strong and perhaps they will only show up in small ways.

Matthew: I know someone who's very mild mannered usually, but behind the wheel of his car he becomes really abusive to other drivers and cyclists, just swearing at them all the time. It's like he becomes someone else altogether.

Jez: The car can become a safe zone for the Shadow to show itself and let off some steam, but that's the mild end of the scale. Emotions can be so strong that they burst through the normal restraints of the Personality and commit terrible acts of violence. I watched a crime programme recently about a teenager in America called Kyle. He was a kind boy, well liked at school, never showed any signs of antisocial behaviour whatsoever...

Matthew: Until...

Jez: Until the night he shot both his parents as they slept in their bed. This story wasn't a 'Who done it?' it was a 'Why did he do it?' The video of Kyle's interrogation at the police station shows that he's as baffled as everyone else by what happened. Although he admitted taking those cold-blooded shots at his parents, he felt that this was not the Kyle he knew himself to be.

He was correct: It wasn't the Kyle he, his parents and friends knew. It was his Shadow, the Hyde to the Jekyll they normally saw. Miraculously his parents survived and gradually a back-story emerged which, if you understand the power of Emotion, explained what had happened that terrible night.

Kyle was an only child. His parents obviously loved him, but there was a strictness to his upbringing which showed in their frequent grounding of him. There was no suggestion he'd done anything really bad to warrant these punishments – it seemed there was a pressure on him to be the perfect son, to live up to their expectations of him. Kyle was a classic 'good boy', who took these restrictions and pressures stoically. It seemed that he'd learned this behaviour from his dad, a very controlled man, as witnessed by his response to the question of how he dealt with the trauma of his son shooting him. 'I repress it,' he said, matter of factly.

The final scene of the documentary showed Kyle's parents visiting him in prison. Although he was now approaching seventeen, from the way they spoke and acted with him, you'd have thought he was seven. You could see the conditions in which this Emotion in Kyle's shadow grew: the needing to be a 'good boy,' the teaching by example to repress difficult feelings which went against that image. With teenage hormones running rampant, one night the Shadow emerged and acted out its fantasy of killing the source of his 'imprisonment.' The logic behind it was: 'Without your parents you will be free.'

Matthew: In France they have the term: 'Crimes of Passion', meaning someone wasn't in their right mind when they killed their wife's lover. You could even use this defence to get away with murder.

Jez: It's the Shadow side of Personality taking over; the repressed Emotion is so strong, it momentarily overcomes any self-control imposed by society's rules.

Some people manage to release negative aspects of their Shadow but keep it hidden from society, such as in cases of domestic violence where physical and Emotional abuse gets played out behind closed doors.

Matthew: And then there's explicit violence: the race riots, the terrorism, the wars...

Jez: As you've shown with your brother, in the Personality, other people can become a threat to us. Outside of the family arena, this is especially true when other people have different beliefs, skin colour and religion. When the 'other' becomes the scapegoat for all our fears, then the violence in the Group Personality becomes explicit. You can see why the Shadow is dangerous: When there's no self-awareness it can lead to wars.

OUTCOMES

28

SUFFERING

The outcome of identifying with Personality

*'You are in prison. If you wish to get out of prison,
the first thing you must do is realize that you are in prison.
If you think you are free, you can't escape.'* – G.I. Gurdjieff

Jez: There are basically two types of suffering. The first is suffering that arises from being human. To be human is to feel, and life throws all kinds of experiences at us. Some of these are painful to our psychological system or physical body and cause feelings that are so intense they become a kind of suffering. I'm talking about what happens when your lover leaves, someone you love dies, you're seriously ill or you have an accident. No one escapes this kind of suffering; it's unavoidable, and why should it be any other way? To experience life in all its manifestations is part of what makes us human.

Also, this kind of pain can carve us out; it makes us look at life in a more mature way. There's an African proverb: 'Smooth seas do not make skilful sailors'. If you look back at the hardest parts of your life, when the seas were roughest, you might find that those were the times that you learned the most.

Matthew: As you said, everyone knows this sort of suffering; so tell me more about the other kind, the Suffering that comes from Personality.

Jez: In the Relative Level, in this phenomenal plane of existence, there is action and reaction, there are events and consequences. This kind of Suffering is a consequence, an outcome of identifying as Personality. To use Indian terminology, you could call it 'karma'. Will you look up the definition of that word?

Matthew: It says here: 'Karma is the spiritual principle of cause and effect where the intent and actions of an individual influence the future of that individual.'

Jez: The word 'karma' can be applied in different ways. It's found its way into Western vocabulary, and here it's usually taken to mean the practical interplay of cause and effect: You work hard to get a promotion, you get the job, it makes you feel good. You put off getting your car serviced, your car breaks down on the motorway, you feel bad. We put it down to karma. But the word has a spiritual root – when they use the phrase 'influencing the future of the individual' in that definition they really mean it! Eastern religions that believe in past lives apply it to the idea of 'earning good karma', which you'll be rewarded for in your next life.

Matthew: What do you think about that?

Jez: It's a belief; all beliefs come from Personality. It's an Eastern spiritual version of 'When I get this I'll be happy.'

Matthew: But you do believe in karma in the more practical sense?

Jez: I don't *believe* in it; cause and effect is an observable fact. No belief is required to see it's true.

Matthew: I've heard some Non-Duality teachers say that there's no such thing as karma.

Jez: I can only presume they're talking about the Absolute Level, which is prior to, and therefore beyond, the arising of opposites such as cause and effect. In Oneness there are no opposites; that would involve the arising of 'two-ness'. However, cause and effect is a fundamental law of nature in the Relative Level. I suggest if you meet any teachers of Non-Duality who dispute this, you carry out this simple experiment: Try gently stepping on their toe as a cause and observe if it has any effect! (Both laugh.)

Matthew: That doesn't sound like a very 'spiritual' thing to do! (Laughs.) So you were saying that Suffering is a consequence of identifying as Personality; it's an example of karma.

Jez: Yes, let's go back further to where this all began: As babies we experience cause and effect in all sorts of ways, mostly as a result of interaction with our parents. When Lucy was a baby being bathed, her skin flushed and became wet in the warm water, and her temperature rose. This is an example of a cause that has minor, short-lasting effects in her life. But there's one significant cause that filters down into all our lives from our parents and, as we get older, has a deeper effect on us. And that's the fact that our parents are identified as Personality.

Matthew: I've asked you this in a previous talk: You're saying this is the case for everyone?

Jez: It's possible it's not, but I've never met or even heard of anyone who grew up with a parent who wasn't identified as Personality. So, for the sake of argument, let's say it's true.

Matthew: So the effect of this is passed onto us?

Jez: Yes, eventually their unhappiness, their Suffering, is experienced in *our* lives in the form of their Emotions: fear, sadness or anger. At first, when we're still in the Natural State, it doesn't make much difference. But once that state has slipped away, our parent's Suffering – a 'cause' – has its devastating 'effect' on us: the Wound.

This effect can last for the rest of our lives, because it creates and underpins the whole architecture of Personality. It creates our beliefs, Emotions, the Mask, the Shadow, the arising of desire, the need for Distraction, the location of ourselves as the mind and so on. All of these collectively add up to the experience of Suffering.

*Matthew: You called the first type of suffering 'natural human suffering'; are you saying **this** Suffering of the Personality isn't natural?*

Jez: Let's look at how the dictionary defines 'natural'.

Matthew: It says here: 'Existing in or derived from nature; not made or caused by humankind.'

Jez: You could argue that humankind *is* nature; I presume what they mean is 'not made or caused by the *mind* of humankind'. By that definition, this kind of Suffering *isn't* natural, because it arises from the mind, from the Personality of mankind.

We all start out in the Natural State, we're in the Original Relationship to Life, which means, in the words of Lao Tzu: 'We are nourished by the great mother.' We receive everything we need to live: We have a body that breathes, a stomach that digests, eyes that see and all the other gifts that are bestowed upon us. Simply living what we are fulfils us and causes us to feel Joy. The Natural State is so called because that's how we come into the world; it's not caused by man's mind.

The Suffering that comes from Personality isn't natural in that it's not how we're made; it's not how we enter this world. We don't arrive here with neuroses, worry, heartache, anger or grief; we come with Love, Stillness, with an innate ability to abide in Oneness.

Matthew: But to lose that is normal?

Jez: Yes, exactly; I'm drawing a distinction between what's normal and what's natural. Just because it's normal doesn't mean it's natural; it doesn't mean that's how it *has* to be. This is why Suffering is avoidable; our early childhoods demonstrate that being a victim of it is not the only way this life can be lived.

It's only after we're identified as Personality that the problem begins – the Personality is a machine of Suffering. That identification can create Suffering out of anything. You once told me, before we started these conversations, that failing a scholarship exam was a devastating event in your life. Remind me what happened.

Matthew: When I was about 11 or 12 our headmaster walked into my classroom and read out six names, including mine. We were walked to a private room and told we were joining Upper Six A – the scholarship class. This was my dream: recognition that I was a member of the school's elite. If I passed the exam my parents would save a significant sum in school fees and my name would be immortalised in gold lettering on the scholars' board in the assembly hall.

Jez: So your sense of security and love was resting on you passing that exam, proving to your parents and peers that you were 'intelligent enough'. But your name didn't make it onto that board; you failed the exam. What I'm suggesting is, your Personality turned this event into a story of Suffering.

Matthew: Can you explain that?

Jez: What made failing your scholarship so painful was your need to prove yourself to your family and peers. If you look at the history of the Group Personality of your family, it's easy to see where this came from. Both your parents pulled themselves out of modest backgrounds by gaining a good education.

Matthew: It's true; intelligence is very highly valued in my family.

Jez: Seen objectively, the exam was simply a practical event in the workings of the school: just a qualification. You turned it into a solution for your need for acceptance and brought that Emotion of fear of failure to it. Had you not aligned your sense of security with that exam then failing it wouldn't have been the cause of Suffering.

This happens for all of us; it's not our fault. You were young; you'd lost the Original Relationship to Life! You were set up, destined to react in this way by fact that you'd been trained to lose the Natural State.

So my point is that identification with Personality creates Suffering not just by making us addictive, neurotic, full of Emotions, subject to the internal dialogue of our minds etcetera. Life brings all sorts of events our way and Personality can *turn them* into Suffering because it comes from a basic sense of insecurity. The Personality is 'a machine of Suffering' because it actually creates it.

So no Personality is immune to the unhappiness of Suffering – everyone has to deal with it.

Matthew: It seems to be a very negative picture you're painting. I can't help thinking that you're demonising the Personality, making it the bad guy. Isn't that just creating more Duality?

Jez: That's a really important question. It may sound that way, but I'm simply describing the function and appearance of Personality. Describing the reality of how something is doesn't mean that you're putting a negative judgement on it.

Matthew: What do you mean?

Jez: The Personality is just a phenomenon that arises in this play of the Relative Level. Put simply, it's an identity that's built around the idea of separation. It's a phenomenon that only occurs in human life, because it requires a developed mind to create that idea and then identify with it.

We think we are the Personality. This is what we're taught to do, that inclination to identify as it is passed on to us in childhood through the Group Personality of mankind.

The Personality becomes a psychological entity; it's not passive, it has its own volition, its own will to survive. In order to survive, it has to keep your identification with it intact. It's so clever, so strong, it can shift shape, it can keep you unaware of its operation, always staying one step ahead of you by making you avoid anything which is going to expose its functioning.

Matthew: You're talking about Personality Awareness?

Jez: Yes. But it's possible to go beyond Personality Awareness and experience Choice-less Awareness; then you can actually watch the Personality. You can see under the hood, you can observe it doing its thing. There's no demonising of it, but there's no misconception either about what it is. You realise it's an amazing phenomenon, but one that has a serious consequence: the obscuring of your Being. As long as we identify with Personality and take on its belief that we're separate from the whole, then Suffering enters the experience of human life.

Matthew: So it's quite a big consequence!

Jez: You could say that! We're born in the Natural State, in the ongoing perception and living of Love. Personality develops; gradually we identify with it and lose the Natural State. That's the normal story of human life.

*Matthew: But if you're right, and identification with Personality has the outcome of divorcing us from our Natural State, that **is** a 'negative' consequence, isn't it? And, if it **is** so negative, isn't it reasonable to cast the Personality as a bad guy?*

Jez: It's all a matter of perspective. From the Relative Level you could definitely say that. From the Absolute Level, the Personality is simply a formation of energy arising in the psychology of man.

Matthew: It seems kind of flippant to say that.

Jez: Not from this perspective – if you take away that 'relative' viewpoint you see things differently. Imagine an artist painting the sky: He's admiring the clouds drifting by, watching them refracting the light, taking on different colours and changing shape constantly. For him, the clouds are a positive. However, for other people, the consequences of those clouds being there could be called 'negative': A golfer trying to enjoy his game will get wet, a holidaymaker won't get her suntan. That doesn't mean there's anything intrinsically wrong with the clouds – they're not 'bad' clouds. Looking at it from the wider perspective, they're just a manifestation of moisture particles in the sky.

Matthew: So, applying this metaphor, you're not saying clouds are wrong, you're just saying you might not choose to live under them?

Jez: Yes, in a way, but now the metaphor has reached the limit of its practical use: The comparison falls apart because it's hard to ever really escape bad weather but, my proposition is, you *can* escape identification with Personality. You don't have to live with the Suffering which identification with it brings – there is another way to live this life. But before we consider that possibility, there are more outcomes to identifying with Personality that we need to discuss.

29

HEALTH

The effect on our health
of identifying as Personality

*'There is more wisdom in your body than in your
deepest philosophy.'* – Nietzsche

Jez: As much as we try, it seems we can't escape the Suffering that results from identifying as Personality. There are mental manifestations of this in unhappiness, moods, depression and Emotions, and there's a physical expression of this in physical health.

Matthew: Are you saying ill health is caused by Personality?

Jez: No. That statement is too broad – it's only partially true. We're not talking about *all* ill health; some of it happens for practical, scientifically proven reasons such as genetic diseases, viruses, eating food that's gone off or simply having accidents. Also, things can go wrong in the body and we don't always know why. Let's be clear: I'm not saying that life beyond Personality automatically guarantees freedom from sickness.

Matthew: So what are you saying?

Jez: I'm saying that the effect of living identified as Personality has a deep impact on the health of our body as well as our minds.

Matthew: So, according to this understanding, a lot ill health is avoidable?

Jez: Yes, definitely. There's unavoidable ill health and there's avoidable ill health. I'm proposing the latter category is much bigger than society acknowledges.

Matthew: You're not just talking about taking responsibility for having a good diet and exercise?

Jez: It goes far beyond all that. That's the top level of healthy living, which is generally agreed on: Eating fresh unprocessed food that's full of energy is just common sense. The avoidable ill health I'm talking about isn't generated by what you do, but what you think you are. Most people think they are their Personality, and there are consequences to that in the body.

Matthew: So how does living identified as Personality create this 'avoidable ill health'?

Jez: To answer this we need to look at what health is. If you break it down into simple terms you could say that health is energy in flow. For example, a healthy plant demonstrates an organic system in flow. During photosynthesis, plant leaves take in carbon dioxide from the atmosphere then, using energy from sunlight, this is combined with water drawn up from the roots to make glucose. Oxygen is also produced in this chemical reaction and it exits the leaves into the surrounding air. All of this is about a healthy flow of energy through the system of the plant. If the conditions in which the plant lives change, for example if the soil is undernourished, there's not enough water or another, larger plant blocks out the sunlight, then the healthy cycle and flow of energy is compromised. As the flow decreases and the systems are not fed satisfactorily, the signs of ill health start to show: Leaves wilt and turn brown, and flowers fail to bloom.

Matthew: I see what you're saying, but lots of people might think it's a little simplistic to compare us to plants!

Jez: I'm talking about principles in nature. We are manifestations of nature. We *are* nature, so the same principles apply even though the cycle of energy, the needs of the organic system and the symptoms are obviously different.

Matthew: OK, so applying this to the human body...

Jez: Our bodies consist of a number of biological systems which carry out the specific functions necessary for us to live. All these systems depend on a smooth flow of energy (or 'chi' in Chinese medical terminology) to function well. Whether it's blood in the circulatory system, hormones in the endocrine system, food in the digestive system, lymph to fight infection in the lymphatic system or oxygen in the respiratory system, it's all about energy flowing. As long as the blood, oxygen, lymph etcetera keep flowing, there is health.

Matthew: I suppose the diametric opposite of this is seen in the body of someone who dies.

Jez: Exactly, the energy flow in all the systems gradually shuts down until there's no flow and, ultimately, no energy. So you have two poles of health: A healthy human baby exhibiting full functioning and flow in all the energy systems, and the same body at the time of death when that flow has ceased. In between the two is the life of that person. The question is, when does that slowing down of flow, that gradual lessening of energy and health, come in and take effect on the human biological system?

There are two related things here: The natural aging process (as opposed to the growth process) and ill health. Once the aging process begins, illnesses related to it can start showing up. This happens in every human life, but the question is, at what point does it begin? On the whole it's true to say that the Group Personality believes this category of illnesses happens in middle age; they're viewed as an unavoidable part of the aging process. Apart from obvious causes, such as overeating or poor living conditions, whatever particular ailment your body exhibits is seen simply as bad luck.

Matthew: But there's consciousness of this out there, isn't there? For example, advice from the Government about exercise, eating well...

Jez: Absolutely, we try to deter sickness in this way, and not just because it's natural not to want to get ill – it goes beyond that. From the point of view of Personality, which wants to survive and maintain our sense of 'I', illness is a threat to its sovereignty. Illness is a reminder that one day the energy in our body will stop flowing altogether and we'll die. Death is the ultimate blow to the belief in Personality. If you're not there – or, I should say, the 'idea of you' is not there – who's going to identify with it and uphold it?

So many people try to eat healthily and exercise, but even with all these efforts to keep illness at bay, statistics show that illness becomes more prevalent as we age. As people get older all sorts of diseases such as diabetes, heart problems and arthritis can start cropping up.

Matthew: But you're suggesting it doesn't have to be like this, that a lot of that illness is an outcome of living identified as Personality? How does that work?

Jez: Just like the plant, when we don't get what we need, our bodies get stressed. The plant needs light; we need Love. The Wound, that first experience of being outside of Love, brought a massive surge of stress to our systems. There we were, bathing in the infinite, receiving Love from our parents, a Love that fed and nourished us, a Love we'd come to depend on. And then suddenly, for the first time, our experience of this Love was lost. I'm not saying it should have been any other way, or imagining some perfect world where it *could* be another way. This is how it was. This is how it is. What's important in *this* enquiry though is to see the consequences of that shock, to recognise the stress that comes into a life which before had only experienced absolute openness, without psychological stress.

Matthew: You mean the Contraction that occurred in response to the Wound?

Jez: Yes, and this is the point I've been leading up to: The Contraction and the repression of our feelings is the opposite of flow. It's a contraction from full engagement with life. This of course shapes us psychologically, but also physically.

The word 'bodymind' is increasingly accepted in society, reflecting an understanding that the mind and body are intrinsically linked. What happens in the mind finds expression in the body. This is not some New Age or esoteric belief system: The understanding of the effect of repressed Emotions on the body has been studied since the 1950s, starting with Wilhelm Reich and carried forward with Alexander Lowen and Bioenergetics. I also find the knowledge of the body found in Oriental medicine to be helpful in understanding symptoms and causes of dis-ease. This connection between mind and body can be quite clearly observed in one's own life, if you're willing to look with honesty and openness.

Matthew: Like when I feel angry, I can get really hot in my body.

Jez: Yes; it raises the question: Where is that anger? Is it a feeling in your head, or is it in the increase in blood pressure in your veins? Is it in the clenching of your fists or the knot in your belly? It's all of those responses and more, and this is why the conjunction 'bodymind' had to be invented. Language has to evolve to catch up with our broadening understanding of life.

Matthew: So you were saying that the stress of the Wound entered our bodymind...

Jez: Yes, and the body registered this stress as a lessening of its effectiveness in functioning. Overall you can boil it down to a lack of flow of energy, and eventually, the resulting blockages of energy, which in turn cause shortages of energy in the biological systems. Over decades, blood vessels become narrowed, oxygen circulates less well, digestion and waste removal become blocked, and so on. In youth the strong flow of energy in our system means that these stresses don't bother our health too much, but as we get older and our vital energy lessens they become more entrenched and we become more susceptible to their effects.

Over time, blocks in energy flow start to manifest in physical matter and that leads to blood clots, hardened arteries, gallstones, ulcers, heart problems, strokes, etcetera.

Matthew: Will you tell me more about how the Contraction can result in us having 'avoidable illness'?

Jez: OK. Let's begin with feelings. Feelings manifest as energy flowing through the brain and the body of a person. To see the natural pathways of feeling in a body, watch a child before the Wound, before they've learnt to repress. It's quite a display. Imagine Lucy in the middle of one of her tantrums when she was a toddler: She's kicking, clenching her fists and teeth, hitting out, making guttural noises, scowling and so on. But as she gets older she, like all children, learns that in society this sort of behaviour is not acceptable. So inside she still feels the anger, but she learns to repress it and, as I've described, that naturally arising feeling eventually becomes an Emotion.

Matthew: And that repressed Emotion is what makes us ill?

Jez: Yes, that repressed anger doesn't just disappear, it goes deep into the body and gets recorded in the tissues, the cells etcetera. It wants to be heard so it comes out in any way it can, even long after the moment of the original feeling. As she grows up, Lucy may develop a permanent scowl, or start clenching her teeth at night, or perhaps develop headaches. These can all be symptoms resulting from liver patterns, which in Chinese medicine is the organ associated with the Emotion of anger; they're the tell-tale signs of the Emotion trying to be heard. Often the symptoms may be at odds with what's shown on the surface. Lucy's Personality may be kind and friendly, but the body doesn't lie: Her repressed anger is recorded, and the symptoms will betray what's going on underneath.

Matthew: This makes me think of a man I met at a social function recently. He appeared confident and outgoing in his manner, but when I shook his hand it was freezing cold and clammy; it didn't seem to match his relaxed demeanour.

Jez: The Personality is expert at projecting a version of itself as it wants to be seen, but the body can tell another story – the one the person wants to hide behind their Mask, the one in which we feel perhaps nervous, or insecure in a room full of strangers.

The cold hand is literally a withdrawal of energy from reaching out, a lack of flow caused by the Emotion of fear. Social occasions can bring out a lot of fear of how we're perceived: Do we look OK? Are we liked and accepted by the tribe? This is the under-story that the body is telling though such symptoms.

It's very straightforward. The body isn't complicated or tricky like the mind; it doesn't give out mixed messages, it expresses clearly what's going on. Once you understand the code, these symptoms can speak volumes about your Personality, and they can be used as a tool for finding out what's really going on, because unlike the mind, the body doesn't lie. The man you met wore a Mask of calm confidence, but his clammy hand contradicted that image.

The cold hand is probably just a temporary example; the party ends, the guy feels more relaxed, by the time he leaves the symptoms have passed. But long-term Personality traits and Emotions, which begin at the Wound, can get stuck and encoded into the body; into muscles, cells and perhaps most damagingly for health, in the organs.

Matthew: How do the organs come into this?

Jez: Chinese medicine teaches that each Emotion has a corresponding organ in which this emotional 'charge' is physically located.

Matthew: You mentioned anger is stored in the liver...

Jez: Yes, and grief is stored in the lungs and fear in the kidneys. Because the backed-up energy is not dispelled, as happens when feelings are fully felt, this results in a progressive build-up of unspent energy, which disrupts the functioning of the organ. This understanding is gradually becoming more known in a few healing traditions in the West, but Oriental medicine has known about it for thousands of years.

Matthew: Traditional Western medicine doesn't recognise this does it?

Jez: Not much; in this society such thinking is labelled 'alternative'. In Western society it's common to view illnesses as bad luck, to see the body as simply a machine we're 'living inside' that can be fixed with the application of science and modern medicine, drugs and surgery. The symptom is treated but they don't seem to be much interested in the cause.

Matthew: It seems quite short sighted, doesn't it? So much funding going into drugs and treatments, but not much understanding of how these illnesses could be prevented, apart from advocating a better diet or more exercise...

Jez: Science is supposed to be all about studying the facts, investigating, and discovering what's true, and yet it's interesting that Western medicine doesn't want to investigate the truth of this. It recognises that the body is run by the autonomic nervous system but to some extent, it ignores the fact that it's also affected by psychology and the Emotions which arise out of that. It seems to me that any system of medicine that ignores one vital part of the picture is incomplete in its model.

When you divorce the body from the mind you start seeing it as just physical matter, as a machine that can be fixed like an inanimate object, like a washing machine or a car. It's such a short-sighted approach because, even when you treat the symptoms with drugs or surgery, the underlying cause of the disease won't just disappear. The Emotion still wants to be heard and will get even more backed up and cause more problems in the future. But of course the drug companies get wealthy, so they're happy, and people are content to be treated in this way, to be just given a pill to give the illusion that all their symptoms have magically disappeared.

Matthew: Why is that?

Jez: It's the same reason that most doctors don't want to think about this: Their Personalities are not interested in looking into repressed Emotions because that's a threat to them. It's much safer to deal in the known, in scientific facts that can be easily quantified, and labelled.

I think it's beautiful how, in the Chinese system, they don't so much label diseases; they see ailments as patterns in energy, and patterns can change, they're fluid. It relates back to what I was saying earlier about health being about the flow of energy.

Matthew: So are you against Western Medicine?

Jez: Not at all, man's understanding of how the body works in both Western and Oriental medicine is a wonderful thing. I feel that Western medicine in general is short sighted in the area of understanding the bodymind and Emotion-based illnesses and this makes it less balanced and leads to reliance on drugs. It seems we'd rather get addicted to the drugs than face the cause of the illness! That's a measure of the degree to which the Personality doesn't want you to become aware of it.

Matthew: You can see that in the sales of anti-depressants – I read the other day that one in eleven people in the UK is taking them now!

Jez: That doesn't surprise me. It's not just physical health that suffers when Emotions are repressed; after years of denial and suppression they can manifest as extreme psychological imbalances. Dammed up anger can turn into hatred and violence, habitual fear can develop into phobias, and grief may crystallise into debilitating depression. We've come a long way from the peace of the Natural State.

30

PERSONAL LOVE

How, in our personal relationships, we seek to
replace the Love we have lost

'The consciousness in you and the consciousness in me,
apparently two, really one, seek unity and that is love.'
- Nisargadatta Maharj

Matthew: I was looking back at our early discussions. When you described the Natural State, you said: 'Before the forgetting of Oneness, all that we see, all that we are, is experienced as unconditional Love. Simply Being, as Love – participating in this play of Duality – is our Original Relationship to Life.' What does that actually mean in our adult lives? Can you explain it a bit more, in practical terms?

Jez: To do that I'm going to have to take the daring step of trying to define what Love actually is.

Matthew: In our first talk you said: 'Love, with a capital 'L', is what is felt when a human being perceives Oneness.'

Jez: I'll try to give a more practical definition – as I always say, it's good to look at things from different angles to get a full picture. So how about: 'Love is the creative, expanding, energy of life that manifests as us and the world in which we live. It is the connectedness of all things'?

Matthew: I like that, but I think many people would argue it's a human projection.

Jez: It *is* a human interpretation. Before man came to this planet there was no one to interpret all this manifestation of energy as Love. But I am a human, and from this viewpoint beyond Personality, this is what is seen.

Matthew: Personally, I'd like to believe that it's true.

Jez: But I'm not asking you to believe it, only that you hold it as a possibility. As I said before, this can't be proved, only known.

Matthew: OK...

Jez: Let's see if we can pin it down any further: Outside of human experience, this Love is absolutely impersonal.

Matthew: Why do you call it impersonal?

Jez: A good way to understand this is to think of animals. When a lion mother raises and cares for its cubs, that's an expression of this connectedness of life, this Love in action, but it's not personal. For it to be personal, there has to be a sense of self to make it that way; and of course the lion doesn't have a sense of self, at least not in the way that humans do.

It's the same for a human baby; before Lucy has learned to be separate she's abiding in a connection to all things which arise in her experience of the world. In the Natural State, you could say that Lucy 'Loves' the wall just as much as she Loves the warm moving shape that she'll one day call 'Mummy'. In the Natural State, this Love has no opposite; it has no choice, no conditions. It can't be absent; it can't be turned off because it is what we are. This is why I call it an impersonal Love.

Matthew: So we're back to the subject of how we lose that Natural State because, after that, love becomes personal, doesn't it?

Jez: Yes. As Lucy's self develops, the Love that was experienced everywhere, in all appearances, becomes more focussed on certain forms of it – for example, gradually the warm shapes that feed and hold her become her Mummy or Daddy. So from the human perspective this universal connectedness is personalised: Sharing, receiving, creating become *personal* experiences of the self. As soon as there's the appearance of separation, there appears to be an '*I*' who can give, receive and perceive this energy. And so Love appears in human life as relationship between Lucy and her mother or her father. It becomes personal love.

Matthew: It all sounds beautiful but as we know, it doesn't stay like that...

Jez: After babyhood, when we're still very young, the self is usually quite good at this loving thing because the self is still pretty pure – meaning, it's untouched by Emotion, repression, a sense of ownership etcetera. At this early stage of development there's very little to obstruct the expression and feeling of that Love. But after the event of the Wound, our relationship to Love changes; we're no longer living *as* that Love. Love becomes a thing, a currency, something you can give or withhold, something that can be overshadowed by Emotion.

Matthew: Like when we talked about Lucy having a tantrum...

Jez: Exactly, that's a good example of personal love being turned off. Lucy is learning to take on the relationship that adults have with Love.

Matthew: Can you tell me about that?

Jez: On the Absolute Level, we *are* Love. But in the Relative Level, we become estranged from the existential experience of that. We've lost our ability to perceive universal Love, to Be it; and so we need to find Love and receive it in the form of personal love from other people. However, as we chase after love, all of the limiting beliefs which developed after the Wound, such as 'I'm bad', 'I'm not worthy, not good enough', or their opposite – 'I am special, I am entitled' – can come into play causing Suffering. But the motivating factor behind all of this drama when it comes to relationship as an adult is our sense of isolation.

Matthew: I presume that starts after the Wound?

Jez: Yes. In the Original Relationship to Life we're *not* isolated; we're connected, not just to other humans but to all of life. This connectedness means that we are already content, *before* relationship to others. Lying in her cot, staring at the sky, baby Lucy can be utterly content and Joyful. She's as comfortable with nothingness, silence, Stillness or aloneness as she is in relationship to her parents.

After the Wound she loses that connectedness to all things; aloneness, which had once been her natural environment, now reflects back her isolation and the feeling of the absence of Love.

We can become estranged from our aloneness. Aloneness can become a place where Emotion can overwhelm us; our aloneness has become loneliness. So as adults when we're alone, we can be confronted directly with the unhappiness within us, in the form of this feeling of isolation: the feeling of separation from Love.

We try to relieve this loneliness through relationships. We need the Love from others to relieve the Suffering that comes from the fact that we've lost our original experience of Love as who we are. However, at the same time, we're also threatened by Love because we learned from the Wound that it can hurt us.

Matthew: It's like a double bind. So what do we do?

Jez: We create a sentimentalised version of Love, based on the romance that's felt when we fall in Love. It's a love that exists in the head; it's built on the Emotion of yearning. It hangs onto the form of Love and reduces it to a cartoon version of itself that's less threatening, but still stimulating and able to distract us from unhappiness.

Matthew: There must be a big need for sentimentalised love, because so many books and films tell stories based around it.

Jez: Sentimental love is what sells; it's packaged and used in advertising because we're all looking and yearning for Love, because Love is the Natural State we lost. The thing is, sentimentalised love will never satisfy – it's a bit like trying to eat a photograph of a sandwich: However glossy and vibrant the colours, there's no nutrition in it. A photograph of a sandwich may stimulate your taste buds and cause your mouth to water, but it's not food.

Matthew: It sounds like, when you live beyond Personality, you wouldn't bother with relationships because you'd already be fulfilled and wouldn't need another person.

Jez: That's not the case at all, because the fullness of life is expressed in the two poles of aloneness and relationship: both are part of the play of life.

Matthew: But there's an archetype of the religious renunciate in isolation in their cave, isn't there?

Jez: This is because there's a stage of spiritual practice in which the aspirant retreats from the world. There's a reason for this, which we'll go into at some point, but that practice of withdrawal is part of searching for this, not of finding it. In the Original Relationship to Life, there's no avoidance of any expression of life, so there's no pulling away from either alone-ness or relationship. Either can happen, or not happen.

Relating to others is a natural outcome of the fulfilment of the Original Relationship to Life; you get filled up and naturally overflow with energy to share in the world with others. That's what I'm doing with you now, and that's what you're doing with me. It's the way we're built; it's a wonderful manifestation of Joy in humans.

Matthew: And yet... We all know that relationships can be the opposite of Joy.

Jez: Yes, governed by Personality, relationships can become dramatisations of our Suffering. Let's talk about that next.

31

RELATIONSHIP

How our Personalities get played out
in our relationships

'Nothing saddens me more than seeing how quickly the dog
grows used to its leash.' – Marty Rubin

Matthew: You were saying that our Personalities seek relationships as a refuge from Suffering, but aren't they also the source of a lot of our Suffering?

Jez: Yes. We've lost our original experience of living as Love, and on top of that we may also have taken on the belief that we're unlovable. This puts us in a position of need. In order to fill that hole in us that was filled with Love, we need to get personal love from other people. That *need* is where the problems come in, because it's an impossible pressure to expect relationship to another person to take the place of the loss of our Original Relationship to Life, and the Love we receive as part of that.

Matthew: But relationships can lead to a healthy union. For example, isn't that what Tantra is meant to be about?

Jez: Yes, we're seeking to find reconnection, union with life. This reconnection is sometimes found momentarily in lovemaking, where the boundaries between the 'two' fall away in the oblivion of communion. There's a quote from Tolstoy about this:

   He did not know where he ended and she began.

Matthew: It's a nice idea but to judge by the predominance of pornography in the world, for many people sex isn't like that, is it?

Jez: Mostly sex becomes a temporary escape from Suffering, an exercise in going unconscious in the same way as when people get high or drunk. There's the goal of the orgasm in the future and the projection of the belief that 'When I get this I'll be happy'. But sex doesn't bring lasting happiness, just a momentary release of stress.

Matthew: I know what you mean. When I've had a lot of sex it doesn't satisfy me; I just want more.

Jez: Or a rest, presumably! (Both laugh.) Sex without the heart is good for the body maybe, if it's not over indulged in, but nothing more than that. There's not much relationship in sex when it's a means of escape; it's more like *using* another person to relieve stress, or at best it's a *mutual* sharing of that stress release. Of course in pornography there's not even the pretence of relationship, so you *could* say it's quite honest in a way.

Matthew: Do you think there's such a thing as a healthy relationship?

Jez: Yes, but not between Personalities. At least, not if you define a healthy relationship as the sharing of Love without Emotion, need or manipulation. If you live identified as Personality then that's what governs and shapes your experience of life and the arena of relationship is no different. In relationship your Personality's particular make up gets dramatised and played out in all its glory.

So for example, your insecurities can influence who you're attracted to: Older men who fear losing their power may seek confirmation of their virility in dating younger women in order to make them feel more confident. Anything that makes you feel more secure – power, money, success, stability – can be the driving force in the choice of your relationship. If you need a mother figure, then a motherly, domineering Personality type will attract you. If you had a violent father, you might be subconsciously drawn to a man who fits that template in order for you to replay that dynamic. Basically this level of relationship is all about fulfilling the psychology of the Personality; it's mostly based on a need to be fulfilled by the other.

Matthew: This all sounds very negative. What about when we fall in Love?

Jez: That's something else altogether. Imagine, in her twenties, Lucy meets a man. He seems to be everything she wants in a partner: strong, sensitive and good looking. She's deeply attracted to him and finds herself falling in Love. Now she experiences a taste of unconditional Love. It comes from beyond Personality, it comes *despite* her Personality; it comes from her heart. It's as if her Personality is suddenly overpowered, disabled by a force higher than itself. Lucy's life begins to overflow with a deep sense of fulfilment and Joy. When we fall in Love it seems we've found the magic cure for the dis-ease of our unhappiness.

Matthew: Falling in Love is often talked about like a sickness or even madness, isn't it? As if you're not in your right mind.

Jez: And that's so true. We say we're madly in Love, but that's the sort of madness you want, isn't it? For once we're not being run by the mind; control has been temporarily handed back to the heart.

Falling in Love is like a free gift, an experience of the Natural State you experienced when you were born; but there's a big difference. When Lucy was a child and she lived in that state, Love was already the case. Now, her Love has a cause: It's triggered by the presence of this man and the Love that arises for him. It's as if she sees his spirit, the very essence of him. If the same happens on his side, a Loving relationship can begin. It's the highest in Lucy, her unconditional Love, connecting with the highest in her partner.

Matthew: I guess what you're describing is the honeymoon period, but that always fades doesn't it? Do you think it has to be like that? Is that just human nature?

Jez: The original stage fades, but the Love that opened up in it *can* go on growing and informing the lives of the couple. However, the identification with Personality doesn't usually let that growth continue very far.

Matthew: You're going to have to explain that.

Jez: If you're willing to learn from the gift of this Love, then it can be a mirror in which to see the games and the Contraction from Love that the Personality plays out. In India this is called Bhakti Yoga: The idea is that by focussing on Love, the Personality is transcended and you return to the Original Relationship to Life. It doesn't have to be the Love of the beloved, it could be a god, a guru, but it's the same principle.

Matthew: I like the idea of transcendence through a focus on Love!

Jez: It sounds good doesn't it, the path of Love? But how many people do you think are ready for that level of surrender?

Matthew: Very few, I should think.

Jez: The Personality doesn't want to surrender; this is where the problem comes in. The Personality wants to maintain its structure, its dominion, its control. Surrendering that control is the last thing it wants to do.

You have to remember that, although Lucy's heart is yearning to be filled with Love, from the point of view of her Personality, Love is still seen as a threat and so, despite her best intentions, its protective instinct of Contraction can be activated. Despite her Love for her partner, subconsciously he can be seen as a threat because, if she opens to him, he can hurt her. The danger is that she can then pull back into the Contraction to protect her heart and, before long, Emotions start disturbing the Joy she found in the Love relationship. Then the misery and trouble begin...

Matthew: Then the partner might experience a fear of her Love going...

Jez: It can be a ping-pong effect. Lucy could then feel fear of him rejecting her. Her belief of being unlovable could be activated and she may project that onto him. When she fell in Love, part of its Joy came from the fact that she felt safe enough to remove her Mask, to show her heart and reveal who she really is. Now her psychological patterns are being triggered, she may start imagining aspects of herself that he doesn't like. Then she'll begin hiding those parts from him behind her Mask in order to produce a semblance of harmony within which she can receive the positive attention she needs from him.

Of course, any Emotions can be activated: fear of losing Love, or sadness or anger at not being loved. Once jealousy enters the picture, the lover is reduced to a possession and most people don't like to feel owned like that, so then more anger can be stirred up.

These are the forces that can get played out in relationships when Personality starts coming into it. In the end, the partners can become each other's gaolers – expecting the other to be how we need them to be rather than allowing them the freedom to be who they truly are. Often couples are willing partners in this; they make each other feel safe but the price they pay is to lose their freedom and stop growing. In the end conditional love reveals its Shadow and the couple can start hating each other.

Matthew: I'm sure most people will know relationships that turned from intense Love to co-dependent battlegrounds like that...

Jez: All the original Emotions brought up by the Wound and stored in our bodyminds can be activated and projected onto our partners, who in turn project their Emotional history onto us. Our adult love relationships then become a stage on which we play out the drama of our primal relationships.

Matthew: When I was in my twenties I had a very intense relationship. We'd have massive rows and then make up, and I remember afterwards the whole flat would feel clearer.

Jez: There's a release involved in this acting out of our pain, a catharsis in which our deepest Emotions get an airing. However, because there's no resolution, no fundamental change, the painful feelings at the root of those Emotions aren't healed. We're condemned to continue dramatising the same patterns in an endless cycle of repeat performances. Even if we start again with a new partner, the same patterns come up and the whole cycle begins again.

Matthew: I always wondered why all my girlfriends turned into the same woman. Then I realised I was the common factor.

Jez: This is where psychotherapy comes in. People try to fix their behaviour by examining their habits in order to improve their relationships. It can help of course, but in terms of this understanding it's like moving the deckchairs around on the Titanic. Without finding the original source of Love, then the relationship patterns will just reform in different configurations.

Matthew: In this culture it's generally accepted that in most cases, as relationships go on, the original spark is lost, as if there's nothing you can do about it. It's a not a very uplifting thought...

Jez: It's not, but there *is* something you can do about it. However, it involves understanding something most people don't want to face.

Matthew: What's that?

Jez: That ultimately we can never find what we seek in the other; that we ourselves have to be full *before* personal relationship...

Matthew: You mean in the Original Relationship to Life?

Jez: Yes. Then personal relationships become something quite different. Without all the need, the other is treated with respect; any Emotions arising are seen for what they are and not projected onto the other. But of course, to do this requires you to go beyond Personality.

32

DISTRACTION

How the Personality distracts itself
from unhappiness

*'Distraction is the only thing that consoles us for miseries
and yet it is itself the greatest of our miseries.'* – Blaise Pascal

Jez: The Personality can be divided into two separate poles of activity: First of all, it's working hard for you to not look at it, to keep you in ignorance of its sovereignty, while at the same time it's doing all it can to stop you feeling your unhappiness by keeping you distracted.

In our discussion about gaining attention we talked about how the Personality Distracts itself from unhappiness by getting attention and approval from society, by obtaining things that the tribe looks up to. This pursuit of happiness from outside ourselves, through desire projected out into the world, is normalised in the Group Personality. This desire is what the popular media sells: Follow this band, drive this car, buy this brand, eat this food and everyone will think you're hip, cool, successful. It's the 'When I get this I'll be Happy' syndrome again.

Imagine Lucy has seen an advertisement for her dream job in the fashion world. She believes that if she can land this position, her life will finally be complete and all her insecurities and unhappiness will disappear.

Matthew: When you put it like that, it sounds silly, but I spend a ridiculous amount of time and energy daydreaming about winning the lottery jackpot and how that will solve all my problems!

Jez: We need these externalised ideas of happiness because we've lost our Joy and sense of fulfilment through our connection to Love. This chasing after our desires gives us a purpose in life: the pursuit of happiness. But it's an ersatz fulfilment – it's not the feeling of being happy now, it's based on the *hope* of achieving happiness in the future.

Matthew: So you're saying in this context, hope is a negative thing? Usually it's thought of as a positive attribute.

Jez: In situations of physical danger it's well documented that a positive attitude and the hope that we'll survive puts our bodies into a higher operating level, and increases our chances of surviving. But the hope our Personalities project onto our desires is a response to our psychological feeling of threat rather than a physical threat. It arises from the Wound and the fear that we're not good enough just as we are. So the hope that's invested in our desires is actually just an anaesthetic, a tranquiliser. It's a false hope.

*Matthew: But it **could** be fulfilled; people do become successful. Lucy might land her dream job.*

Jez: That's true, but will it really bring the fulfilment and happiness she's attached to it? She might be distracted from the Suffering of her Personality for a while, but the job won't ever make her unhappiness go away. And then she'll need to get more from the job; perhaps she'll start seeking a promotion, and her happiness will then be pinned on that. The goal keeps moving further away on the horizon.

Whatever our form of Distraction, it seems it never quite delivers its promise – we can never be rich, famous or successful enough. We're so busy trying to fill up our bucket that we fail to notice it has a hole in the bottom.

Matthew: Are you saying that anyone who strives after success and achieves it won't be fulfilled in the long term?

Jez: It *could* happen, but not by the achievement of the success itself. It would take a change of orientation, away from the Personality that desired success, to fill that hole. Chasing happiness in the form of success is a never-ending cycle of hope and failure. Not necessarily failure of the desire, but failure to quench the need to fill the hole. Then, even the happiness of the achievement transforms back into its opposite, unhappiness. But the Personality is used to this ongoing tussle back and forth between hope and disappointment. It takes a lot for it to give up.

Matthew: But why won't it give it up, if it always ultimately leads to disappointment?

Jez: Because the chase after success or happiness is, in itself, *a part* of the Distraction. As long as Lucy's occupied in the chase – the desire for, and hope of, success – she's distracted from the Suffering of her Personality, from her unhappiness, her Emotions. The desire can be very strong; we often use the word 'lust' for it, for example a lust for success or money. Desire stimulates, hence the connection between sex and success, which advertising exploits. Stimulation, not just the sexual kind, plays a big part in Personality's Distraction techniques. It started when we were very young. As a child the self learned that, when we were stimulated or excited by a new event, we were, at least temporarily, not feeling any of our painful feelings.

Matthew: Like when my Mum announced that she was taking my family to the zoo.

Jez: Yes. In the same way, objects can become totems of Distraction. I mentioned earlier how, when I was a boy, one of the things that brought me a lot of Joy was my love of football. I remember receiving a football as a birthday present; it became linked with the promise of happiness. For a while I even slept with it by my bed. It was just a football, but it's not about the object, it's about what you project onto it. We take this link between stimulation and Distraction with us into adulthood, and of course, when you grow up, your toys can get more expensive: a Ferrari, a Rolex watch, the latest designer handbag... Often it's about things that make us more desirable to the opposite sex.

Matthew: The subject of sex keeps cropping up, doesn't it?

Jez: It's bound to when you're talking about escape. During adolescence we learned that sex, or even masturbation, temporarily takes us out of our minds and away from our Personalities.

Matthew: When I was younger and single I used to love going out on the pull almost as much as doing the act itself. There was the thrill of the hunt; there was affirmation when someone attractive was interested. I can see now that I wanted to go unconscious, to get lost in the sensation and forget my problems.

Jez: It's all going on there: stimulation, searching for approval and attention, all in the service of Distraction from your Suffering. Rather than the expression and sharing of our love, sex can become just another desire. And of course sex without love is where the Distraction of pornography comes in. Sex then becomes divorced from the body and stays in the mind. For Personality, sex in the mind is a lot safer than opening up to another human being. Feelings are dangerous; they can lead where Personality doesn't want to go: in the direction of the Wound. So being in the mind is very safe for the Personality; that's why we get addicted to thought.

There are other ways of distracting ourselves: You mentioned just now the desire you had to go unconscious; this seems to be widely accepted by the Group Personality as a normal way of dealing with the stresses of life. Anyone who's been to college or university knows there are two parts to student life: the stresses of studying for exams and the relief of going unconscious to get away from all that through the use of alcohol, drugs or sex. This is never questioned; it's just how it is.

Matthew: I'm not sure it's the case nowadays, but when I was at university people would've thought you were religious or there was something wrong with you if you didn't get drunk on a Friday night.

Jez: Or 'out of your head' – that's the phrase we used to use. That was the intent: to get out of your head. When you're out of it, your mind's internal dialogue is easier to ignore.

Matthew: So are you against using drink or drugs to relax?

Jez: Not necessarily, it's not about the activity; it's about what you're using it for. If you're using the activity not just for pleasure but to go unconscious then it becomes just another manifestation of your Suffering. Gradually our systems become so insensitive to stimuli that we need an ever-increasing amount of stimulation and our Distractions can turn into addictions. I heard that now there are clinics to treat people who are addicted to being on the Internet; sometimes they're on it up to 14 hours a day! That's an extreme example, but it's symptomatic of what's happening in the Group Personality.

You can get addicted to anything. I read an interview with an ex-soldier recently; he was being asked what he missed about being in the army. I was expecting him to say something like: 'The camaraderie of working with my mates,' or 'The feeling of doing a worthwhile job for my country', but what he missed most was the adrenaline rush of combat. There's no limit on what the Personality can distract itself with – even war!

Everyone is making their own choices of Distraction: for some people it's drugs, for others it's eating, doing yoga, or going to the gym. (Some methods of addiction are more socially acceptable than others!) Whatever the Distraction, it's all going on unconsciously. When it comes to re-finding your Original Relationship to Life, you need to become *more* conscious, not less. This is not a moral judgement, from this point of view it's just about whether your activities are part of you re-finding freedom or continuing the Suffering. In which case it's all just 'Doing' with a capital 'D'.

Matthew: What do you mean by 'Doing'?

Jez: This use of the word refers to any action that arises from the strategies of Personality to carry out its functions and maintain its dominance. Anything that arises from the need to prove oneself worthy, loveable, acceptable, good enough: That's all Doing.

Matthew: At the start of a personal development course I attended we were asked what our goals were, what we wanted to achieve by the end of two years. One guy said he wanted to have a two-million-pound business up and running. Is that Doing or is it just healthy ambition?

Jez: It could be either; it depends where it's coming from. If he has nothing to prove, it could be a simple statement of intent with no Emotion attached. If that's the case, there's a possibility he *could* achieve it. If it arises from his Personality needing to prove its self-worth, then that would be Doing.

Matthew: This guy has a quite an unsupportive Dad; he doesn't always show it, but I've seen him really upset about it. I suspect he wants to prove himself to his Dad.

Jez: I think you've answered your question. There's another tell-tale clue in there: Whenever there's Doing, Emotions are always lurking in the background.

Matthew: Why is that?

Jez: Because Emotion is the driving force of so much of Personality. Any need to prove oneself ultimately arises from fear; the fear of not being good enough, which of course originates from the Wound.

Matthew: So what do you think of his chances of reaching his goal?

Jez: Not very good. He can try all the techniques, say all the positive affirmations he wants but the Emotion behind his ambition will impede his clarity, his creativity and his ability to make his dream a reality.

Imagine if three months into his plan his business suffers a major setback. Frustration will start kicking in; there'll be anger at the obstacles that are arising. Pretty soon stress is going to start showing in his body and mind, impeding his clarity even more. When the realisation hits that he isn't going to reach his goal, his original pain around the lack of support and Love from his father is really going to come up.

Matthew: It all sounds really negative.

Jez: Don't get me wrong, ambition can be positive and useful; amazing things can be achieved with clarity behind one's intent. But the result of any Doing will always be more Suffering in the end.

Matthew: Why's that?

Jez: Because Doing is the playing out, the dramatisation of Suffering. If you're approaching anything with the energy of Suffering, it can only create more of itself. If you make a cake with stale ingredients you end up with a stale cake, no matter how positive your intentions.

Matthew: Is this why, when I kept trying to give up smoking, you weren't interested?

Jez: I could see it was coming from your Personality, from willpower. That works for a while but then the addiction creeps back in, you need the cigarette and you start all over again. So I knew it was Doing, and I don't have any inclination to support that, to be a cheerleader to that delusion. To use the psychoanalytic jargon, that would make me a co-dependant: you needing me to encourage you to believe that *this* time it's different, *this* time you'll really give up. I'm only interested in supporting you in becoming more aware, because that's the only way addictions can fall way.

Matthew: So you think that it's possible to go beyond addictions?

Jez: Yes, absolutely. To go beyond Personality opens up whole worlds of possibilities which were previously closed to you.

Matthew: But how does it happen?

Jez: When you see through your Personality, you go beyond Doing; then it's possible that the cigarettes give *you* up. I have a friend who used to drink two glasses of wine every night. Not much you might think, but it had become a habit, an addiction which took the edge off the stresses of her life. Once she faced those problems head on, the drinking suddenly stopped. There was no Doing in it, no willpower, no effort. An awareness that was bigger than her Personality, Choice-less Awareness, took over and that addiction just fell away.

Now we're touching on the subject of 'Non-Doing', which is a huge topic that doesn't fit here, because here we're focussing on all the manifestations of Personality, not what lies beyond it. So we've discussed Distraction in general, but one of the biggest Distractions is the chase after happiness. That's the subject of our next talk.

33

CHASING HAPPINESS

How we pursue fulfilment in the world

'Happiness is your nature. It is not wrong to desire it.
What is wrong is seeking it outside when it is inside.'
– Ramana Maharshi

Jez: We're going to start by talking about the Group Personality and how it operates, not with the intention of criticising it, but of understanding it. The Group Personality is the collective expression of the Personalities that make it up. What you see out there in society is very likely going to be a reflection of something in yourself. So seeing what's going on out there in the Group Personality is an opportunity to understand those unconscious habits of escape, Distraction and identity strengthening arising in your own Personality. So with that in mind, let me ask you a question: What do you think is the predominant idea of what constitutes a fulfilled life in Western secular society?

Matthew: I'd say it's to live life fully, to squeeze every drop out of it. The acronym YOLO sums it up: You Only Live Once.

Jez: The YOLO idea has permeated modern western culture; you can see it promoted in the media, self-help books, advertising and lifestyle programmes on TV. It's supported by the popular quasi-spiritual idea of 'living for the moment'. On the surface it seems quite a sensible viewpoint, certainly preferable to living a sluggish, uneventful life in which you don't engage fully with your aspirations and your goals.

This worldview can be most clearly demonstrated by looking at social networks, which were originally designed as platforms to enable people to share and connect. That means they're all about Love, right?

Matthew: I wish they were; we both know they're not! But in principle, connecting with people all over the world has got to be a good thing, hasn't it?

Jez: Of course, and maybe in the beginning they *were* used simply for sharing, but then the Personality discovered they're a great way to go about its business of maintaining and strengthening its identity.

Matthew: I think I can see where you're going with this.

Jez: If you look at social media these days you'll know that some people use it practically, as a promotional tool for their business. But in general, most people use it as a sort of notice board on which to demonstrate their success in living that YOLO philosophy.

Imagine Lucy, like most of her generation, has taken to using a social network. When she goes on a trip to Thailand, she posts photos of herself on perfect beaches, drinking cocktails with her boyfriend, living the good life. When she's at a sales conference she posts photos of herself and colleagues celebrating their company's success. When she's with her friends she posts photos of them smiling, having fun, looking hot, partying. Don't misunderstand me; I'm not saying there's anything wrong with having fun. The problem only comes when the posts are simply the *projection* of a life of fun, a way for Lucy to gain attention and be Distracted from her anorexia, her self-esteem issues etcetera. So there's a gap, a disassociation between the life that's presented and the reality of the life that's lived.

The message being promoted in many of the social media posts out there seems to be a composite of some, or all, of the following: 'Here I am in this amazing location. See how I travel the world. Don't I look attractive? See how many friends I have. Don't I have a wonderful family? Aren't I living a fabulous life?'

The general idea of success in the world as seen in social media is to look like an ideal of beauty presented in fashion magazines: to never grow old, to be constantly busy, and to have lots of money, houses and possessions. This idea of success pretends to be about 'living in the moment', but actually, it isn't doing that at all. This moment doesn't need an advertisement, it doesn't need continually updating posts to prove it's OK, to prove it's a 'fulfilled moment.'

My point is: This mentality, which needs to constantly prove you're doing OK, is an expression of Personality. Lucy needs to feel loved and accepted by the tribe out there on social media because she doesn't love and accept herself. It's just another form of the 'gaining attention to feel OK' strategy she learned as a child.

If Lucy was *really* fulfilled and happy, she'd be sharing that Joy with whoever was around her, in that moment. There'd be no need to broadcast it to friends and strangers all over the world. So paradoxically it actually highlights the fact that she's *not* doing OK. What she presents in her posts is an *image* of fulfilment rather than fulfilment itself.

Matthew: It's bit like the popular idea of having a 'bucket list', a checklist of things to see and do before you hit a certain age – or before you die.

Jez: Yes. The idea of fulfilment is always in the future: When Lucy's run a marathon, bungee jumped over Niagara Falls and climbed Mount Kilimanjaro, *then* she'll be a fulfilled person. *Then* she'll be ready to die!

Matthew: But wait a minute, isn't there something admirable in that philosophy? To think positively and strive for success can't be all bad can it? Isn't it a kind of self-empowerment?

Jez: What that way of living really represents is 'Personality empowerment'; a way for the Personality to refortify its self-image by seeking recognition from other Personalities in the world looking at their posts. It's a massive game of ego stroking played out in the Group Personality via the medium of the Internet. At the same time, it provides incredibly rich potential for Distraction.

Matthew: What do you mean?

Jez: As long as Lucy's Personality is engaged in this game of looking for attention in the form of 'Likes', she's Distracted from her Suffering, from the unhappiness of her Personality. None of this has anything to do with 'living in the moment'. Like I said, these attempts at living life to the full are actually orientated towards the future. *When* Lucy gets 'x' amount of followers she'll be really liked. (The number of course is always increasing.) *When* she ticks off all the adventures on her bucket list, *when* she's thin enough, then she'll finally be loveable and start to love herself. Her fulfilment is not 'here now', it's actually 'out there', in the future, in the world, in potential achievements, and it all rests on the erroneous belief that 'When she gets 'this' (whatever 'this' happens to be) she'll be happy.'

Also, though it may look like a celebration of positivity, there's a negative side to this lifestyle that's starting to be recognised now.

Matthew: I know what you're going to say: In the race to reach this idealised life, some people inevitably get left behind.

Jez: Exactly. The idealised life being projected by the Group Personality can become a pressure, and some people can't keep up. By comparison with those succeeding in living that projection of a fulfilled, successful life, of being 'someone', Lucy might see herself as inferior and then patterns of self-criticism and unworthiness latent in her Personality could be shown up. However, failure to live up to the projected ideals of the Group Personality doesn't always lead to such a negative reaction; it can lead to a positive breakthrough.

Matthew: Failure can lead to a positive breakthrough?

Jez: Yes, whatever Lucy's aiming for in the future to make her happy never quite arrives. No matter what she does, her goals seem to be forever beyond her reach. This was always the case but now, because of the repeated failure, something happens: Lucy becomes *aware* of the whole game. Instead of being pulled back into that hope of getting the reward in the future, she becomes conscious of the fact that it's not working. She's no longer fooled into thinking it can deliver its promise of happiness to her.

   Conversely, the whole game of future desire can also collapse through success, i.e. when you reach your goals and are aware enough to see that they haven't delivered the happiness and fulfilment they promised.

Matthew: I know a few people who've 'made it' on every objective measure – they have great jobs and salaries, they live in big houses in the best parts of town and have apparently perfect families. But they're still not happy – none of it brings them lasting Joy...

Jez: A classic case of success failing. But whichever way the game collapses, through success or failure, the outcome is the same: There's a hole left in the life of the person and there can be a realisation that they've been looking in the wrong place. They've been looking out there in the world to find happiness, but they need to look at themselves.

Matthew: You mean by looking at their own part in creating the lives they live? There are many self-development courses built on the idea that you can create the life you want if you change your beliefs.

Jez: Yes, self-development is one way we start looking inside ourselves for answers to our problems. Let's talk about that next.

PERSONAL GROWTH

34

PERSONAL DEVELOPMENT

How we try to find happiness by rearranging the Personality

'When I went to school, they asked me what I wanted to be when I grew up. I wrote down "Happy."' – John Lennon

Matthew: I've been doing Personal Development courses for many years. I find them useful in terms of helping me live a more peaceful and productive life. How does this type of course fit with what you're talking about here? Do you think this sort of work could lead to a life lived beyond Personality?

Jez: Not in itself.

Matthew: Why do you say that?

Jez: Personal Development courses are, by nature, not designed to go *beyond* Personality. As the name suggests, they're there to develop and *polish* the Personality, to get rid of negative habits and make you more effective – *as* a Personality. Polishing or reshaping the Personality is not the same as seeing *beyond* Personality. That's something else altogether.

Matthew: So do you think that people who run such courses don't know this?

Jez: Anyone who's discovered life beyond Personality would never offer a course in Personal Development because they wouldn't be interested in 'polishing the Personality'; their focus would be on pointing out what Personality *is*.

Matthew: One organisation I find especially effective actually does that – I've come to see certain aspects of my Personality, such as my 'good boy' act, very clearly.

Jez: And what do you do then?

Matthew: When I see I'm being driven by one of those patterns, I acknowledge that, let the pattern go and generate a new way of being in the space it leaves.

Jez: So a new, more authentic, confident Matthew is adopted?

Matthew: I wouldn't put it quite like that, but I guess so, yes.

Jez: I'd suggest to you that's not something *beyond* Personality, that's just a new, improved configuration of your Personality. As I said, these courses are about making you more effective but the

Personality is like a Hydra, the many-headed serpent of Greek mythology: If you cut one head off, more appear in its place. They may be more positive, helpful faces, but underneath it's all coming from the same root, from Personality, which wants to distract you from really seeing its operation by numbing you with a sense of positivity or self-improvement.

Matthew: Now I'm feeling slightly defensive...

Jez: Great, now we have a clear example of your Personality at work! If you're feeling defensive, that's an Emotional reaction from Personality.

Matthew: Isn't it natural for me to defend an organisation that's given a lot to me?

Jez: It's natural to the Personality, because of what it's invested in that group. As we've discussed, the Personality builds its identity partly through its allegiances. It says: 'I'm with this group, this is part of my self-image,' and that association with a Group Personality makes it feel stronger.

Matthew: So you're not saying that defending something is wrong?

Jez: No. I'm pointing out that in this case you had an Emotional reaction: You wanted to defend your group. Without your investment in the group as part of your self-image, you might still defend it, but that would be a *response* rather than a reaction.

Matthew: What's the difference?

Jez: Emotion.

Matthew: You're going to have to expand on that a bit.

Jez: When you reacted, you came from the Emotion generated by the perceived assault on what you needed to defend. If you think someone's discrediting your group, you feel threatened because that group represents part of your identity. So all sorts of Emotions can be stirred up: hurt, anger or maybe fear. Defending your group helps make you feel secure and safe. By contrast, a *response* would not be charged up with Emotion, so it has a measured calmness about it.

Matthew: I feel embarrassed, like I screwed up and I'm being told off.

Jez: You didn't screw up at all; you simply had an Emotional reaction. That's what Personalities do! Your Personality showed itself and I pointed it out. So what? If you take it personally and start feeling bad because you feel you've been reprimanded, that's just the Personality coming in again with another Emotional reaction. It's fed by all the times in your life when you've been told off and not felt good enough; it comes from the Wound and the original feeling of being unloved.

To engage in this enquiry you have to *get used* to the Personality being exposed; that's what this is all about. Whatever the Personality does is fine; just let it do its thing. If you try and push down those Emotions you'll just be feeding your Shadow.

Matthew: Feeding my Shadow? What do you mean?

Jez: Where do you think those Emotions exist? In your Shadow, and further repression of them only makes them stronger. So rather than pretending your Emotions aren't there, I'm suggesting you watch them and become aware of *why* they're there. Become aware of the pain they're built around, the hurt they're defending.

Matthew: So what happened just then is really an opportunity to see my Personality?

Jez: Yes, absolutely. As far as this enquiry's concerned, anything that shows up your Personality should be welcomed, whether it be something I say eliciting a feeling of hurt, the person who cuts in front of you in the queue provoking anger or maybe trouble in a relationship making you feel depressed. Whatever happens in your life is a mirror in which you can see your Personality reflected.

Matthew: And if I keep seeing it, that will help?

Jez: If you know your Personality and all its ways, you'll begin to understand, from your own experience, the themes I'm addressing in these talks. So for example, the next time I bring up the subject of how Personality reacts, from this exchange, you'll know exactly what I mean and what I'm saying may make a little more sense to you. Becoming aware of your Personality is essential if you want to go beyond it.

Matthew: We've taken a bit of a detour there.

Jez: Sometimes detours are the best bits of a journey. So where were we?

Matthew: I was feeling defensive because you were questioning the validity of my Personal Development work.

Jez: I wasn't questioning its validity in terms of how it's helped you in certain areas. Within the remit of what they're setting out to do, Personal Development courses can be very helpful. Your group is, I think, concerned with models of behaviour and applying strategies for dealing with life, achieving goals etcetera. I've seen some ways in which you've changed: You've become a bit clearer in your communication and more reliable. So there's definitely a level on which it works, but I'm saying, in relation to this enquiry, that level is quite superficial.

Matthew: I'm feeling defensive again now! (Laughs.) Why do you think it's superficial?

Jez: Because it seems those changes have proved to be temporary. There have been periods where you've been acting like a new, efficient version of yourself and then, usually due to stress, that improved behaviour pattern falls away. For example, you'd start smoking again and stop following through on your work commitments to me.

Matthew: I don't really want to admit it but that's true. It seems to be a pattern: I go to the course, apply the principles and experience a period of improvement. Then, despite my best intentions, the old habits re-emerge. Why is that? Why doesn't it work long term?

Jez: Because it's all Doing.

Matthew: Remind me again: What do you mean by Doing?

Jez: Let's take giving up smoking as an example. First of all I should make it clear: I don't care if you smoke or not, it's your freedom to do what you want with your body and it's nothing to do with me. However, you've expressed an intention to give up smoking and that intention comes from willpower. It arises from the desire to create a healthier, improved version of 'you' in the future, so you can feel happier and better about yourself.

Matthew: But there's nothing wrong with that, surely?

Jez: Of course not, it's totally logical: You feel trapped in a habit that doesn't serve you; it has negative effects on your health, so naturally you want to change it. But does it work? No, because it's all Doing.

Matthew: I'm still unclear on why you call this Doing.

Jez: Let me ask you this: Who's trying to improve himself?

Matthew: Me.

Jez: Who do you mean by 'me?'

Matthew: The 'me' that wants to improve his life.

Jez: I'm suggesting that the one who wants to improve his life is your Personality. 'Doing' is action that springs from Personality. That means it doesn't come from Being or Stillness; it comes from tension, from the Wound, from the need to lessen Suffering.

There's nothing wrong with Personal Development, but if it comes from the idea that 'When I give up smoking/When I lose weight/When I become more assertive then I'll be happy' – it's destined not to last.

Matthew: But why? Why doesn't it work?

Jez: Because the intention behind it comes from Personality and Personalities, by nature, are untrustworthy.

Matthew: Whoa – that's a big statement! What do you mean by that?

Jez: You intend to give up smoking. I know you really mean it... Every one of the many times you've tried!

Matthew: All right, don't rub it in!

Jez: What sabotaged your goal of giving up was the needs of your Personality, the unseen patterns and Emotions that lie *behind* your addiction to smoking. All addictions lead back to the Wound; they're a reaction to the loss of our Natural State. Before the Wound, there were no addictions; nothing was needed to make you happy. The Natural State needed no improvement.

Addictions become hardwired into the Personality; they run deep in the subconscious. Unless their root is exposed, the addictive impulse will still be there. That's why Personalities are basically untrustworthy: because of their hidden structures in the subconscious. All the agendas you're not aware of are the programmes that are actually running the show, the machinery creating the story of 'you' and the life it lives.

I'm not just talking about addictions like smoking; this relates to all Personality habits: desires, Distractions, self-hurt etcetera. Unless you become aware of the root of why these patterns are there, which is the loss of your Natural State, then their presence and influence in your life, despite your best intentions, remain active.

That's why Personal Development always has a limit on its effectiveness: You're looking to create more freedom in your life but you're looking in the wrong place. You're trying to rearrange the Personality into a more acceptable configuration, but it never works long term because, whatever formation you change it into, it's *still* Personality. And Personality will always have its own agendas beyond your good intentions to change.

Personality is untrustworthy because it follows its own agenda; in this case, distracting you from your Suffering by giving you the impulse to smoke. In the end that agenda will usually override your good intentions to give up.

Matthew: I feel you're painting me into a corner with no way out: It's frustrating.

Jez: There *is* no way out, as long as you're looking for it through the Personality. When people realise this, they often become what we call 'Seekers'.

Matthew: What do you mean by that exactly?

Jez: The word relates specifically to the search for spiritual answers to the problem of Suffering and the quest for happiness. (We'll give it a capital 'S' to distinguish it from seeking in other areas, such as self-help, personal development etcetera.)

Seekers hear about gurus or eastern religions offering a kind of liberation that comes from a completely different worldview from the one they know; it seems higher, it's 'spiritual.' Someone's had some sort of awakening and this is promoted in their teaching, which promises the same outcome for the Seeker.

Matthew: Which, in essence, is what's happening with you and me. I've started to become disillusioned with finding a permanent way out of my Suffering through Personal Development courses, and you seem to be offering some kind of liberation by helping me see beyond my Personality.

Jez: Yes, that dynamic *is* appearing here. I'm playing the role of teacher and – by our definition – you're a Seeker. Seekers are all basically coming from the same place of not knowing this; that puts all Seekers in a vulnerable position.

Matthew: Why?

Jez: Because not all teachers are the same: They may all offer the same promise of liberation but that doesn't mean they're all speaking from this viewpoint.

Matthew: Are you saying this viewpoint is higher, that your viewpoint is valid and theirs isn't?

Jez: It's not a case of higher or lower; it's a case of: 'Is what's being taught coming from a viewpoint beyond Personality or not?' If it is, then it will be coming from the same root as this.

Matthew: Isn't that the idea, that those teachers and gurus are enlightened, and so beyond ego or Personality?

Jez: That's the idea that's promoted, but it's not always the reality.

Matthew: As I know only too well... One of my friends went to India and joined a sect. I did some research into her guru and, from some of the stories I've read about his abusive behaviour, he doesn't appear very enlightened.

Jez: How and why this inconsistency happens with some teachers is a massive subject; we'll go into it in detail in our next collection of talks.

*Matthew: How do I know that **you're** not one of those teachers?*

Jez: You don't. All you can do is trust your feelings, and know that you're doing this in freedom; you're choosing to explore this subject. There's no pressure on you and you can stop anytime.

Matthew: That's true; I'm doing this because it feels right.

Jez: Yes, there's a feeling side to this, an instinct that pulls you towards it. But engagement with the Spiritual teaching itself, with what I'm actually saying, usually happens first through the mind. You don't know if what I'm saying is true, but you can understand it intellectually and hold it as a concept. This, of course, is not the *experience* of seeing life from beyond Personality but openness to the fact that a radically different way of living *could* be true is a small crack in the edifice that *is* Personality.

Matthew: So what happens next? How do you get beyond that intellectual understanding? Is this where spiritual practice comes in?

Jez: Yes, let's discuss this next.

35

SPIRITUAL PRACTICE

What is it and does it work?

'All spiritual practices are illusions created by illusionists to escape illusion.' – Ram Dass

Matthew: Spiritual Seeking usually involves adopting some form of spiritual practice, such as meditation, mindfulness, chanting or fasting. Is having a spiritual practice necessary or helpful in this enquiry?

Jez: There are two very different views on this: One asserts that it's essential and another holds the opposite opinion, that you don't need to do any practice at all because liberation happens all by itself.

Matthew: So, according to you, which is right?

Jez: In a sense, both are right. Let's open that up by asking a couple of basic questions. First of all: What do you think is the point of having a practice?

Matthew: To solve the problem of Suffering – isn't that the classic Buddhist viewpoint?

Jez: Where does this Suffering come from? Why is it there in the first place?

Matthew: I think the Buddha said: 'Desire is the root of all Suffering.'

Jez: But to go further, where does the desire come from?

Matthew: You always say it comes from Personality.

Jez: Yes, and identification with Personality is a consequence of the fact that we've forgotten where we came from. We've forgotten that we are Love, we believe we are this appearance of an 'I', this Personality. It's a huge narrowing down of what we take ourselves to be. This fundamental misidentification, this gap between what we *are* and what we take ourselves to *be* creates the Suffering: the unhappiness, depression, worry etcetera. So what all spiritual practice seeks to do is return you to your original state of Being, to remind you who you are.

To embark on this spiritual journey isn't mainstream. Fulfilment in the world is all about celebrating and indulging Personality, spiritual Seeking is supposed to be about the opposite: By taking on a practice, the intention is that you stop *indulging* your Personality and start *undermining* it by focusing on what's beyond it. Essentially you're questioning it, exposing what it is, what its motivations are. That's the theory anyway.

By association, this means that you're also questioning the Group Personality in which the Personality arises. So someone who commits deeply to this, who's really trying to question that whole paradigm in this way, is not supported by being within the setup of the Group Personality. It doesn't fit any more. This is where the archetype of the religious retreat, the monastery and the ashram comes from. To facilitate that search *beyond* Personality, it helps to withdraw, at least to some extent, from the tribe in which the Personality is indulged and facilitated. So you enter smaller subgroups, sects, movements, religions, which share the same intention to look within, and each of these Group Personalities has its own prescriptions and practices.

Matthew: Meditation is probably the most common spiritual practice. How useful is it in finding life beyond Personality?

Jez: Before we get into that, let's look up a definition of 'meditation'.

Matthew: It says here: 'Meditation is a practice where an individual trains the mind or induces a mode of consciousness, either to realise some benefit, or for the mind to simply acknowledge its content without becoming identified with that content.'

Jez: That's a bit of a mouthful! There are two parts there: The first defines meditation as a means for *gaining* something. Usually it's peace, Stillness, clarity, relaxation or even enlightenment. The second part is quite different: To paraphrase, it's simply the action of observing, objectively, what is. These are very different meanings; let's start with the first.

Matthew: Meditation to become more still, more peaceful... That's a good thing, surely?

Jez: It's great if you want to have more relaxed, spiritual Personalities. My dentist is a very spiritual man: He prays, meditates and chants and this produces a very fine energy. He's peaceful, focussed and exceptional in his work, but all of that doesn't mean he's seen through, or is living beyond, Personality. That's a different step altogether, one that would require him to drop that spiritual identity, drop his beliefs and his religion. He might still meditate but it wouldn't be to *reach* anywhere, it would simply be to sit still and Be. So what I'm saying is that a spiritual life, as it's come to be known, has little to do with discovering life beyond Personality.

Matthew: I still don't really get this. Why isn't it?

Jez: Before I answer, I need to pose another question: Who is doing this Seeking after peace, Stillness, enlightenment?

Matthew: You mean who is the Seeker?

Jez: Yes.

Matthew: It's the same question that you asked when we talked about Personal Development: 'Who is the 'me' that wants to develop itself?'

Jez: Yes. To answer this you have to understand where the Seeker comes from. The Seeker doesn't arise from nowhere to start a spiritual search; the Seeker has history. It used to chase success and happiness in the world, but then this was seen through. When it fell away, this was a blow to the Personality: If it can't distract you in this way then it's lost its control of you. As we know, the Personality's principle objective is to be in control; therefore it doesn't like this situation one bit. So what does it do?

Matthew: Try to regain control?

Jez: Exactly, and it does this by letting you *think* that you're in control, that it's you who's pursuing this higher spiritual ideal of Stillness or enlightenment. The Personality has won back its control over you by very cleverly replacing one set of desires for another.

Matthew: So you're saying that Personality is the Seeker? It's another form of Personal Development?

Jez: Not in all cases, but I'd say in most cases, yes.

Matthew: But why? It doesn't make sense. Why would the Personality, which wants to survive, pursue goals that are beyond itself?

Jez: In order to pull you back into one of its most trusted control techniques: Distraction. As long as you think you're in control, and you're pursuing this hallowed state of perfection, then you're not actually questioning the Personality itself. The collapse of your desire for fulfilment in the world was dangerous to the Personality, because it lost one of its biggest Distraction techniques, but in the guise of the spiritual Seeker, it cleverly replaces that desire in the world with desire in the spiritual arena. 'When I get this I'll be happy' is now applied to the idea of enlightenment.

So you can see how meditation, in this first definition as a *pursuit* of Stillness, peace, enlightenment, is actually not helping you find life beyond Personality at all. In fact, it's the action of Personality keeping you asleep in its Dream, by entrancing you with the *promise* of achieving all these spiritual goals in the future. If Personality, in the guise of the Seeker, is behind those practices of meditation and mindfulness, all that's happening is you're being fooled into thinking you're 'being spiritual' and 'advancing spiritually'.

*Matthew: But if you meditate you **can** become very peaceful, can't you? Surely this is beneficial?*

Jez: Yes, the bodymind can become more peaceful, which is beneficial, but that's not the same as what I'm talking about.

Matthew: So what's the difference?

Jez: One of the outcomes of life beyond Personality is Stillness because, if you remember, it's one of the attributes of Being. What this means, as an adult, is the mind is no longer frantically running after desires or going round and round in well-worn grooves of thought patterns.

When practiced by the Personality, meditation is like doing an *impression* of that Stillness. It's a practice to still the mind and it works. As a tool for enhancing your experience of life it's surely one of the finest and purest. No equipment is needed, no teacher is really needed, it's simply between you and life. But it's not *necessarily* connected to this enquiry. I know someone who meditated regularly for 30 years; it gave her some good experiences, and a lot of calm was brought into her life, but she would be the first to admit that her Personality was still in control. The calm was only skin deep. Arranging the Personality so it's a bit calmer, or more effective in the world is not freedom.

There's no bridge between the practice and the actual living of all the attributes of Being: Stillness, Choice-less Awareness, Joy and full-feeling engagement with life. The imitation of Stillness is still an imitation. If an actor studies the films of Charlie Chaplin, observes his mannerisms and works tirelessly to perfect a flawless impression of him, would that actor ever actually turn into Chaplin himself? An impression, no matter how finely honed, remains a counterfeit of that which it imitates. Stillness cannot be practised; it arises spontaneously when the Personality is seen through.

Matthew: Are you saying that meditation, in this first definition of the word, can be counterproductive?

Jez: Not when it comes to mental and physical health; in that regard I'd say meditation is wholly beneficial. But, as I've said before, this enquiry is not about Personal Development; it's about seeing beyond Personality. The belief that 'When I meditate, when I go into the spot where I sit cross-legged, then I'll be peaceful' is just a more spiritual version of 'When I get this I'll be happy'.

Imagine Lucy's taking a bus home from work in heavy traffic. It's stuffy, polluted and crowded. The person next to her has a heavy cold and she's convinced she's going to catch it from him. Feeling stressed and annoyed, she starts looking forward to sitting in her meditation room at home, bowing to the statue of Buddha, lighting a candle and closing her eyes. She's not in Stillness now, on the bus: She's projecting peace and happiness into an idea of meditation, an abstraction in the future.

The danger is, this idea of meditation becomes just one more bauble for the Personality to play with, just another Distraction. As long as Lucy's engaged in that game, she's pulled away from the present moment, which is of course the only place that this can be found. Where else?

Matthew: So ironically, you have a situation in which the search for this becomes the thing that stops you finding it?

Jez: Yes, it's like a dog chasing its own tail. You get caught in an idea of liberation in which Personality gets to hold onto its identity while taking on some spiritual beliefs and practices. The Personality has simply found a new role, a new identity to take on – 'I practice mindfulness/ meditation', 'I'm a yoga master now' – new stories to tell, new goals to achieve, to keep you occupied in your sleepwalking.

Matthew: But you're not saying that all practice is a waste of time?

Jez: No, because that's an incomplete assertion. It's true from the Absolute Level; there's no question about that. You can't go beyond Personality while simultaneously being identified *with* it and its projections of freedom in an imagined future. But the thing is, although no practice can *cause* an Opening to life beyond Personality, it *can* prepare the ground. This may seem like a subtle distinction but it's important. If you're the soil, and a glimpse of liberation from the Personality is a seed, then having a fertile, rich soil doesn't create the seed; it doesn't make it appear, but it sure helps the seed to take root and flourish when, through grace, it does appear.

Matthew: Why is that? How do such practices help the seed grow and flourish?

Jez: First of all, you have to understand that this liberation from Personality can happen to anyone, not just 'spiritual/pure people' who do years of practice, yoga, meditation and chanting. This means that a thief is just as likely to find this as a monk who's spent the last ten years meditating in a cave or studying Holy Scriptures. The fulfilment of this can happen *despite* the Seeking, but not because of it.

Matthew: But your average monk would be far better prepared than your average thief...

Jez: Yes, there's a big difference between suddenly seeing the world from a viewpoint beyond Personality in someone who's heard the teachings, understood the concepts, and got their bodymind used to meditation, and someone who knows nothing about it.

Matthew: Why is that?

Jez: Discovering this can be a profound shock to the bodymind system, like landing in a totally new reality. It's the same world but all the rules have changed; everything's different. It can be disorientating, shocking, even traumatic, and so having some kind of physical and mental preparation, as well as a map, can be helpful.

Imagine Lucy wants to go to Timbuktu: She meets someone who used to live there, and he draws a map of it for her. Looking at the map, Lucy can imagine the place: Where the hill, the roads and the town centre are. She can dream about going there but it's conceptual; the map only informs her imagination. The map never claims to take Lucy to Timbuktu; it can't make her really experience that location.

However, if Lucy actually travels to Timbuktu then the symbols used in the map become relevant and useful. They can help her find her way around, help her understand the geography of where she is.

Matthew: What happens if someone finds this viewpoint beyond Personality without being acquainted with its 'geography'?

Jez: You can be utterly overawed – it can be such a shock to the body and mind that some people get derailed. There are a lot of people who've glimpsed beyond Personality who end up in psychiatric hospitals; society has deemed them to be mentally unwell. In fact they've discovered something the Group Personality doesn't want to see, but they don't have the grounding, the stability to be able to contain and live it.

So though that map of life beyond Personality is just symbols and concepts, knowing something of it before you experience it can make the acclimatisation to it a lot easier.

Matthew: So this book is a kind of map of life beyond Personality?

Jez: Yes, a map of a place you once knew as a child but have forgotten. Exposing yourself to this map won't necessarily take you to that place, but if you're ready, it might stir up some memories of it, which can lead you on a journey to find it again.

Because stirring up memories or following a regime of spiritual practice is not necessarily going to get you there, some Non-Dualist teachers use the words 'Seeker' and 'practice' in a slightly derogatory sense. But, if you look at the history of those teachers, what do you think they did before they had this understanding? Most of them engaged in some form of practice, or at least enquired after this subject. It's how we're built as humans: You have a passion for something and you follow it. It's the same if that passion is Spiritual in nature: It appears as a yearning to find out who you really are. Availing yourself of the true teachings of this, understanding the concepts, is a start, and meditation creates some peace in the bodymind as this takes place.

LIFE BEYOND PERSONALITY

36

TEACHING THE UNTEACHABLE

Pointing to what you already know

'The root of all desires is the one desire:
To come home, to be at peace.' ~ *Jean Klein*

Matthew: In our previous discussion you said that it's good to meditate, practice and immerse yourself in the teachings of this realisation of life beyond Personality, but you warned that none of that actually helps you have the realisation itself. Isn't there anything you can suggest I do to help discover this?

Jez: It's a Catch-22 situation: If you're given something to do, your Personality can use it to project freedom into the future and the whole Distraction game of Seeking begins again. You're back in the trap of: 'When I get this I'll be happy'. You're replacing Being, in this moment, with the promise and hope of happiness in an imaginary future.

The point is, you are what you Seek, you are *already* Being. At your centre you already have what you're looking for. It is in fact who you are, but you *don't know* that. That 'not knowing' is the problem; that misconception is where the Suffering comes in. So I have to address you where you are now, in the not knowing of that. I have to address you as someone who *thinks* they are their Personality. You're looking perturbed…

Matthew: I think I'm experiencing some of that Suffering in the form of frustration!

Jez: Tell me about that.

Matthew: We've had all these talks, I've learned about the Wound, the Personality, the Dream and all the rest of it. It's been really interesting, even inspiring but… I feel like a hopeless case, like I'm never going to get it. You've said: 'You're not the Personality' so many times… I hear the words, I get the concept but… It doesn't seem to change anything…

Jez: No, because that belief that you are your Personality is so firmly rooted in you. It was planted early in your life and it's established itself, in your case, over four decades. You've forgotten that it's only a belief: You forgotten that it isn't real.

Matthew: There you go again, saying the same thing! It doesn't make me feel any better because I'm powerless to do anything about it.

Jez: You're right; when it comes to this, 'you' are totally powerless.

Matthew: I think we're at a kind of impasse: You have something to teach me, but despite my desire to learn, I seem to lack the ability to comprehend it.

Jez: You *can't* learn it; this isn't like a course in plumbing.

Matthew: It would be easier if it was! (Both Laugh.)

Jez: That's for sure; even a course in rocket science would be easier! Not all teaching is the same; there are different categories of teaching depending on their subject matter. The first category is simply the passing on of facts. That's the easiest type to engage in; anyone with a functioning brain can put facts into their heads and store them. It's not so much learning as memorisation.

Then there's the passing on of skills, for example musical skills. This is more difficult and requires some aptitude in the Character, a certain kind of brain that responds to music. Studying something like science or philosophy is different again: They require a higher level of intelligence, clear thinking and logic because they involve the intellectual *understanding* of concepts.

Whether it's facts, skills or understanding concepts, all of these types of learning are based on head-knowledge. Even music learning, which obviously involves the body learning to physically play an instrument, is based around understanding music theory.

Teaching about this enquiry, which deals with metaphysics, is another thing altogether: I'm imparting information to you yes; but that's just preparation, it's preparing the soil in which the seed grows. In a subject like science, learning and understanding the concepts is the end result; the teaching has done its job and reached its fulfilment. With this enquiry, understanding the concepts isn't the end of the process; in fact, it's just the beginning. The only real fulfilment of *this* teaching is when the student has first-hand, *existential* experience of what's being taught. The germination of the seed is when you actually *taste* life beyond Personality – but that doesn't happen as an outcome of learning the concepts.

Matthew: So how does it happen?

Jez: Anyone teaching this understanding finds themselves in a paradoxical position. They're teaching something which the student already knows, but they've forgotten.

Matthew: It's another one of those 'two opposite things being true at the same time' scenarios.

Jez: Exactly. You *know* this, but you don't know that you know it. So you could say that you do know it, but at the same time, you *don't* know it. This is obviously not the case in most teaching situations. Normally the setup is: The teacher knows, the student doesn't know, the teacher passes on the knowledge until the student knows it too.

Because, somewhere inside, you know this, your interaction with this teaching is not really about learning; basically it comes down to you *finding* it inside yourself. I'm trying to remind you that it's there.

Matthew: So when you keep talking about Being, Joy and seeing beyond Personality you're trying to jog my memory?

Jez: Yes, I'm approaching the same thing but from many different angles. I'm throwing all this 'knowledge' at you, waiting for one part of it to be the trigger. I've no idea what that part will be, when or even if it will happen. But the fact that you're still here listening is a good sign; many people would have made their excuses and left by now.

Your Personality doesn't want you to engage in this enquiry: Why would it? This is a teaching which points to life *beyond* Personality; the last thing it wants you to do is get involved with this teaching which spells the end of its control of your life. So I have to somehow reach *past* your Personality; I have to find a connection to the one in you who knows. Understanding the concepts is easy; the fulfilment only begins when that one in you who knows starts to wake up and respond.

Matthew: I don't think that's happening; I think I must be stuck at a conceptual level and it's making me feel despondent. It almost makes me want to give up.

Jez: I think that would be a good idea.

Matthew: What? Giving up?

Jez: Yes. Take all the striving to get it, all the trying and reaching and let it all go.

Matthew: I don't want to let it go...

Jez: Why not?

Matthew: Because... I don't know... Because then I'd be left with just this feeling of lostness and failure.

Jez: So you're using the teaching as a way to avoid this feeling, as a form of Distraction?

Matthew: You're not making me feel any better!

Jez: I'm not *here* to make you feel better. Personal development courses and self-help are there to make you feel better about yourself, but that's not the job of a teacher of life beyond Personality. My job is to make you see *what is*, not to distract you from it. The way 'in' is through whatever's happening in this moment. There's no 'enlightenment', no great revelation or breakthrough going on. What's happening in Matthew right now is the experience of helplessness and frustration. Take away your mind's judgement of what you *should* be feeling or what you'd *like* to be feeling and you're left with just that. That's the truth of Matthew right now. You could even say it has a kind of beauty because it's a true response to your experience, to where you are in your life.

Matthew: What do you mean?

Jez: You're aware that you're Suffering, that there's something missing in your life, but you also have a feeling that there's another possibility, another way to be which doesn't involve that Suffering. Somehow, life has brought us together: I'm sharing this 'story' with you and you're trying to understand it, to get 'inside it'. However, apart from on an intellectual level, which is a very safe place for you to be, you can't 'get it'. Frustration and helplessness are very natural responses. Why *wouldn't* you feel that right now?

Matthew: But isn't that frustration all part of the Suffering I'm trying to get away from?

Jez: No, no, no! (Laughs)

Matthew: But...

Jez: That's exactly where you're going wrong. This is a *really* important point; it's perfect that it's come up. This is exactly what you need to learn right now.

Matthew: I don't understand.

Jez: You said: 'Isn't that frustration what I'm trying to get away from?' Yes, in the end it will be left behind, but not by such a response to it. Frustration is what's happening now. Rather than push it away, you need to encounter it, to face it. Just take away all judgements about it; feel it and let it be. It's like when you felt defensive when we talked about your personal development course; it's just a reaction coming up. You don't need to get caught up in Emotion about it, you don't need to dramatise it. Just let it do its thing in your bodymind without any interference from your Personality.

Matthew: I can't help feeling that this frustration has been there for a while during these talks, but I've been resisting it because I didn't think it had any part in this.

Jez: Think of it like this: Anything that arises as a response to this teaching is a part of it. Fear, anger, frustration, confusion, sadness: It's all the theatre of the Personality, that's what's being shown up and that's what needs to be seen. What's vital is your response to what arises; you need to feel it. It's called acceptance.

This enquiry has nothing to do with your ideas of how you *want* things to be or how you think they *should* be; it deals with what *is*. Wherever you are, however you are, that's the entry point. But to go through it and enter, you have to stop resisting whatever's happening, you have to accept those conditions and feel them.

37

RESISTANCE

The habit of not feeling

'I exist as I am, that is enough.' – Walt Whitman

Jez: So you're still here? Despite the frustration that's come up in the last few discussions, you've showed up for our talk; I haven't driven you away.

Matthew: Not yet! (Both Laugh.)

Jez: But it used to happen: Early on in our friendship, you used to suddenly disappear from my life, sometimes for up to half a year.

Matthew: Yes. It's odd to think about it now. I didn't even know why I was doing it.

Jez: If you'd started to back away once we'd begun *this* project, if your commitment had tailed off and you'd started cancelling, it would have been clear that this enquiry wasn't for you. You can go so far intellectually agreeing with me, staying safe in that conceptual level, but there'll be times when what I say provokes resistance in you. Then our talks will become more confronting. If they *don't* start becoming more confronting there are two possible reasons: The first is that identification with your Personality is very thin; there's nothing much left of it to put up a fight…

Matthew: I don't think that's the case with me.

Jez: You're right, and you're aware enough to know and acknowledge it. That's a good sign, as I've said before; arrogance is a severe hindrance in this enquiry: It's going in the opposite direction to where you need to go. Arrogance is a puffed-up Personality; that's just more resistance to get beyond.

*Matthew: So if the talks **aren't** confronting me, what's the other possible explanation?*

Jez: If you're not being challenged beyond an intellectual level then I'm not doing my job as a teacher of this. Personal growth and self-help are there to soothe you, to encourage you to be a better person and make you feel better about yourself. There's no conflict involved, that's what you sign up for and that's what you get. But somehow, you've found yourself engaged in *this* enquiry. You strayed from the normal pursuits of personal development; you've left the well-worn route and taken this unknown path that had no signpost telling you where it was going. Why did you do that?

Matthew: When I met you, I thought you had an interesting perspective on life: one I'd not encountered before. Also, I'd known lots of people who, like you, are successful, but none of them had the contentment I saw in you...

Jez: This led to us having some talks on this subject and, without meaning to, you found yourself walking in this weird and wonderful foreign land. Unlike with your personal development courses, you didn't know what this enquiry involved. It's almost as if you entered into it without realising what you'd done, without choosing it. You didn't research this subject; you don't know what the rules are. You didn't read the manual, because there isn't one. There are rules of engagement, but there's no manual. You only find out what those rules are by actually walking this path.

Up until recently you've been in the first stage of that engagement: the easy bit. It's an engagement through the mind: You're simply entertaining the concepts; it's all on a conceptual level. So far, the only 'rule', if you want to call it that, is that you've needed to stay open to the concepts, while not believing them. You had to be willing to entertain the possibility that they *could* be true. That's the passport needed to continue the journey at this first stage. You've done that, and everything's been relatively easy. It's made you feel pretty good, at least some of the time – am I right?

Matthew: It's true, I often leave here feeling kind of content: inspired and peaceful.

Jez: That's because, through the concepts, you've tuned into your Natural State and awakened some primal feelings of Joy. You could almost see it as proof that you already know this. Because I keep pointing you back to your original state of Being, something in you is remembering it. So there'll be times when that Joy becomes your main experience of coming here. This is why people can get hooked on being with spiritual teachers: They want the high; it's like getting a fix. Teachers don't *give* the Joy to you, they just remind you of what you have, what you are inside.

Over the last few discussions I'd say you've started to enter the second stage of this enquiry where, every now and then, what

I'm saying will be offensive to your Personality. Your niceness and goodness will be penetrated; you'll show glimpses of what's behind that public Mask. Things will get a bit more personal, a bit more real: You won't be able to just entertain what I'm saying intellectually; it will hit up against deeply held beliefs. You'll start experiencing Emotions: What I say may make you angry, sad, annoyed or scared for reasons that you won't at first understand.

The question isn't whether uncomfortable, disturbing feelings are going to arise. The question is: How are you going to respond when they do? This is the challenge, this is the test: If you start disappearing again or closing down, then you'll know this isn't for you. If something in you makes you continue and keep coming here, *despite* the discomfort, that will be a sign you're ready to continue on this journey.

So the fact that you came back, after hitting that frustration in our last talk, is a good sign. You left here in the middle of it. Tell me how it was: What happened?

Matthew: Not much really. When I stopped trying to push it away I just felt sadness, which I think was underneath the frustration. I realised that this situation, feeling like 'I'm not getting this' was something I already had inside me from years ago. I remember the feeling from school days; a fear that I'm being left behind, like I'm not going to make the grade.

Jez: Your repressive response to your feeling of frustration was an example of Personality Awareness. When we have painful, difficult feelings, the Personality says: 'Don't go there; it's going to be too painful to bear.' It becomes so engrained *not* to go there, you don't even know you're repressing something. But the point is, it's the repression itself that causes the Suffering, not the act of *feeling* what's repressed. As you described, that often comes as a relief.

Full-feeling engagement with life is part of the original state of Being. When a baby's feeling stressed and it screams and cries, it's not Suffering (meaning it's not feeling the angst, neurosis etcetera of the Personality). It *has* no Personality yet, so it's just feeling that feeling; and because it does that, the feeling passes.

Matthew: That's what happened with me: Once I'd connected with the frustration, I could feel my mind and body start to relax.

Jez: A feeling just wants to be heard. If you feel hunger and you ignore it, it's not good for the body in the long term, because we need to eat to survive. The body will keep trying to tell you that you're hungry until you eat. But a feeling is not a survival issue, so you can repress it and go on repressing it your whole life. You won't die, but it will have all sorts of consequences – mainly in creating more Suffering as it becomes an Emotion and eventually creates mental and physical health issues.

Matthew: So whatever comes up, I just have to feel it?

Jez: Yes, don't fall into the trap of using conceptual understanding as just another mental occupation to avoid feeling. There's a good quote from W.B. Yeats on this:

> *We taste and feel and see the truth.*
> *We do not reason ourselves into it.*

Life is happening now, in the heart of this experience, not in an idea of a peaceful experience that begins in an imaginary future.

Matthew: It sounds so obvious when you put it like that...

Jez: It *is* obvious, but who lives like that? We're constantly judging, editing and adapting our experience of ourselves. A feeling arises, then the mind comes in and judges it. It says: 'Don't feel that, you shouldn't be feeling that.' So we block it, we repress it and then we're in this strange divided position of being one thing, but pretending we're something else. We're in conflict with what we are.

As I said in an earlier talk, animals don't have this. What they are is what they are. A lion roaring and strutting in front of its pride doesn't think: 'Am I coming on a bit too strong here, a bit too powerful? The other lions might think I'm being big headed, too dominating. I'd better tone it down a bit.'

Matthew: But humans have self-awareness.

Jez: Yes, like animals we have consciousness, but our consciousness includes self-awareness. We can be aware of our actions and, with

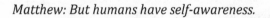

our highly developed minds, we have the ability to reflect on those actions. This is a mark of man's civilisation; it's what raises us above being just animals.

If a chimpanzee gets really enraged with a rival, there's no thoughts or conditioning to stop him expressing that rage so fully that it leads to him attacking and killing the rival. In the human world, if extreme anger rises up towards someone we have a safety valve. The primal, animal part of us may feel like killing someone but there's another part, this self-awareness, which can take a rational overview and decide that following those primal instincts might not be the best course of action. That's the part of you that says: 'Take a deep breath, count to ten, walk away.'

Matthew: That's a good thing, surely.

Jez: Yes. Self-awareness gives us the ability to feel something fully without acting on it: If you feel like killing someone, you can feel the feeling without it leading to murder. Self-awareness provides a safety valve.

Matthew: But that safety valve isn't there in everyone...

Jez: Yes, Personalities can be psychopathic; they can be devoid of that safety valve; then the possibility of murder arises. Also, as we've discussed, that awareness can be temporarily switched off in the heat of the moment, and then you end up with crimes of passion.

Matthew: So this ability to reflect on our actions and behaviour, which is a central part of being a civilised human, is also responsible for making us so screwed up when it comes to our feelings?

Jez: I wouldn't say it was responsible. It's just a function, but it became hijacked by Personality and was used to avoid Suffering. This started after the Wound when we learned to Contract, to pull in from painful feelings and consign them to the subconscious. At that moment, awareness, which previously had been Choice-less and impartial, became partial. That partiality came from Personality; it chose what we should feel and what we shouldn't feel.

This is what happened to you the other day: A strong feeling came up and your Personality said: 'Don't feel it, push it away.'

When that happened, you became divided, split. Your mind was able to carry on engaging with these concepts, but you weren't living what they were pointing to. I'm continually directing you back to that original state of Being, and part of that is this full-feeling engagement with life.

The Story of 'You'

38

AWARENESS

Consciousness encountering what is

'Empty yourself of everything,
let the mind rest at peace.
The ten thousand things rise and fall
while the self watches their return.' – Lao Tzu

Jez: You've asked me what you can do to help discover life beyond Personality. From my experience I'd say there are two things: The first is what we covered in the last talk; you have to remember how to feel.

Matthew: That's an odd statement; I want to say: 'Of course I know how to feel.'

Jez: Yes, you know how to feel, but your feeling isn't inclusive; it's selective. You don't know how to feel without selectivity. You've forgotten what it's like to fully encounter whatever's happening. To do that you have to go beyond the Contraction, you have to wake up the whole feeling system of the bodymind. That's what you did: You felt frustrated but you were repressing that feeling. The solution was simple: I pointed out what was happening, then you got in touch with that feeling and felt that frustration.

You see what I mean? It's not difficult; it's just a little shift. It's like dropping a bad habit. But it's a habit that's totally incompatible with finding this, because *losing* that full-feeling engagement with life is one of the outcomes of *losing* your original state of Being. Trying to find this without full-feeling engagement with life is like trying to get in the sea without getting wet. It can't be done.

But feeling on its own is not enough; you could train your body and mind to get used to feeling everything, but that won't reveal this understanding to you. In fact, to be endlessly tossed around by your feelings and Emotions like a ship in a stormy sea without a rudder would probably make you even more confused!

Matthew: So what's the other thing I can do?

Jez: To get to the root of Suffering you have to go further; the first step is feeling, the second is *awareness* of what is felt. Usually when there's pain in our life, our attention is increased; awareness rises up and becomes more acute. For example: If you've ever twisted your ankle, you'll know how the excruciating pain draws your attention to the injury. There's no way you *can't* be aware of what's happened, all other bodily sensations fall into the background; your awareness becomes totally focussed on that pain. This is a physical example but it's the same with mental pain; you become pre-occupied with a problem, you try to solve it, you look at it from many different angles, you can't stop thinking about it. When there's pain, suddenly awareness increases.

Matthew: And when there's pleasure...

Jez: We're too busy having a good time to be aware. The Indian teacher Nisargadatta Maharj said:

> *Pleasure puts you to sleep and pain wakes you up.*
> *If you don't want to suffer, don't go to sleep.*

So what I'm talking about is having awareness *all* the time, awareness that's not dependent on conditions, on our moods, on what is happening. In other words: 'Don't go to sleep.'

Matthew: (Pause.) Let me just take that in for a moment.

Jez: I love it when you pause.

(Pause.)

Matthew: Sometimes you explain something and it hits me deep inside. When you said that, it seemed so obvious. It feels like I already knew it. It's a bit like experiencing déjà vu.

Jez: I said something and it woke that knowledge up in you. It's important to stop when that happens. My statement produced a feeling in you, and you want to feel it, so naturally you pause to let that happen. It's beautiful: You're already practicing the first step.

As you indicated, you're receiving the information on a different level; you're not just intellectually entertaining a concept. The concept is pointing to something that's true; when you get hit like this it means the concept has 'landed'; the truth it points to is being perceived – understanding is opening up in you. Then, rather than your engagement with this just being in your head, your whole body becomes involved.

I used to get this a lot in my twenties when I browsed in a spiritual bookshop near where I lived. I'd just read a quote from someone like Buddha or Lao Tzu, and the words would hit me so hard I used to have to find a seat somewhere, sit down and close my eyes for a while as the understanding that the quote encapsulated opened up in me. Like I said; it's not just the head, it's a whole-body thing.

I know someone who, when we talk about these understandings, is occasionally mentally knocked out by something one of us says. She goes into a kind of swoon and has to lie down for a while. It's the whole system expanding as it takes on, makes conscious, new levels of knowledge.

Matthew: So these talks are like verbal boxing matches; you're trying to land punches....

Jez: Yes, while your Personality is ducking, diving and weaving to avoid them!

Matthew: Now and then you get through my defences and land a good punch...

Jez: One day maybe I'll knock you right out!

(Pause.)

Matthew: That comment itself was a bit of a blow! I don't really know what it means, but it landed.

(Long pause.)

***

Jez: Are you ready to continue?

Matthew: Yes, I think so. Where were we?

Jez: We were talking about what you can do to help discover life beyond Personality. I'd just said there are two steps... The first step is feeling and the second is *awareness* of what is felt. This takes us back to that definition of meditation you found about the mind 'acknowledging its content without becoming identified with that content'.

Matthew: You're referring to Choice-less Awareness.

Jez: Yes, we discussed this in our talk about Being. There are four attributes of Being: full-feeling engagement with life, Choice-less Awareness, Joy and Stillness. They're all intimately related; you could say that Stillness comes first; it's the ground in which the other attributes arise. Joy is an outcome of full-feeling engagement with life. The baby plays with Mummy, experiences the mashed-up banana being spooned into its mouth or lies in silence in its cot watching the shadows in the room, and this interaction with life produces the feeling of Joy.

Choice-less Awareness and feeling are like a double act; one follows the other. We become aware of our surroundings *through* our senses, through feeling. When Mummy spoons the banana into the baby's mouth her senses experience it: She feels the mushy, wet texture and the sweet taste on her tongue. Then she becomes *aware* of those feelings: She becomes conscious of the fact that the banana tastes good and she wants more of it.

The fact that the baby hasn't developed a sense of self yet gives the awareness a certain character: it's Choice-less. With no self, there's no 'centre' that could make a choice about what awareness falls on. If Mummy brings a banana into the baby's world, then that's what the baby will experience.

As I said in the previous talk, awareness is a function of consciousness. Animals have full-feeling engagement with life, and a capacity to become *aware* of what is felt. For example, a chimpanzee eats a certain leaf, finds that it has a taste that it likes; and it becomes conscious of that. It can remember that pleasurable taste and the tree on which that leaf grows, and it can go back and find it so it can eat it again.

Because of our superior brains, Awareness in humans is obviously on a different level to our animal cousins, but in newborn babies it hasn't reached its potential yet. It's still on that primitive, animal level. So although the baby can have some recollection that eating banana is pleasurable, it doesn't have the self-awareness that could say 'I like bananas.' How could it? There isn't a sense of self in which that point of view could arise. So in a baby, awareness is primitive and because of that, it's Choice-less, meaning it doesn't choose what it falls on.

As we grow up our awareness changes: We develop a sense of self (which eventually becomes our Personality) and with that sense of self comes self-awareness. This allows us to watch our responses to what we encounter and become aware of those responses. We learn that some things are distasteful to us and some things are pleasurable: We develop likes and dislikes. We also find that, in the World of Separation, we have the power of choice, and this has a huge influence on our experience because we can have some control over what appears in our lives.

Matthew: You mean we can choose one experience we like and reject another we don't like.

Jez: Exactly. So awareness is no longer Choice-less. And this is a natural part of being a functioning adult: We can make choices, we have a certain level of control over our lives and we take responsibility for it.

Matthew: I can feel a 'but' coming...

Jez: You're right. It's a natural and central part of human adult life, but... at a certain point, that ability to choose is no longer applied just to the world out there; it's applied to aspects of ourselves. We have the *ability* to look at ourselves, but we *choose* not to look at some parts. The reason we do this is because we've found that to look in certain places means going in the direction of pain. Even if we *do* look at ourselves and have a bit of self-awareness, we only go so far and we have blind spots. We don't see Choice-lessly; we only see parts that are not too confronting.

As we've discussed, all this begins at the Wound, that's when Choice-less Awareness is generally lost. The pain of that first encounter with the absence of Love in the Relative world is consigned to the subconscious. So the feeling is repressed, but so is the consciousness of what happened. Just as we can choose to *not* feel things, we can choose not to be aware of something. It's like pretending that it never happened. It's a self-protective mechanism that happens instinctively, and then becomes a habit. Then Choice-less Awareness becomes Personality Awareness.

So just as you have to get into the habit of feeling, you also need to be bringing awareness to those feelings. When you felt that frustration after the last talk, was there some part of you watching what was happening?

Matthew: Yes, that was when I realised that this was a feeling I'd been having a lot during our talks.

Jez: But there was something else you became aware of...

Matthew: Yes, that behind that feeling was a fear of not 'making the grade', of being left behind.

Jez: From what you told me, you had this fear in your schooldays. We discussed how it comes from the fact that in your family, intelligence was highly prized and love was linked with demonstrating cleverness.

Matthew: So whenever I'm in a situation where I feel I'm not making the grade...

Jez: It becomes a big thing for you: You get frustrated; you're hard on yourself. Why? Because the whole thing has become overlaid with the idea of not being loved. If you don't 'get' it, if you aren't 'clever enough', there's a voice inside that says you won't be loved. All this is part of the theatre of your Personality; it's programmed with all these beliefs. You're not aware of them but they're running all the time.

This is why you need to become aware of the shape and form of your own particular Personality; all the pain and Emotions in the Shadow, the beliefs, the patterns and thought forms. As long as you're not aware of them, they continue to create the Dream of your Personality. They create the Story you are living.

Matthew: So becoming aware of your Personality can wake you up from its Dream?

Jez: Not in itself no, but the more awareness you have of the Personality, the more likely it is that you come to a point where you see through your identification with it.

The Story of 'You'

39

WHO ARE YOU?

The ultimate question

'Let come what comes.
Let go what goes.
See what remains.' – Ramana Maharshi

Matthew: I've asked you what I can do to help discover this experience of life beyond Personality. To summarise, so far you've said: 'Immerse yourself in the great teachings of this, have a spiritual practice if you're that way inclined, and feel – and observe – whatever's happening.'

Jez: Yes. If you want to have a spiritual practice, if you're moved to meditate, then get into that. Help the body and mind relax. But don't fall into the trap of believing: 'When I practice long enough or seriously enough then I'll be happy, then I'll be really spiritual.' This enquiry isn't concerned with '*What* I can achieve' or 'How can I be better?' Those thoughts won't lead to *this* answer.

This enquiry is built on the much more fundamental question of 'Who am I?' Instead of looking at changing the Personality – which is what self-help and personal development do – you have to look at the one who wants to change it: the Personality. It's a shift of focus. That shift is what I've been nudging you towards in all these talks. You've forgotten who you are; if Suffering or just innate curiosity has pushed you to realise this, then it's natural to respond by asking the question: 'Who am I?'

Matthew: So asking that is also something I can practice?

Jez: I wouldn't call it a practice. If it's just a practice it won't get you very far. For it to be useful, the question 'Who am I?' has to rise from deep within your bones; it has to be the most important pursuit in your life. It's why I advise you to feel and watch. In the Prologue I quoted Socrates:

The unexamined life is not worth living.

Apparently that isn't true for everybody, but it *has* to be true for you if you want to discover this. Answering the question 'Who am I?' has to become a quest; so that everything in your life reflects it back to you like an echo:

Am I...

...the thoughts in my mind?'

*

Am I...

...the opinions that judge, comment and direct my life?

*

Am I...

...the ever-changing Emotions that control and dictate my moods?

*

Am I...

...the beliefs that give my world a sense of security?

*

Am I...

...the Suffering that I can't seem to escape?

*

Am I...

...the sum of my successes or failures?

*

Am I...

...what my parents, family and friends think I am?

*

Matthew: I'm guessing the answer to all of these questions is 'No.'

Jez: You see: This is a good example of head knowledge...

Matthew: I know, my comment was just based on what you've said.

Jez: You have to ask that question and '*live*' that question yourself; that's the only way you'll find any answer that's meaningful to you. It's not about guessing, or just accepting what I say. I've been leading and guiding this enquiry, but there's a point where you have to step up and be proactive; otherwise this just remains on an intellectual level. Rather than something you know in your bones, it's just head knowledge. Head knowledge is superficial; there's nothing at stake and nothing essentially changes in you apart from the fact that your mind holds a few more concepts or facts than it held before. Without a deep, full-feeling engagement this whole enquiry is reduced to a series of theories and concepts. These can make you feel safer, and perhaps a little more important, but when it comes to this enquiry all of that has no value whatsoever.

You could immerse yourself in the understanding I've shared in these discussions; you could learn all the arguments and answers and reproduce them in a cohesive manner when questioned, but that would be nothing more than the *impression* of understanding. From the outside it might look the same as if you'd actually had this realisation. You could make a listener who's seeking this believe you've seen beyond Personality. You could fool other people with that impression; you could even fool yourself – in fact, this is what some teachers actually do!

Head knowledge means that Personality is still controlling the experience of your life. Finding life beyond Personality begins with a questioning of the one who's running the show. It's not that we have to learn anything; we have to take away, or see through, that which is blocking our clear vision of this.

Matthew: Which is the belief that we are this Personality.

Jez: Yes. That's what separates you from your original state of Being. Until the Personality formed, that's what you lived. So if you want to remember and re-discover this, you're going to have to see through the Personality.

Matthew: When we started this series of discussions you talked about this as a story you were telling. Have we come to the end of that story?

Jez: We've discussed how that 'Story of You' began, how it was influenced by its environment, how it grew and all the outcomes of identifying with it. So we've come to the end of describing that 'Story of You', yes, but we're at the very beginning of how to be free of it. Do you want to continue?

Matthew: Yes – you can't leave me here!

Jez: There's a lot more to say.

Matthew: I think we're going to need another book...

THE INFINITE JOURNEY

*The next book in this series, **The Infinite Journey**, describes how identification with Personality can break down, and what is revealed in its place. It examines what it really means to Wake Up from the Dream of Personality: how the original state of Being manifests in an adult life, how it differs from the image of enlightenment that's been passed down to us and how life beyond Personality relates to the sometimes-confusing world of spiritual Seeking and teaching.*

GLOSSARY

*Words in **Bold** refer to other Glossary entries*

ABSOLUTE LEVEL – *A level of reality where energy exists in an unmanifest form (as a potential to be something). This formless ground of everything manifests as the phenomenal world – the Relative Level – in which time, space and form appear. From the point of view of Non-Duality there's only the Absolute Level (the Relative Level simply arises within it) but from the human perspective there appears to be these two Levels of reality. (See Chapter 3)*

BEING – *The essential nature and essence that we come into this world as (rather than the Personalities we become). It has four attributes: **Joy**, **Stillness**, **Choice-less Awareness** and full-feeling engagement with life. (See Chapter 5)*

CHARACTER – *The qualities that make you individual: your talents, quirks etcetera. All this comes with you at birth; it is your nature. By contrast your Personality is the product of nurture.*

CHOICE-LESS AWARENESS – *Perception that sees with absolute clarity because there's no Personality involved selecting what awareness falls on or whether it's turned on or off. We all start our life with Choice-less Awareness; it is one of the four attributes of **Being**.*

CONTRACTION – *A spontaneous reflex action of self-protection, a pulling back from full-feeling engagement with the world which originally arises in childhood to protect us from painful feelings of **the Wound**. (See Chapter 15)*

DISTRACTION – *A strategy the Personality uses to prevent us engaging with unwanted feelings. By being occupied in activities that we like, that make us happy, we temporarily escape our unhappiness. Whereas the **Contraction** cuts us off from painful feelings, Distraction simply turns our attention away from them. (See Chapter 32)*

DOING – *Any action that arises from either the need to **Distract** oneself from feeling or to prove oneself worthy, loveable or acceptable. (See also **Non-Doing**)*

DUALITY – *Refers to the **Relative Level** in which the formlessness of **Oneness** becomes form. In Duality there is the appearance of separation, relationship, cause and effect. (See Chapter 2)*

DREAM OF PERSONALITY – *The building blocks of Personality – desires, beliefs, hopes and **Emotion** – combine to produce the particular psychological reality you inhabit. This version of life seems real to the Personality and in a sense, it is real because it is being experienced. But it is subjective – no one else is experiencing that version of life – so in that sense it is like a Dream. (See Chapter 23)*

EMOTION – *In their effort to be heard, over time, repressed feelings become exaggerated, distorted and incessant; they become Emotions. (See Chapter 17)*

GROUP PERSONALITY – *The tribe we're born into and its collective consciousness; an amalgamation of its constituent Personalities. There are many levels of, and factors influencing, Group Personality including: species, race/nationality, gender, geography, income, politics and religion.*

HEART CENTRE – *The centre of Love in a human being. While still in the **Natural State** we are located primarily in the Heart Centre.*

JOY – *The original feeling that arises simply from the enjoyment of living what you are. A natural outcome of **Being** interacting with life in all its different forms.*

LOVE – (With a capital 'L') *refers to the unconditional Love that is perceived beyond the perspective of Personality. What Rumi is referring to when he says: 'Love is the bridge between you and everything.'*

LOVE – (With a small 'l') *The Personality's version of love, which is what Love becomes once we've lost touch with unconditional Love. It's based on need, it's often sentimentalised and romanticised, and it's conditional, meaning it can be turned on or off.*

MASK – *The false face that all Personalities, to a greater or lesser extent, wear to hide the parts of themselves they do not want others to see. 'Persona' is the Greek word for 'mask'. (See Chapter 26)*

MYSTERY (THE) – *Knowledge can take you so far, then you're left in The Mystery: the inexplicable wonder of life.*

NATURAL STATE – *The experience of **Oneness** in which we enter this world. An umbrella term encompassing the **Original Relationship to Life** and **Being**. (See Chapters 4 & 5)*

NON-DUALITY – *While **Duality** relates to the **Relative Level** of form and separation, Non-Duality points to its opposite: The non-separate, **Oneness** of the **Absolute Level**.*

ONENESS – *Before energy manifests as something, it starts out as undivided, potential energy. A more metaphysical word for describing that potential is 'Oneness'. (See Chapter 1, also **Non-Duality**, **Absolute Level**)*

OPENING – *A short glimpse beyond Personality.*

ORIGINAL RELATIONSHIP TO LIFE – *Before any human relationship our primal connection is to life itself, which fulfils and sustains us. The Original Relationship to Life is one of surrender; we are all children and life is the mother. As Lao Tzu puts it: 'I am nourished by the Great Mother'. (See Chapter 4)*

PERSONALITY – *The Personality is the construct of 'you'; an identity built on the building blocks of the **Contraction**, **Emotion**, beliefs,* *desires and hope. The Personality has a function of self-preservation; it is programmed to maintain its sense of absolute authority. In Personality, the mind is king and all of the Personality's thoughts, beliefs and Emotions, which are mostly the product of your past, are in control of your life. (See Chapters 19 & 20)*

PERSONALITY AWARENESS – *Perception that is governed by the* **Personality**. *Unlike* **Choice-less Awareness**, *it can be turned on or off – i.e. it is personal. If we don't want to feel something we can distance ourselves from our experience by cutting off from our feelings. If we don't want to see something we can look away from it. (See Chapter 21)*

RELATIVE LEVEL – *The level of existence where the potential energy of* **Oneness** *manifests as physical matter. In this level of reality there is the appearance of separation, relationship, and cause and effect. (See Chapter 3, also* **Absolute Level***)*

SEEKING – *Searching for spiritual answers to the problem of Suffering and the quest for fulfilment. Usually involves adopting some form of spiritual practice such as meditation, mindfulness, chanting, fasting etcetera.*

SELF – *Our original sense of separateness which allows us to operate in the world. This begins as a neutral, functioning centre but as we grow up it becomes burdened with Emotion and beliefs and turns into the Personality. (See Chapter 10)*

SHADOW – *The hidden side of the Personality, the subconscious where we consign everything we do not want to confront. What is hidden behind the* **Mask***. (See Chapter 27)*

SPIRITUAL – *Connected to something bigger than ourselves; beyond Personality.*

STILLNESS – *One of the four attributes of* **Being** *which we come into* this world with. Not just the lack of action but also the absence of thought.

SUFFERING – *Psychological pain or ill health which originates from the loss of our **Natural State**. The Personality's illusion of thinking that we are separate manifests as neurosis, worry, emotional states, depression, addiction or self-hatred. (See Chapter 28)*

WORLD of SEPARATION – *The Relative Level as seen in the manifestation of form, people and events.*

WOUND (THE) – *Having lost our **Natural State** we begin needing to receive **Love** from other people (such as our parents). The Wound is the moment we experience that, unlike Love, such personal **love** can be absent. At that moment we feel, for the first time, the existential pain of being in the world yet outside of Love's embrace. (See Chapter 13)*

CPSIA information can be obtained
at www.ICGtesting.com
Printed in the USA
BVHW081829220421
605634BV00002B/159